TONE, SEGMENT, AND SYLLABLE IN CHINESE:

A Polydimensional Approach to Surface Phonetic Structure

A. Ronald Walton

China-Japan Program
Cornell University
Ithaca, New York 14853

The Cornell East Asia Papers publishes manuscripts
on a wide variety of scholarly topics pertaining to
East Asia, principally China-Japan, which, in the
opinion of its editorial board, merit wide
circulation. Manuscripts are published on the basis
of camera-ready copy and without copy-editing by
C.E.A.P. The volume author (or editor) is thus
responsible for the necessary editing.

Inquiries should be addressed to Editorial Board,
East Asia Papers, China-Japan Program, 140 Uris
Hall, Cornell University, Ithaca, New York 14853.

Preface

This monograph is an expansion of my Cornell University Ph.D. dissertation (1976). The first twelve chapters, which constitute the original work, have been left in tact, for while phonological theory continues to change and evolve, the specific analysis offered in the dissertation seems to me to remain timely. Two chapters devoted almost exclusively to theoretical concerns have been added, partly to provide a broader perspective of the original analysis and partly as a response to suggestions by colleagues in the field of Chinese linguistics that the earlier treatment be expanded through a comparison with some very recent theoretical trends, particularly Autosegmental Theory.

While the additional chapters reflect a considerably deeper and more far-ranging concern with theoretical issues, I have not attempted to address every specific recent publication on relevant topics individually (an undertaking well beyond the limitations of this expansion), but rather have addressed the general theoretical underpinnings characteristic of such works. No specific current work surveyed invalidates, in my opinion, the theoretical orientation presented in either the original study or in the newly added chapters.

TABLE OF CONTENTS

TABLES

INTRODUCTION

Considerable concrete detail on the aims and organization of this work are presented in the first
and final chapters. Rather than recapitulating the
information offered elsewhere in this study, I should
like, in this introductory section, to touch upon a number
of fundamental themes which recur both explicitly and
implicitly throughout the body of the study so as to
provide a general perspective of the analysis presented
herein.

Following the established canons of typological
language classification, I assume that Chinese and other
monosyllabic morpheme, lexical tone languages within the
Sino-Tibetan language family manifest certain phonological
features or traits that uniquely distinguish the sound
systems of these languages from other human language sound
systems. In approaching an analysis of Chinese, the
phonologist's task, as I see it, is two-fold: 1) to offer
a principled analysis of the Chinese phonological system
that captures these unique, defining features by way of
an explicit model or theory, and 2) to ground this model
or theory within the larger context of what is known
about human sound systems generally. The effect of these

two considerations is to offer an analysis that is at once universal, such that Chinese can be seen to have much in common with other languages, and yet to offer an analysis that reveals exactly why Chinese can be defined as a separate and distinct language within the pool of the world's languages. The logical procedure in such an analysis is to present and defend a description of the unique traits of Chinese phonological structure and then to explore the power of existing, universally oriented theories in characterizing these defining traits, with the understanding that such theories rightly require modification if they cannot adequately account for the structure of any language sound system, in this case, Chinese.

A major theme of this study is that no existing phonological theory can adequately characterize the nature of the Chinese sound pattern, that theoretical revisions are thus required and, by extension, that any universally oriented theory must therefore include the mechanisms required for describing Chinese and other Sino-Tibetan languages.

A second theme in this treatment concerns the locus of the "defining" or "unique" phonological features mentioned above. Here, it is useful to distinguish between what I suggest are primary, as opposed to secondary, defining features. I strongly advocate the position that the primary defining features of Chinese are to be found in the internal structure and organization of the Chinese monosyllable.

While all Chinese languages and dialects have different inventories and arrangements of phonological units, these languages nevertheless share a remarkable similarity with respect syllable organization. Maximum syllables can be analyzed as having initial, medial and final components, accompanied (with some exceptions) by a tonal component. The number of consonants in syllable initial position far outweighs the number of consonants in syllable final position, there are no consonant clusters in either initial or final position, the number of possible medials will be less than the number of initials or finals, the number of tones will range from at least three to no more than ten, etc.

Likewise, in examining the historical development of Chinese, the monosyllable figures prominently. Factors internal to the syllable, such as the nature of syllable onset and coda, may have played a key role in the evolution of tone and such factors have certainly influenced the nature of tones in the various Chinese languages and dialects. Syllable final stops and nasals have persistently merged and disappeared in a seemingly patterned manner and, the process continues today as does the persistent devoicing of voiced initial obstruents. All the while, the monosyllable has manifested a remarkable resistance to assimilation across syllable boundaries (though some such sporadic assimilation has indeed occurred), a fact that persuasively argues for an analysis of the Chinese sound system focused heavily on the internal composition of this unit.

Thus, it would seem that as one seeks to pinpoint those features that characterize Chinese phonological structure, both synchronically and diachronically, one is drawn again and again back to the monosyllable, to its internal composition, to the interplay between its prosodic and non-prosodic features.

Under the label of "secondary" defining features I include such extra-syllable phonomena as intersyllabic assimilation, tone sandhi, stress, intonation, and the like. Among these secondary features, tone sandhi (the changes individual syllable-tones undergo when the syllables are combined into larger units such as phonological words and phrases) is perhaps the most complex phenomenon in Chinese. However, I characterize tone sandhi as secondary rather than primary for several reasons. First, some

Chinese languages evidence very little tone sandhi (e.g.,
Cantonese, Mandarin). Furthermore, while tone sandhi in
some languages seems independent of the segmental composition of the syllable (e.g., Mandarin) in other languages
(e.g., the Wu languages), tone is intrically linked to
syllable-internal, segmental features and thus tone changes
may be related to certain largyngeal configurations within
the segmental make-up of the syllable, thereby suggesting
a prior necessity of analyzing the monosyllable before
embarking on an analysis of tone change. This last point
is of more than minor importance theoretically: approaches
to tone sandhi without regard to a prior analysis of the
monosyllable can distort and misrepresent the internal
structure of the syllable (see Chapters 9 and 10 for
examples of this problem).

In sum, I have concentrated in this study on the
monosyllable rather than on tone sandhi simply because an
analysis based primarily on tone sandhi would do little
to reveal the essence of the Chinese sound pattern while
the reverse procedure, attempting an analysis of the
syllable in isolation, not only accounts for a much greater
range of features (with respect to both theory and to the
various languages and dialects within the Chinese family),
but also makes the implicit claim that an understanding

of tone sandhi requires a prior account of internal syllable structure.

Of course, a complete analysis must indeed account for the monosyllable and extra-syllable processes as well. Suffice to say that simply attempting to analyze the Chinese monosyllable in a rigorous manner is a challenge that has yet to be mastered despite what could be interpreted as some preliminary steps put forth in this essay.

Yet another critical theme concerns not just the fundamental unit of analysis, as discussed above, but also the level of analysis. Phonological theories commonly distinguish between various underlying levels (phonemic, morphophonemic) and a phonetic level. Generative phonological theories and various modified versions of this theory distinguish between an underlying phonological level and a so-called "surface phonetic" level. The latter is derived from the former by various layers and types of phonological rules. The distance between the two levels, it would seem, is in direct proportion to the phonological complexity of word formation, and, in fact, the need for the two levels and the intervening rules seems necessary just to account for the phonological nature of word formation. It is accurate to claim, I believe, that current theories are much more concerned

with the nature of underlying structure and the nature
of phonological rules -- or, what is termed morphophonemics -- than with the nature of surface phonetic structure. This latter level, I suggest, is often seen as the
starting point for inquiry into the nature of the underlying level and processes, or conversely, is seen as the
output of such processes. In and of itself, however, the
surface phonetic level is contantly portrayed as secondary
and derivative as a level of analysis.

Yet, it is widely recognized that aside from tone
sandhi (and some cases of segmental assimilation across
syllable boundaries), there is little morphophonemic
variation in Chinese word formation. In fact, the general
absence of segmental morphophonemic variation can itself
be seen as a primary defining feature of Chinese. Moreover, even when tone sandhi is considered, since some
Chinese languages have so little tone variation in word
formation, it would be difficult to argue in favor of
a strictly or even heavily morphophonemic approach to the
analysis of the Chinese sound pattern. Thus, a recurrent
theme in this work is that the key to describing and analyzing the primary (as opposed to secondary) defining
features of Chinese resides in the surface phonetic
structure of the language rather than in the abstract
underlying representations and phonological rules. Since

most current theories include a surface phonetic level
somewhere within the theoretical model, the particular
analysis offered herein should have implications of a
theoretical nature for phonological theory generally.

A final theme which underlies all the others is that
the predominant phonological theories have been and continue to be ill-equipped to characterize the defining
features of Chinese and of Sino-Tibetan languages in
general, not just because of purely linguistic factors
but rather because of the cultural milieu within which
these theories have evolved. It seems fair to say that
the majority of current phonological theories have been
developed within the confines of the Indo-European cultural and linguistic tradition, have drawn their impetus
from initial work on Indo-European languages, and have
then been modified when applied to non-Indo-European
sound systems. No clearer case for this interpretation
can be made than the intuitive acceptance of the segment
as the key unit of phonological structure accompanied by
a persistent ambivalence with regard to the status of
the syllable and by the relegation of prosodic features
such as tone, intonation, etc. to the back corners and
upper reaches of mainstream phonological inquiry.

One could argue that we need not look far for the
rationale behind this state of affairs. Our Western

phonological tradition has naturally drawn on its linguistic roots. Alphabetic, letter-sized units, i.e., segments, of course have intuitive appeal to users of alphabetic languages. Likewise, the syllable naturally has a less intuitive appeal in a language family and native linguistic tradition where words and morphemes are commonly polysyllabic and where no satisfactory mechanism has yet been developed even to determine syllable boundaries. In a similar vein, it also seems natural that the Indo-European linguistic tradition and theories to which it gives birth should have poorly developed intuitions about such features as lexical tone. Even such a commonplace prosodic phenomenon as word stress is not marked in Indo-European writing systems. Indeed, the term "suprasegmental" itself seems to imply a primary, trustworthy segmental base with a secondary over-lay in contrast to the equally plausible notion of a primary prosodic base with secondary "sub-prosodic" features.

Likewise, the case could be made that the current emphasis on morphophonemic phenomena -- the intense inter-est in underlying representations and the nature and order-ing of phonological rules -- is the predictable perspective for phonological theories emanating from an Indo-European base, that is, from a language family characterized by complex morphological phenomena. The fact that the theories so developed are enriched and modified by application to

non-Indo-European languages does not necessarily imply that
the initial assumptions, the most basic of assumptions,
the deepest and seemingly most reliable of intuitions are
somehow free of the biases and influences of the Indo-
European ethnolinguistic paradigm.

While I certainly would not advocate that each human
language or language family be "approached in its own
terms," I question the accuracy of assigning the label
"universal" to a panoply of assumptions and intuitions
that seem so clearly to be culturally and ethnolinguisti-
cally biased. Should the predominate linguistic theories
have evolved within the Sino-Tibetan cultural and linguistic
milieu, we might well be confronted today with a situation
where prosodic phenomena and the syllable are intuitively
and theoretically acceptable and well defined, but where
the focus of inquiry is on the nature, reality, even the
necessity, of the segment as a viable theoretical construct.

In sum, I would suggest that the interest in deep,
morphophonemic structure (as opposed to surface phonetic
structure), the reliability of intuitions about the segment (but not about the syllable), the secondary stature
of prosodic pheonomena, etc. are not the consequence of
linguistic reality but rather of the perceptions of this
reality as filtered through the Indo-European cultural,

language and linguistic tradition. If nothing else, I
hope to demonstrate in this study that an understanding
of surface phonetic structure, of the monosyllable, of
lexical tone, of the relationship between tone, segment
and syllable are as complex, as theoretically challenging,
as worthy of scientific inquiry as the more orthodox
approaches which tend to dominate phonological analysis
at the present time. In short, I hope to have made a case
for another reality.

Chapter One

BACKGROUND

1.1 Introduction

This work originally began as an attempt to present
a phonological analysis -- based on field-collected data[1]--
of several dialects in the southern branch of the Wu language
of Chinese.[2] Of course, any such analysis or characterization presumes to account for the "relevant facts" of the
language at hand. However, the "relevant facts," as so many
philosophers of science have been quick to point out, are
relevant only to theories or hypotheses: "Empirical 'facts'
or findings, therefore, can be qualified as logically relevant or irrelevant only in reference to a given hypothesis,
but not in reference to a given problem" (Hempel 1966: 12).

----

1. The data was collected under the auspices of a Fulbright-
Hayes Fellowship during 1971-72. The study is based on
work with native speakers presently living in Taiwan
and covers five sites in the south of Zhejiang province -
Wen-Zhou, Rui-An, Li-Shui, Tai-Shun and Yi-Wu.

2. The major language divisions of China are often referred
to as "dialects," though in terms of mutual intelligibility
and variability in phonological structure they resemble, for
instance, the Romance "languages." In this essay I will
follow the convention of terming the major divisions (e.g.,
Mandarin, Cantonese, Wu, etc.) as "languages" and reserve
the term "dialect" for subdivisions within each language.
Geographically, the Wu language then, is spoken in Zhejiang
province and in the southern part of Jiangsu province.

Indeed, one can only assume that "the facts" were
actually collected with a number of hypotheses and underlying assumptions already well at hand and that in the course
of the field work, such hypotheses were constantly modified
and tested. Hempel (1966: 13) maintains that this is inevitable in scientific inquiry:

> In sum, the maxim that data should be gathered
> without guidance by antecedent hypotheses about
> the connections among the facts under study is
> self-defeating, and it is certainly not followed
> in scientific inquiry. On the contrary, tenta-
> tive hypotheses are needed to give direction to
> a scientific investigation. Such hypotheses
> determine, among other things, what data should
> be collected at a given point in a scientific
> investigation.

By virtue of the linguist's formal training in the science
of linguistics and by virtue of working on a particular language or language family over a period of time, it seems
safe to assume that the linguist develops a set of "quasi-
intuitions" about how the language works -- how it is put
together. Another critical factor at stake here is the influence of the linguist's native language and native language tradition in shaping these quasi-intuitions. This
entails more than just the linguist's own personal language
background. The native language tradition makes its impact
felt in the formal linguistic training of the linguist. For
example, one theme I shall present several times in this
essay is that linguists in the West are so accustomed to

working within an alphabetic language tradition that their intuitions sometimes lead them to an extreme "segmental" view of phonological structure.

Phonological analyses, then, are carried out and presented with reference to some particular (though not necessarily explicit) phonological theory and hopefully the theory will capture those quasi-intuitions which the linguist has come to consider the "valid linguistic generalizations" of the language under examination.

However, several of my colleagues and myself have increasingly come to feel that neither the modern structuralist (so called "taxonomic") theory of phonology nor the more recent theory of generative phonology (as expressed in say Chomsky and Halle (1968), Postal (1968)) are adequate to characterize what we feel to be the valid linguistic generalizations of Chinese phonological structure. This is simply a case of lack of fit between theory on the one hand and data (tempered by quasi-intuitions) on the other. The closer the examination of the latter, the more significant and radical the proposed revisions of the former.

As a result of what seem to me to be serious inadequacies in the theoretical framework, my initial concern with the description of Southern Wu was at first subsumed under and finally replaced by an in-depth exploration of the source of these theoretical inadequacies.

1.2 Some Alternative Approaches

In Walton (1971), I argued for the abandonment within generative theory of morpheme structure _rules_ and for the adoption of morpheme structure _conditions_ (as proposed by Stanley (1967)) as a step toward matching certain facets of Chinese phonological structure with the standard theory. By far the most emphasis was placed on establishing the notion of the "Positive Condition" as a formal device for expressing the canonical shapes of Chinese syllables (the particular Chinese dialect under study was Shanghai) and on establishing a set of conventions to express the constraints on the possible sequential arrangements of systematic phonemes within the Chinese syllable. In the same phonotactic vein, conventions were proposed to express the relationship within the syllable between segments and tone.

Sherard (1972) went outside of both the structuralist and generative traditions in his study of Shanghai. The main reason for this, it seems, stems from a feeling that these theories placed undue emphasis on segment-sized "phonemes" as the key subsyllabic elements in phonological analysis. Sherard's analysis tends towards that of the Firthian pro-sodic school. Taking the syllable as basic unit, he pro-poses five minimum syllable types differentiated by such "features" or "components" as vowel length, glottal constric-tion at onset, glottal constriction at cessation of phona-

tion and register and tone contour (Sherard 1972: 51-53).
He states, in fact, that such features as tones, syllable
shortness and final nasal "... affect the entire syllable
nucleus and are clearly features which are relevant to more
than a minimal segment -- i.e., they are very reminiscent of
Firthian prosodies" (1972: 42).

The phoneme is rejected outright: "I have not used
the phoneme here as a structural component in my analysis of
Shanghai phonology; the syllable is taken instead as the
basic building block" (1972: 30). Furthermore, even the notions of "features" and "components" are seen as syllable-
wide phenomena: "... I have not concerned myself with their
relative size or subsyllabic status" (Sherard 1972: 43).

Light (1974) attempted to show that neither modern
structuralist theories, generative theory nor Sherard's
quasi-prosodic analysis were adequate for the analysis of all
Chinese languages. He proposed a relativistic approach to
phonological analysis which would allow the use of autonomous
phonemes, systematic phonemes, prosodically defined syllables
and other units that would be appropriate to the language
under study. Light, drawing on Pike and Pike (1947) and
Hockett (1955), proposed that differences in syllable constituent structure are at the root of phonological typology.
Light's particular emphasis was on establishing the subsyllabic unit, the "rime," as a key concept in the analysis of

at least some Chinese languages.

1.3 The Syllable

It should be apparent that each of the studies mentioned above sought to revise current theory or go outside
modern structuralist and generative theories. Moreover, in
each case, the proposed approach centered on the proper phonological treatment of the syllable in Chinese. In Walton
(1971), I was trying to establish a formal device for expressing syllable structure and for expressing phonotactic
constraints within the syllable. Sherard (1972) proposed a
quasi-prosodic approach to the internal structure of the
syllable and rejected the notion that there were discrete
subsyllabic units corresponding to the "phonemes" of structuralist or generative theories. The syllable was thus com-
posed of syllable-sized features and components. Light (1974)
took the syllable as the basic typological unit. Particularly, he was concerned with the constituent structure of
the Chinese syllable, especially notions such as Initial,
Medial, Final and Rime. The fact that all these studies
were so concerned with the syllable deserves some discussion.

Current phonological theory, especially the various
versions of generative theory, has been in my opinion, chiefly concerned with morphophonemic alternation. Current issues
center on such problems as abstract versus concrete morpho-

phonemic representations and on the nature, type, ordering and interaction of the phonological rules necessary to map correct morphophonemic representations into surface representations. For example, it is interesting to note that in Anderson's recent work, <u>The Organization of Phonology</u>, eleven of the thirteen chapters dealing with current generative theory are solely devoted to problems in morphophonemics (whereas the syllable gets some treatment in the "problems for the future" section near the end).

However, one of the most characteristic features of Chinese is the relative lack of morphophonemic alternation. This is not to say that there is <u>none</u>, there is definitely some (e.g., tone sandhi) but relatively speaking, there is very little. This fact has often been emphasized by linguists working with Chinese within the generative framework. For instance, William Wang (1968) has suggested that there is a type of "phonemic" level intermediate between the morphophonemic and surface phonetic levels. Wang (1968: Fn. 19, p. 707) states: "The morphemes which neither undergo nor cause alternations simply have phonemic representations and are exempt from morphophonemic rules."

As a consequence of this structural fact of Chinese, i.e., the lack of morphophonemic alternation, the "organization of phonology" (to use Anderson's words) is seen as involving a set of theoretical problems quite different from

those being currently debated within generative theory.
Since there is very little "deep" phonology in Chinese, a
great deal of emphasis is put on surface phonetic organization, and, as it turns out, the smallest and most accessible
unit of phonetic organization is the smallest pronounceable
unit - the syllable. This concern with surface phonetic
organization leads to deeper and deeper examinations of the
syllable as a structural unit and ultimately, as in the case
of Walton (1971), Sherard (1973) and Light (1974) to dissatisfaction with the way in which the internal structure of
this unit has been handled in phonological theory.

I believe that it is especially in this area, the continuing examination of the syllable in Chinese, that the
phonological study of Chinese can make significant contributions to phonological theory. In recent years the syllable,
a unit ignored for all practical purposes in standard generative theory (e.g., Sound Pattern of English, Aspects of
Phonology) has become increasingly important in theoretical
formulations - especially in that brand loosely called
"natural generative phonology" (e.g., Hooper (1973, 1974)).
Anderson's recent discussion of the syllable with respect to
current generative theory is worth noting. After devoting
the bulk of his work to what might be termed a "segmental"
conception of phonology, he admits that the notion that
phonological and phonetic structures should be regarded as

a string of segments, makes the implicit claim that "...
there are no necessary units with their own structure which
are either larger or smaller in size than the segment" (1974:
252). He goes on to state: "A fair amount of evidence has
accumulated that this assumption is untenable, and that our
notion of a representation is in need of revision." (1974:
252). This then leads to the significant conclusion: "The
first phonologically relevant unit other than the segment
for which an argument can be given is the syllable" (1974:
252). Anderson gives a rather comprehensive argument for the
formal inclusion of the syllable in generative theory. Here,
I should like to quote several statements which I consider
to be the essence of his argument:

> The consistent attempt in generative phonological
> studies to ignore the syllable as a structural unit
> has not been based generally on a refusal to re-
> cognize the existence and potential articulatory
> and psychological integrity of such elements. A
> case against the inclusion of syllables in phono-
> logical representations has never been made in any
> detail in print, but it has generally been assumed
> that the sort of facts associated with syllable
> structure can in fact be attributed to the strictly
> segmental representation, and do not require addi-
> tional elements.
>
> If it were generally true that phenomena associated
> with the syllable as a structural unit could be
> recorded satisfactorily without reference to
> elements other than segments and morphological/
> syntactic boundaries, this would be an interesting
> result... This does not, however, appear to be
> the case, and some revision of our attitude toward
> the syllable seems called for. (p. 253).

Given the above stated goal concerning the "revision of our attitude toward the syllable," it would indeed seem that the continuing examination of the structure and nature of the Chinese syllable will contribute significantly to this revision. As noted earlier, the lack of morphophonemic alternation clears the way for examining other facets of phonological organization. In Chinese, the syllable is a natural focal point. It is fairly isolatable - the smallest tone-bearing unit, the smallest pronounceable unit. It is, moreover, both historically and synchronically a unit characterized by strong internal cohesion and resistance to extra-syllable language processes (tone sandhi aside). For example, the joining of syllables into larger units, such as phonological words has, with few exceptions, not resulted in consonant clustering or even in a significant amount of cross-syllable assimilation. The internal structure of the maxi - mum syllable can still be characterized as it was in 600 A.D. - a unit consisting of an initial, a medial, a final, and a tone.

Furthermore, the total number of syllables is rather small compared to Western languages such as English. Modern Mandarin is said to have approximately 1,300 syllables (including tone); the greatest number ever estimated was 3,877 in the Ancient or Middle Chinese and this number is considered exaggerated.[3] Compare these figures with one estimate I have seen for English: 200,000 syllables (cited in Fromkin 1968: 63).

In sum, given the basic phonological structure of Chinese on the one hand, and the "attempt to ignore the syllable in generative phonological studies" on the other, it seems only natural that the theory-data conflict mentioned in 1.1 and the alternative approaches discussed in 1.2 ahould arise.

The theory-data problem, however, has not been restricted simply to the segmental facets of the Chinese syllable. The characterization of tone in the syllable has also presented a great many problems as will be discussed in the next section.

1.4 Tone

A concern with the characterization of tone in the phonological analysis of Chinese follows quite naturally from a concern with the syllable as the pivotal unit of phonological organization in Chinese. Since Wang's (1967) proposal of a set of tone features for characterizing tone in Chinese, there has arisen in the field a much more vigor-
_____
3. Estimates of the precise number of syllables in modern Mandarin and in Middle Chinese vary slightly; these figures are taken from Chao (1948: 14).

ous theoretical approach to tone within the framework of
generative phonology.

Indeed, the situation has become quite complex. It
would be senseless to maintain that there is a basic theory-
data matching problem here simply because there is no "standard theory" within which to approach the data. This is, in
fact, the real problem. Concern over the correct set of
tone features, though important, does not constitute a theory
of tone.

Recent attempts to formulate a vigorous, explicit
characterization of tone within generative theory have
raised the very important question of whether tone is to be
regarded as segmental, suprasegmental, or perhaps both - that
is, segmental in some languages, suprasegmental in others.

With respect to Chinese, it has been proposed (Woo
1972) that tone is to be characterized as being segmental.
Again, my own quasi-intuitions derived in part from field
work and observation is that this approach is misguided.
However, I do not believe the problems in this area derive
so much from artifices of the theory or from inadequate phonological theories but rather from the truly inexplicit way
tone has been treated phonetically. In the concern for
deep phonology, the surface characteristics of tone have
largely gone ignored or else have been assumed unimportant.
Thus, with respect to tone in Chinese, the problem seems not

to be one of revising inadequate theories (as proposed above for the syllable) but rather one of basic theory construction.

Again, then, early attempts to apply the generative model to what seemed to me "valid linguistic generalizations" about tone in Southern Wu eventually led to the conclusion that the entire area of "tonology" in Chinese - even when restricted to the tone of individual syllables - merited a much closer examination than originally seemed necessary.

1.5   Aim of the Present Essay

The aim of the present essay is essentially two-fold: to present and defend an analysis of the fundamental, distinguishing characteristics of the Chinese sound pattern, particularly the relationships among segmental, tonal and syllabic features, and to propose a variety of theoretical revisions necessary to overcome what I perceive to be serious inadequacies in a range of theoretical approaches as they are applied to this sound pattern. A concomitant aim, implicit throughout the essay, is to demonstrate that the issues raised herein, while stemming from an analysis of Chinese, have implications for the phonological analysis of all languages.

In the following chapter I will examine some data drawn from a previous study (Walton 1971) with the goal of explicitly formulating a set of generalizations concerning the

syllable structure of this particular language. Having
formulated this set of generalizations for a specific Chinese
language, I will then show that they are valid for all Chinese
languages. Chapter 3 will be concerned with reformulating
these structural generalizations into a set of requirements
which a phonological theory must meet in order to express the
generalizations.

In Chapter 4, I will examine how standard generative
theory has met such requirements and in Chapter 5 an attempt
will be made to demonstrate that even in the light of recent
revisions, the present framework of generative phonology is
incapable of meeting the requirements on syllable structure
stated in Chapter 3.

Chapter 6 will be concerned with formulating, at least
tentatively, an approach that can match the requirements.
Such an approach represents a synthesis and reformulation of
notions discussed in Chapters 4 and 5. In Chapter 7, the
Shanghai phonetic data is re-examined in light of the proposals set forth in Chapter 6.

Whereas the first part of the essay is concerned with
the characterization of the segmental dimemsion of the
Chinese monosyllable, the latter part focuses on the characterization of the prosodic dimension of this unit. Chapter
8 outlines the basic problems of representing tone within

the framework of generative phonology and introduces two
recent attempts at characterizing tone within this framework;
the Sonorant Feature approach and the Feature Assimilation
approach.

In Chapter 9 it is argued that the Sonorant Feature
approach to tone characterization is phonetically unmotivated,
is incapable of capturing certain generalizations and unnec-
essarily complicates the characterization of tone sandhi.
Chapter 10, in turn, examines the Feature Assimilation approach
and concludes that such an approach suffers exactly the inadequacies of the Sonorant Feature proposal.

In Chapter 11 it is argued - as in the first section
of the thesis - that if tonal phenomena are approached from
a surface phonetic point of view rather than from a deep
phonological orientation, then the Sonorant Feature and
Feature Assimilation approaches can be seen as oversimplifi-
cations of the nature of tone in Chinese. To accentuate the
independence of tonal from segmental phenomena and to empha-
size the importance of characterizing tone in its own terms,
I introduce the heuristic notion "Tone Program."

Chapter 12 explores in a rather abstract way the interface of the segmental syllable as described in Chapter 6
with the tonal components of the syllable as characterized

by the Tone Program (introduced in Chapter 11). The segmental and tonal facets of the Chinese syllable are seen as constituting different, separate dimensions neither of which is mapped onto the other. Rather, the interface of the two dimensions is based on the sharing of certain glottic features common to both dimensions and on the various phonetactic contraints which hold among these features.

Chapters 13 and 14 constitute the third and final part of this work. To this point, the characterization of Chinese phonological structure and the discussions of theoretical approaches have been undertaken with primary reference to Generative Phonology and particularly to the inadequacies of this approach when applied to Chinese. This emphasis on Generative Phonology seems justified simply because this particular theory, in all its various versions and with its ongoing revisions is widely accepted as the dominant approach to the analysis of human sound systems. The last two chapters are intended to provide a perspective of Chinese phonological structure, as it has been outlined in the first two parts of this essay, which lies outside a strictly generative frame of reference.

Chapter 13 explores the appropriateness of three interesting alternatives to standard generative theory as possible theoretical models for analyzing the Chinese sound system.

In examining these three approaches, Autosegmental, Prosodic
and what I have termed 'non-synchronic,' the thesis put forward is that while each of the three provides partial solutions to the inadequacies of the more standard Generative
treatment, each also has serious problems when applied to
Chinese. Particularly, as useful models of surface phonetic
structure, Autosegmental and Prosodic theory are seen as too
abstract whereas 'non-synchronized' phonology is, conversely,
too concrete.

Chapter 14 is at once a logical extension of - and yet
radical departure from - the rest of this work. As an extension, the aim of this chapter is to formulate what at
most could be considered a plausible framework for resolving
the inadequances of the theoretical approaches explored
earlier in a chapter-by-chapter fashion. As a departure
from the tenor of the earlier portions of this essay, the
final chapter is quite speculative and tentative. Thus, in
a sense, the final chapter is a rather natural conclusion
to what has come before but is likewise the sort of explora-
tory probing more characteristic of the starting point for
an entirely new line of inquiry.

More specifically, this chapter sketches an outline of
what I have called a 'polydimensional' perspective, an
attempt to formulate the groundwork for a more coherent

approach to providing a theoretical account not just of
Chinese but of the kind of segmental, prosodic and syllabic
integration presumably reflected in human languages generally.

Chapter Two

SYNTAGMATIC STRUCTURE: THE SYLLABLE AS SYNTAGM

2.1 The Syllable in Shanghai

A fruitful way to begin the discussion of the syllable
in Chinese is to examine the structure of the syllable within some specific Chinese language. Consider Tables 1 and 2.
These are respectively a phonetic and a phonemic syllabary
of the Shanghai dialect of Wu Chinese (see Appendix I for
background and phonetic details).

The Chinese syllable is traditionally divided into
an optional Initial (a consonant or "zero") and a Final,
which includes a tone, an optional medial glide, an obligatory nuclear vowel and an optional terminal offglide or consonant.[1] A "syllabary" then is simply a systematic way,
based on traditional Chinese phonological practice, of looking at the structure of the Chinese syllable.

Each form in these tables is also the representation
of a morpheme since for the most part Chinese morphemes are

----
1. In addition to this traditional division, many modern
dialects have syllables consisting of one consonantal segment, such as syllabic m or ṇ. These are identified in
Table 1 as having "zero final." In Table 2 these syllables
and several others are identified simply as "syllabic."

-19-

monosyllabic. For the present, I shall not try to "define" the syllable but shall state that probably all linguists working in Chinese phonology assume the existence of such a unit. For practical purposes, one can assume that it is the smallest tone-bearing unit in the language. A characterization of the syllable will be given in sec. 2.5 below.

The "phonemic" syllabary (Table 2) is based on an analysis of the data in the phonetic syllabary (Table 1). Since there is no significant segmental morphophonemic alternation in Shanghai, the phonemic analysis is based largely on distributional factors. In any case, this particular analysis is not relevant to the present discussion - it is simply presented as a given. In generative terms since the phonetic syllabary represents surface phenomena, the phonemic syllabary would correspond to the systematic phonemic level. Unless otherwise stated, I will use the terms "phonemic" and "phoneme" to refer to the underlying level of representation and the units there regardless of whether these terms are taken in the generative or structuralist sense.

In addition to the segmental information given in Tables 1 and 2, each syllable in the syllabaries would have one of the following five tones:

-21-

TABLE 1

The Phonetic Syllabary of Shanghai
Finals

Initials	·ɿ	ɿ	ʮ	·i	ʅ	ːo	o	a	ia	ua	ɿ	uɿ	o	ue	ɤ	iɤ	ɔ	iɔ
p				X	X	X	X	X			X		X				X	X
p'				X	X	X		X			X		X				X	X
b				X	X	X	X	X			X		X				X	X
t				X	X	X		X			X		X		X	X	X	X
t'				X	X	X		X			X		X		X		X	X
d				X	X	X					X		X				X	X
ts	X	X		X	X	X	X	X	X		X				X		X	X
ts'	X			X	X	X	X	X			X				X		X	
k					X	X	X	X		X	X	X		X	X		X	
k'					X	X	X	X		X	X		X	X	X		X	
g								X				X		X			X	
h					X	X	X	X		X	X			X	X		X	
ɦ		X		X	X	X	X	X	X	X	X	X		X			X	X
tɕ		X	X	X				X								X		X
tɕ'		X	X	X												X		X
dʑ		X	X	X												X		X
ɕ		X	X	X												X		X
s	X	X		X	X	X	X	X	X		X		X		X		X	X
z	X	X		X	X	X	X	X	X		X				X		X	X
f				X	X						X				X			
v				X	X						X				X			
m		X		X	X	X	X	X			X		X		X		X	X
n				X	X	X	X	X			X		X			X	X	
ñ		X	X	X												X		X
ŋ				X	X	X	X				X				X		X	
l		X		X	X	X					X		X		X	X	X	
ʔ		X	X	X	X	X	X	X	X		X	X		X	X		X	X

TABLE 1 (Con't)

The Phonetic Syllabary of Shanghai
Finals

Initials	ʔa	iã	ʔɒ	uɒ̃	iŋ	oŋ	uəŋ	oŋ	ioŋ	aʔ	iaʔ	uaʔ	əʔ	iɕʔ	uəʔ	oʔ	ioʔ	zero
p			X		X	X				X			X	X		X		
p'			X		X	X		X		X			X	X				
b	X		X		X	X		X		X			X	X		X		
t	X		X		X	X		X					X	X				
t'			X		X	X		X		X			X	X		X		
d			X		X	X		X		X			X	X		X		
ts	X	X	X		X	X		X		X			X	X		X		
ts'	X	X	X		X	X		X		X	X		X	X		X		
k	X		X	X		X	X	X		X		X	X		X	X		
k'				X	X		X	X	X		X		X			X	X	
g				X				X										
h			X	X		X	X	X		X		X	X		X			
ɦ		X	X	X	X	X	X	X	X	X	X	X	X	X	X	X	X	
tɕ		X			X				X		X			X			X	
tɕ'		X			X						X			X			X	
dʑ		X			X				X					X			X	
ɕ		X			X				X					X			X	
s	X	X	X		X	X		X		X	X		X	X		X		
z	X	X	X		X	X		X		X	X		X	X		X		
f			X			X		X		X			X			X		
v			X			X		X		X		X	X			X		
m	X		X		X	X		X		X			X	X		X		X
n			X			X		X					X					
ɲ		X			X				X		X			X			X	
ŋ	X		X							X						X		
l	X	X	X		X	X		X		X	X		X	X		X		X
ʔ		X		X	X	X	X	X	X	X	X	X		X		X		

TABLE 2
The Phonological Syllabary of Shanghai
Finals

Initials

	:ɿ	:ʮ	ɿ	ɹ	:o	o	ɑ	iɑ	uɑ	ʅ	uɛ	ɵ	ue	ø	ei	ɔ	iɔ	ã
p			X	X	X	X	X			X		X					X	X	
p'			X	X	X		X			X		X					X	X	
b			X	X	X	X	X			X		X					X	X	X
t			X	X	X		X			X		X		X	X	X	X	X
t'			X	X	X		X			X		X		X		X	X	
d			X	X	X					X		X				X	X	
ts	X		X	X	X	X	X	X		X				X		X	X	X
ts'			X	X	X	X	X			X				X		X		X
k	X	X	X	X	X	X	X	X	X	X	X		X	X	X	X	X	X
k'	X	X	X	X	X	X	X		X	X		X	X	X	X	X	X	
g	X	X	X				X				X		X		X	X	X	
x	X	X	X	X	X	X	X	X		X	X		X	X	X	X	X	
ɦ	X		X	X	X	X	X	X	X	X	X		X			X	X	
s	X		X	X	X	X	X	X		X		X		X		X	X	X
z	X		X	X	X	X	X	X		X		X		X		X	X	X
f			X	X						X				X				
v			X	X						X				X				
m	X		X	X	X	X	X			X		X		X		X	X	X
n			X	X	X	X	X			X		X				X		
ŋ	X	X	X		X	X	X			X				X	X	X	X	X
l	X		X	X	X					X		X		X	X	X		X
ʔ	X	X	X	X	X	X	X	X		X	X		X	X		X	X	

TABLE 2 (Con't)

The Phonological Syllabary of Shanghai
Finals

Initials	iaŋ	ɑ̃	ɤn	iŋ	ɤe	ɤen	oŋ	ioŋ	aʔ	iaʔ	uaʔ	əʔ	ieʔ	ueʔ	oʔ	ioʔ	Sylla-bic
p		X		X	X				X			X	X		X		
p'		X		X	X		X		X			X	X				
b		X		X	X		X		X			X	X		X		
t		X		X	X		X					X	X				
t'		X		X	X		X		X			X	X		X		
d		X		X	X		X		X			X	X		X		
ts	X	X		X	X		X		X			X	X		X		X
ts'	X	X		X	X		X		X	X		X	X		X		X
k	X	X	X	X	X	X	X	X	X	X	X	X	X	X	X	X	
k'	X	X	X	X	X	X	X		X	X		X	X	X	X	X	
g	X		X	X			X	X					X			X	
x	X	X	X	X	X	X	X	X	X		X	X	X	X		X	
ɦ	X	X	X	X	X	X	X	X	X	X	X	X	X	X	X	X	
s	X	X		X	X		X		X	X		X	X		X		X
z	X	X		X	X		X		X	X		X	X		X		X
f		X			X		X		X						X		
v		X			X		X		X			X			X		
m		X		X	X		X		X			X	X		X		X
n		X			X		X					X					
ŋ	X	X		X				X	X	X			X		X	X	X
l	X	X		X	X		X		X	X		X	X		X		
ʔ			X	X	X	X	X	X	X	X	X		X		X		

Tone	Contour	Description
1	53	High Falling
2	34	Mid Rising
3	14	Low Rising
4	5	High Level (Short)
5	2	Low Level (Short)

Restricting our attention to the segmental aspects of the syllable in the phonemic syllabary, a number of observations can be made about the arrangements of phonemes into syllables. To begin with, it is obvious that syllables may have one of the following basic five shapes:

(1)	#C#	#ŋ# (Tone 3)	"fish"
(2)	#CV#	#mi# (Tone 3)	"uncooked rice"
(3)	#CVV#	#hue# (Tone 3)	"great, heroic"
(4)	#CVC#	#loʔ# (Tone 5)	"sex"
(5)	#CVVC#	#xuaŋ# (Tone 1)	"marriage"

This, of course, presupposes an analysis in which syllable-initial glottal stop has been considered a phoneme; otherwise, based on distributional criteria it would be possible to consider all such syllables as having a "zero initial" - i.e. no initial. In such a case, then, there would also be a syllable type #V#. There are arguments pro and con for the various analyses but I will not enter into this problem here since it is ultimately not important to the discussion.

Given these syllable shapes, it is possible to formulate the first generalization regarding Shanghai syllable structure: the overall phonological structure of the syllable can be characterized as particular arrangements of two classes of sounds, consonants (contoids) and vowels (vocoids); the number of syllable types based on this classification will be small. One way of formulating this generalization is with a canonical shape formula:

$$\#C((V)V(C))\#$$

An examination of Tables 1 and 2 reveal that an even more explicit formula can be given as:

$$\#C\left(\left(\left\{ \begin{matrix} i \\ u \end{matrix} \right\}\right) V \left(\left\{ \begin{matrix} ? \\ \eta \end{matrix} \right\}\right)\right)\#$$

Beyond this, further analysis will show that there are additional patterns in terms of the sequences of particular consonants and vowels. For instance, in any CVV(C) sequence, if the first vowel is /u/, then the second vowel must be non-high and non-round, that is, the second vowel must be of the class /a, e, E, ə/. This means that sequences such as /Cua?/, /Cuaŋ/, /Cue/, /CuE/, /Cuəŋ/ (where C = Consonant) are permissible whereas sequences such as */Cui/, */Cuu/, */Cuɔ/, */Cuo/, */Cuö/ and */Cuü/ are not permissible. Other restrictions will apply between certain vowels and the final consonants /ŋ/ and /?/, some will apply between the initial consonant and the following vowel, etc. (see Walton 1971: 88 for additional examples). Such facts of patterning can be summarized as the second generalization on Shanghai syllable structure: the phonemes of Shanghai do not pattern in a random sequential order; there are definite constraints on sequential patterning. This then would cover the fact that certain syllable types are impossible, others occur as morphemes and still others are possible but do not occur as morphemes (i.e. they are "accidental gaps").

Another interesting aspect of the Shanghai syllable is the tremendous imbalance between the number of consonants which can occur in syllable-initial position (twenty-two) and in syllable-terminal position (only two, /?/ and /ŋ/). In fact, the data from Table 1 shows that phonetically /aŋ / and /ɔŋ / are realized as [ã] and [ɔ̃]. This indicates that, if anything, there is a tendency towards even more reduction of syllables ending in a final nasal - thereby creating even more imbalance between the number of consonants occurring in syllable initial and terminal positions.

This leads to a third generalization with respect to Shanghai syllable structure: there is an extreme imbalance in the structure of the syllable in terms of initial and terminal consonants, and the tendency seems to be toward even more imbalance.

Finally, let us examine Table 2 to see if any particular relationships hold among the phonemes which make up the syllable. Another way of phrasing this is to ask if

there are any patterns of bonding between contiguous segments.
As the structure of the syllabary itself indicates, the least
amount of bonding occurs between the initial consonant and
the following segment, be it onglide or nuclear vowel. This
is not to say that there are not some obvious bonds between
the initial and post-initial segments. For example, the
medial /u/ is only preceded by velar and glottal consonants.
Nevertheless, structurally speaking, if one were to make a
break in the syllable in terms of paradigmatic substitution,
it is obvious that the most likely break would be between
the Initial and the rest of the syllable, the Final. Let
us examine some Shanghai finals:

	a	E	e	ə	ɔ		
	ia			iə	iɔ		
	ua	uE	ue				

	aŋ	ɔŋ	əŋ	oŋ	a?	ɘ?	o?
iŋ	iaŋ	iɔŋ		ioŋ	ia?	iə?	io?
			uəŋ		ua?	uə?	

These finals have been arranged so that the patterning is
more obvious. It seems quite clear that if one were to analyze these finals in terms of structural patterning, that is,
in terms of the paradigmatic substitutability of the various
elements, the pure vowels /a, E, e, ə, ɔ / would be seen as
isolatable and independent. Likewise in the closed syllables /a/, /o/ and /ə/ would be isolatable since they occur
before either /ŋ/ or /?/. Furthermore, these same vowels

plus /ɔ/ can also stand alone. In three segment combinations,
other aspects of bonding can be seen. The groups /aŋ, ɔŋ,
əŋ, oŋ, aʔ, əʔ, oʔ/ can also stand alone so that they too
are isolatable as units within three segment sequences.
Furthermore, /i/ and /u/ are isolatable since they are the
only segments which can occur initially in three segment finals. Suppose these facts could be diagrammed as follows
for the syllable /liaŋ/:

#liaŋ#

where the longer the line, the looser the bonding between
successive elements. These observations lead to the conclusion that in speaking of the structure of the syllable, it
is clear that the syllable is not simply a linear arrangement of C's and V's nor even of particular C's and V's.
Rather, the segments within syllables enter into relationships with one another such that sub-groupings exist. That
is, the syllable is not simply a linear sequence of segments
such as

#l│i│a│ŋ#

where each segment of the segments has equal status with regard to every other segment and to the overall structure
of the syllable. Instead, the segments bond in various
arrangements. Thus /liaŋ/ might be represented like this:

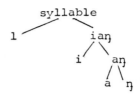

This aspect of phonological structure leads to the final generalization concerning Chinese syllable structure: sub-syllabic segments enter into various structural relationships with one another; the linear sequential notions "comes before", "comes after" are not adequate to express these relationships.

2.2 The Syllable in Chinese Languages

The four generalizations on syllable structure arrived at in the above discussion do not apply simply to Shanghai but to all Chinese languages.

The first claim is that the syllables of any Chinese language can be grouped into a small set of syllable types based on the various possible arrangements of consonants and vowels. That is, such a statement of "canonical shape" defines a set which characterizes all and only the well-formed syllables of the language. Among other things, such a statement gives the size, in terms of segments, of the smallest syllable and the maximum syllable.

The second claim is that in any Chinese language

there will be restrictions on the sequences of particular consonants and vowels such that only a small number of the total
possible combinations will occur.

These two claims are rather straightforward and uncon-
troversial. Analyses of various Chinese languages typically
include canonical shape formulae - this is true of both structural and generative descriptions. One can only conclude
that such formulae are included because they make certain
structural facts about the syllable more explicit.

The restrictions on sequential combinations are likewise normally considered an integral part of Chinese language
descriptions. In structural phonemic studies, such restrictions on the sequences of phonemes were often restricted to
stating the possible combinations of Initials with Finals in
the form of a syllabary. Such syllabaries then revealed
which initials may occur with which Finals. Within generative studies of Chinese languages such constraints have been
stated in terms of morpheme structure rules and morpheme
structure conditions (see Walton 1971 for a survey of these
notions applied to Chinese). Within both approaches such
statements on the constraints of segments define the notions
"occurring" form, "admissible but not occurring" form ("accidental gap") and "inadmissible" form.

The third claim is that there exists a significant imbalance in the number of consonants which can occur in sylla-

ble-initial position as opposed to syllable-final position.
Examination of a number of Chinese languages and dialects, as
well as a brief examination of certain historical facts will
allow us to refine this claim somewhat.

Consider Table 3. It is quite obvious that not only
are there very few consonants that can occur in terminal position, these are moreover restricted to a very small class:
m̱, ṉ, ŋ̱, p̱, ṯ, ḵ, ʔ.[2]

Historical evidence suggests that the system of terminal consonants was at one time much richer. Moreover, the
disappearance of the terminal consonants has been steady and
systematic in many languages since Middle Chinese times (ca.
600 A.D.). Chen (1973) has outlined the schedule of attrition of these terminal consonants. The Middle Chinese end-
ings [-p, -t, -k] first went to two consonants then to one,
then to glottal stop and then disappeared leaving a short
preceding vowel which eventually lengthened. Parallel to
this [m, n, ŋ] went to two, then one, then to a weak nasal
ending. The next step was complete loss of the weak nasal
ending with nasalization of the preceding vowel and finally

----
2. The data in Table 3 is drawn from Hanyu Fangyan Cihui
(1964). Professor Bodman (personal communication) would
analyze the Min dialects somewhat differently. Nevertheless, these other analyses would not significantly
alter the thrust of the argument being made here.

TABLE 3

Consonant Distribution in Chinese Languages

Language	Dialect	Number of Initial Cons.	Number of Terminal Cons.	Consonants
Mandarin	Peking	21	2	n, ŋ
	Jinan	23	1	ŋ
	Xi-an	26	1	ŋ
	Taiyuan	20	2	ŋ, ʔ
	Hankou	18	2	n, ŋ
	Chengdu	20	2	n, ŋ
	Yangzhou	17	2	n, ŋ
Wu	Suzhou	26	3	n, ŋ, ʔ
	Wenzhou	27	1	ŋ
Xiang	Changsha	22	2	n, ŋ
	Shuangfeng	27	2	n, ŋ
Gan	Nanchang	18	4	n, ŋ, t, k
Hakka	Meixian	18	6	m, n, ŋ, p, t, k
Cantonese	Guangzhou	19	6	m, n, ŋ, p, t, k
S. Min	Amoy	18	6	m, n, ŋ, p, t, k
	Chaozhou	18	3	ŋ, ʔ, k
N. Min	Fuzhow	14	2	ŋ, ʔ

denasalization of the vowel.

Thus, Table 3 not only confirms the family-wide initial-terminal imbalance in syllable structure, but also reflects an ongoing diachronic process of syllable-terminal consonant attrition which continues to increase this imbalance.

The fourth generalization is that within the syllable in all Chinese languages the relationship between consonants and vowels is not simply linear - there are sub-syllabic relationships of various sorts holding between these elements. Let us consider the traditional Chinese analysis of the syllable as given below.

Tone			
Initial	Final		
	Medial	Rime	
		Nucleus	Ending

Table 4 - The Chinese Syllable

Such an analysis of the syllable can be termed "hierarchical" as opposed to linear. Each "cut" shows the natural bonding tendencies of the syllable.

Light (1973) has argued that these various types of subsyllabic bonding reflect important typological facts -

both in comparing Chinese with other languages and in comparing Chinese languages and dialects with one another.

In particular, Light demonstrated that the traditional concept of the Rime in Table 4 must be incorporated as a coherent, single unit within any phonological theory characterizing Cantonese and perhaps, to some extent, in characterizing other Chinese languages as well.

In any case, this traditional, hierarchical concept of the Chinese syllable is still followed implicitly if not explicitly in most modern analyses, structural and generative, of various Chinese languages. For example, in Cheng's (1973: 11) recent generative analysis of Mandarin phonological structure he cites just this conception of the syllable as applicable to Mandarin.

2.3 The Syntagmatic Dimension

The four generalizations formulated in 2.1 for Shanghai and expanded in 2.2 for all Chinese languages can be briefly summarized as follows:

(i) The basic syllable structure of Chinese languages is most explicitly stated by the possible arrangements of consonants and vowels

(ii) given (i), there will be further constraints on the possible concatenations of specific segments within the syllable.

(iii) there exists a systematic imbalance in the structure of syllables such that many more consonants occur
in initial than in terminal position; this imbalance
seems to be part of an ongoing process.

(iv) the syllable in all Chinese languages has a hierarchical structure reflected by the tendency of subsyllabic segments to bond into various configurations.

These four generalizations are all concerned with one
specific aspect of phonological analysis - the sequential arrangement of segments. That is, statements (i)-(iv) are not
directly concerned with establishing the correct set of phonemes, nor with allophonic variation nor with morphophonemic
alternation. Rather, such statements are concerned with the
various configurations which such units as autonomous and
systematic phonemes enter into after they have been established.

Another way of viewing such statements is to say that
they are concerned with the syntagmatic dimension of phonological analysis rather than with the paradigmatic dimension.
However, even this claim must be clarified: such statements
as (i)-(iv), at least as presently formulated, are concerned
with the syntagmatic dimension of the underlying level of
representation, not the surface level. Thus, such statements
concern themselves with the syntagmatic patterning of under-

lying phonemes rather than surface segments.

In any phonological analysis there exists two syntagmatic planes - one phonetic and one phonological (or phonemic). Although this distinction is critical, it seems to me that it has not always been made clear and this has resulted in some confusion. Before exploring the theoretical nature of statements (i)-(iv) above, it will therefore be necessary to discuss the notion "syntagmatic."

The concepts "paradigmatic" and "syntagmatic" have long been a part of linguistic theory, having been first introduced in modern form by Saussure (1949) as "associative" and "syntagmatic." These terms have been defined and elaborated upon at length in linguistic theory. For the discussion here, I will simply give two capsule definitions taken from current handbooks. The first is from Lyons (1968: 73):

> By virtue of its potentiality of occurrence in a certain context a linguistic unit enters into relations of two different kinds. It enters into <u>paradigmatic</u> relations with all units which can also occur in the same context (whether they contrast or are in free variation with the unit in question); and it enters into syntagmatic relations with the other units of the same level with which it occurs and which constitute its context.

Robins (1964: 48-49) gives a similar definition:

> Essentially the relations between linguistic ele-
> ments are of two kinds or dimensions, usually
> designated syntagmatic and paradigmatic. <u>Syn-
> tagmatic</u> relations are those holding between ele-
> ments forming serial structures at a given level,
> referable to, though of course not identical with,
> the temporal flow utterances of linear stretches of
> writing.
>
> Paradigmatic relations are those holding between
> comparable elements at particular places in struc-
> tures... and more generally between the comparable
> elements of structures in classes (e.g. consonants,
> verbs) or in the language as a whole (e.g. phonemes
> (phonological elements), word classes ('parts of
> speech')).

In these definitions, it is clear that it is theoretically

impossible for one dimension, e.g. the paradigmatic, to have

some sort of precedence over the other dimension vis-a-vis

arriving at the units of a phonological description. The

two dimensions apply, as it were, simultaneously:

> The point is, therefore, that one cannot first esta-
> blish the elements and then state their permissible
> combinations. The elements are determined by taking
> account simultaneously of their paradigmatic and
> syntagmatic relations (Lyons 1968: 75).

Yet, if this statement is true, then both structural phonemic

and generative theories of phonology directly violate it.

The entire notion of "phonotactics" in structural phonemics

and the entire area of morpheme structure rules and condi-

tions in generative theory is exactly to state the permissi-

ble combinations of phonemes which have <u>already</u> been esta-

blished.

It would seem that Lyons' statement is concerned with
the role of the syntagmatic plane in <u>determining</u> elements
whereas phonotactics and morpheme structure rules are concerned with the arrangement of previously determined units
within the syntagmatic plane.

The confusion resolves itself once the notion of levels
is introduced. There are two syntagmatic planes. At the
phonetic level, the intersection of the syntagmatic and paradigmatic dimensions results in the postulation of phonemic
(or phonological) units. At the phonemic (or phonological)
level, the syntagmatic dimension characterizes the possible
sequential arrangements of these postulated units.

Given this distinction, consider the following statement by Light:

> While the existence of both syntagmatic and paradig-
> matic planes is generally accepted in linguistic
> thought, in American theory, little attention has
> in fact been given to the syntagmatic plane. Our
> fundamental units in both generative and structural-
> ist linguistics are entirely paradigmatic.
> (Light 1974: 12-13)

Light's statement is, I believe, in error without some quali-
fication. It is quite easy to demonstrate that American
theory devoted a tremendous amount of attention to the syntagmatic dimension, <u>but at the phonetic level</u>. The units
of the autonomous phonemic level, for example, are postulated
in part with regard to the distributional patterning, i.e.

syntagmatic patterning of phones. However, it is true that the same approach was not terribly concerned with syntagmatic patterning <u>at the phonemic level</u>: phonotactic statements on the sequences of phonemes seem to have been considered much less important than formulation of the phonemes themselves.

The distinction established here between the phonetic syn- tagmatic plane and the phonological syntagmatic plane will be important in the following discussion of the notion "syn- tagm" and with respect to some major revisions being cur- rently proposed in generative theory (discussed in Chapters 5 and 6).

2.4 The Syntagm and the Syllable

In the preceding section, it was argued that the statements (i)-(iv) on Chinese phonological structure are concerned with the syntagmatic dimension of linguistic anal- ysis. Moreover, stated in their present form, these struc- tural generalizations refer to the phonemic plane not the phonetic plane. That is, such generalizations are concerned with the arrangement and patterning of phonemes.

In phonological theory, it has long been implicit that the combinations of phonemes within higher-order units is not random. Moreover, I believe it is safe to assume that the highest order unit within which sequential patterning is considered significant is the "word." That is, phonologi-

cal theory normally assumes that the sequential concatena-
tion of phonemes across word boundaries is random. Likewise, it would seem an implicit assumption that the smallest
unit within which sequential patterning is significant is
the syllable. Still another unit commonly cited with respect
to phonemic patterning is the morpheme, especially in generative theory.

This does not mean, however, that in a particular
language phonemic patterning within the word or morpheme must
be significant, only that it may be. One could argue, as I
shall, that phonemic patterning is never random within the
syllable but of course, this presupposes some rather clear
notion of what a syllable is. If we assume that the syntagmatic patterning of phonological units in a language is random beyond a certain sized unit (e.g. is random in the phrase
or the sentence) and yet constrained below this unit, then
we need some cover term for the unit. Rather than make use
of notions such as syllable, word, or morpheme, let us call
the unit a _syntagm_. This term is borrowed from Malmberg:

> We must now turn our attention to the chains of
> phonemic units which occur in utterances and which
> in turn, suppose the existence of models or
> patterns of sequence here labeled _syntagms_. The
> structure of the syntagm consequently is the
> distribution, that is, the selection and arrangement,
> of the phonemic units within it. This kind of
> structure like the paradigmatic one, has both
> general and specific aspects. There are certain
> features which appear to be general in human lan-
> guages, and which we may thus take as fundamental

to their structure. But any syntagmatic system,
as a whole, is characteristic of and specific to,
a particular language (Malmberg 1970: 209)

The syntagm then is a "unit" but it is a unit of structure and of variable "size." It is not tied directly to any
one such notion as word, syllable or morpheme. It might
correspond in some one language to any of these notions or
to all of them. Within one language it might correspond to
one or several of these units at various levels of analysis.
Thus, the syntagm is a relativistic notion; it characterizes
all units within which significant syntagmatic patterning
occurs.

2.5 The Syllable

It has now been established that the generalizations
on Chinese phonological structure (i)-(iv) apply to the syntagmatic pattern of phonological (phonemic) units and it has
been assumed that these generalizations apply within a unit
of phonological structure termed the syllable. We are now
in a position to discuss the status of this unit in phonological theory.

The approach of the present work is to treat the syllable as a syntagm - a structural unit of syntagmatic patterning. As such, it is not directly tied to the physical unit
"syllable". Phrased in this manner, the syllable is taken

as a theoretical construct in phonological theory. As such, it manifests all those characteristics that accrue to a construct in any scientific theory. For example, constructs may defy precise definition and may not be directly observable. On the other hand, they are not completely abstract and arbitrary; they must be justified.

This approach to the syllable seems not only desirable, as I shall argue below, but also inevitable. All precise, universal, physical definitions of the syllable have ultimately failed. As Pulgram (1970) has discussed, scholarly research on the syllable in the past has been focused almost exclusively on the phonetic properties - acoustic and physiological - of the syllable.

> Thus we find attempts to define and bound the syllable by means of vocal sonority (Jesperson), articulatory opening of the vocal tract (de Saussure), physiological tenseness and laxness of the speech organs (Grammont), thoracic pressure (Peterson), chest pulses induced by muscular activity (Stetson, Durand), voice (Rosetti). The choice of such parameters makes the syllable not a functional, linguistically pertinent unit, but a physical one (Pulgram 1970: 17).

Pulgram's own point of view is that the search for the physical syllable should follow from a linguistic definition of the syllable rather than vice-versa. This approach, as noted above, seems desirable since it follows the usual canons of scientific inquiry - physical data or "facts" are data or facts only in terms of some higher level hypotheses - in this case linguistic ones.

The understanding of this physical-phonological dichotomy is critical in the present essay since there still
seems to be some doubt about operating with a unit which
"can't be defined."

Consider the following statement by Lyovin (1973) reviewing Kao's monograph <u>The Structure of the Syllable in
Cantonese</u>:

> Her claim (13) that 'the syllable in Cantonese is
> a basic phonological unit' is not supported by
> any formal arguments. Like most linguists work-
> ing on Chinese dialects, K probably considers such
> arguments to be superfluous; nevertheless, a clear
> statement of relevant factors motivating this claim
> would be of great theoretical interest, at least
> to those linguists who are not familiar with Can-
> tonese or other languages of the same phonological
> type.

Such comments tend to throw what seems to me quite unwarrant-
ed suspicions about any linguistic undertaking which purports
to treat the syllable as a central unit of analysis, description or even explanation. Is this unit to be defined,
defended and "supported" in every linguistic treatise which
must openly make use of it? There seems to be little agreement on any sort of precise definition of such notions as
segment, phone and allophone and yet these units are seldom
questioned with the sort of caution displayed in discussing
syllables. Even the most defined and redefined unit of American structural phonology - the phoneme - was never defined

with the sort of preciseness that so many investigators seem to require of the syllable.

There is, however, at least one plausible explanation as to why the syllable has been approached with a rigor qualitatively different from other phonological units. That explanation is that segment-sized units have an intuitive appeal to Western (Indo-European) linguists since they were raised, became literate and even learned their linguistics, all within an overwhelming pervasive alphabetic tradition. So much of Western phonological analysis has been - to no small degree - substituting more refined, sophisticated, scientifically motivated alphabetic symbols for the ones acquired as a part of the cultural heritage of the investigator.

To put it another way, it is conceivable that a Chinese or Japanese linguist uninfluenced by an alphabetic tradition would be much more prone to accept the syllable intuitively but would demand precise physical, acoustic, physiological definitions of those very units so readily accepted as imprecise givens in Western linguistics - such units as "segments" and "phones." There is some doubt as to whether satisfactory "definitions" could ever be given to the Chinese or Japanese linguists.

Thus, the lack of a precise, physical definition of the syllable has often led to a sort of linguistic schizophrenia in which investigators either use the syllable as a

unit but refuse to talk about it (e.g. Chomsky and Halle
(1968)), or recognize it formally but apologize for its scientifically nebulous nature in an otherwise rigorous investigation. I shall not in this paper attempt to defend or
"support" the notion syllable as a necessary linguistic unit.
If linguists are to use such concepts as "segment," "phone,"
"allophone," "phoneme," "morphophoneme" without total agreement on the definition and without unique physical, psychological, physiological, acoustic, neurological correlates,
then the only argument against formal adoption of the syllable as still another theoretical construct is that it is
unnecessary. To date, just the opposite seems true: the
syllable is critically necessary (see Anderson 1974 for
recent discussion; see also sec. 1.4 above).

For the applicability and necessity of the syllable
specifically in Chinese language analysis, Sherard (1972),
drawing on, among others, Sampson (1970), Andersons (1969),
Fudge (1969), Hoard (1971), Woo (1970), McCawley (1968),
Ladefoged (1967), Lehiste (1970), has summarized the cogent
arguments and rationale.

2.6 Summary

This chapter has been an attempt to present a number
of generalizations about the phonological structure of Chinese and then to explore the nature of these generalizations.

It turns out that such statements as (i)-(iv) above pertain to the syntagmatic dimension in phonological theory. Furthermore, the syntagmatic dimension is characterized by various patterns of sequence which can be termed syntagms. The particular syntagm which statements (i)-(iv) characterize is the syllable.

The present chapter has examined the underlying nature of such syntagmatic statements as (i)-(iv) as they apply directly to Chinese. To provide a broader theoretical perspective, the following chapter will be concerned with examining such generalizations as they apply to all languages.

Chapter Three

CONSTRAINTS ON SYNTAGMATIC STRUCTURE

3.1 Introduction

If the four generalizations on phonological syntagmatic structure formulated in the previous chapter are valid
linguistic generalizations, then we should expect of a theory
of phonology that it express them explicitly and adequately. If, moreover, these generalizations are simply reflec-
tive of four types of generalizations characteristic of the
structure of all languages, then we should be able·to reformulate the four generalizations as four requirements on phonological theory. The present chapter is concerned with reformulating the four generalizations characteristic of Chinese phonological structure into a set of four requirements
on phonological theory.

3.2 The Global Constraint on Syntagmatic Structure

The first generalization formulated as characteristic
of all Chinese languages concerns the explicit statement of
canonical shape. Actually, the statement of canonical shape
has a traditional place in phonological descriptions. Generally, canonical shape formulae have been presented as a

part of an analysis to reveal the canonical shape of morphemes (e.g. Nida 1949) or syllables or even words, even
though the status of such statements has always been rather
nebulous. Harms (1968: 86) in discussing certain problems
in generative theory has stated:

> In another sense the MS rules lie close to the tra-
> ditional concern for canonic forms of morphemes
> (c.f. Nida 1949: 65-66), <u>the motivation for which</u>
> <u>has never been clearly stated</u>. (Emphasis mine).

Within generative theory, this "traditional concern for canonic form" has become increasingly important. The theory
of morpheme structure (MS) rules and MS conditions are very
closely tied to formulating this canonic form and the Positive Condition (Stanley 1967) is an attempt to express it
formally and integrate it into the phonological component.

Moreover, the theory of markedness has also tried to
capture such generalizations. In fact, the very first four
marking conventions suggested by Chomsky and Halle (1968:
408) concern canonical shape and are seen as somehow
different from the other marking conventions:

> Conventions (I)-(IV), which express the universal
> constraints on syllable structure, thus differ from
> the other marking conventions not only in content
> but also in the principles governing their applica-
> tion (Chomsky and Halle 1968: 408).

There are three observations which can be made with respect

to informal canonical shape statements regardless of whether they are stated within structuralist or generative theories. First, such statements deal only with the major categories Consonant and Vowel.[1] Secondly, the syntagm for stating the arrangement for C's and V's ranges from syllable, to morpheme, to word. Thirdly, such canonical statements state the arrangements of C's and V's for the entire syntagm not simply the arrangements of C's and V's at the beginning, middle, and end of the syntagm. Thus, for instance, any such canonical statement gives the entire structure of the syntagm and moreover gives the possible varying lengths in terms of C's and V's (or segments) of the syntagm.

Let us say that a canonical shape statement is "global"[2] in its application, that is, it applies to the structure of the entire syntagm. Furthermore, such a statement represents a "constraint" on syntagmatic structure in that it states which arrangements are characteristic of the language and which are disallowed.

----

1. Liquids and glides are sometimes included in canonical shape statements, but these ultimately are interpretations of 'contoids' and 'vocoids', so the terms consonant and vowel still seem to underlie liquids and glides.

2. "Global" here is specifically restricted to syntagmatic structures; it is not to be confused with "global phonological rules" which are concerned with changing (mapping) paradigmatic units.

The above observations then lead to the first requirement on phonological theory: The Global Constraint requirement on syntagmatic structure. The essence of this requirement is simply that phonological theory should capture the
notion "canonical shape of syntagm."

3.3 Local Constraints on Syntagmatic Structure

In addition to providing canonical shape statements,
an inherent part of phonological analysis is to state restrictions on phoneme sequences - thus the phonotactics of
structuralist theories and the MS rules of generative theory.
These restrictions, too, are generally stated with reference
to some particular syntagm. In addition, the syntagm is
seen to consist of three positions - initial, medial, and
final - and phonetic constraints are stated in terms of these
positions. This notion of stating restrictions on phoneme
combinations in terms of "positions" has been standard practice in modern linguistics. In Language, Bloomfield states:

> ...the simplest way to describe the phonetic struc-
> ture of a language is to state which non-syllabic
> phonemes or groups of non-syllabic phonemes (clusters)
> appear in three possible positions; initial, before
> the first syllabic of an utterance; final, after
> the last syllabic of an utterance; and medial
> between syllabics. (p. 131).

Bloomfield refers to "utterance" but his examples make it
clear that his "utterance" is the word.

Trubetskoy (1971) unlike Bloomfield, states that before the combinatory rules for stating phoneme sequences can
be studied, the unit within which these combinations occur
must be determined. These he calls "frame units" (1971:
249) which will be either morphemes or words. Frame units
are then divided into "structural types" (249-250). Then,
the combination of phonemes in initial, medial and final positions of the structural types or frames (if frame and type
coincide) are to be stated.

Pike (1949) assumes a variety of units would be possible for stating phonotactic constraints. Pike (1949: 130)
admits that a complete statement of the distribution of the
phonemes of the language would be "too bulky" and concludes
that a minimum statement of phoneme distribution "should
include a presentation of those single consonant phonemes
which may occur at the ends of syllables, at the beginning
of syllables, at the end, beginnings and middle of utterances
(or words etc.)".

I cite these works because they seem representative
of the traditional approach to stating phoneme combinations.
Moreover, they bring out two important facts with respect
to phonotactics: (1) the syntagm is variable (syllable, word,
morpheme) and (2) constraints are stated in terms of the
three positions initial, medial and final.

Although these observations are based on more tradi-

-53-

such as initial or final. It simply states that English
syllables have this shape (among others). The fact that
/brIk/ and /blIk/ can occur in English while /bnIk/ cannot
is not captured by a global constraint. The initial cluster
*/bn-/ is not allowed in English. A local constraint is
necessary to allow initial clusters such as /br-/ and /bl-/
while disallowing */bn-/. Such a constraint is local in
that it pertains to syllable-initial position and that it is
context-sensitive, i.e., n is not allowed after b in initial
position but is allowed, for example, after s in initial position.

The second requirement on a phonological theory can
now be stated. A phonological theory must provide a mechanism for expressing local constraints on syntagmatic structure
such that impossible sequences of phonemes are not permitted.
Let us term this the Local Constraints Requirement on syntagmatic structure.

3.4 The Inherent Structure Requirement

The imbalance of syllable structure discussed with regard to Chinese languages and dialects - the differences in
the number of syllable-initial and syllable-final consonants
and the tendency for the latter to decay - can likewise be
considered a structural fact not just of Chinese syllables
but of syllables in all languages. If this is true, then

it is necessary that a phonological theory explicitly account for this structural fact.

Malmberg, in defining the syntagm (see Chapter 2) suggested that some facets of the structure of syntagms may be universal: "There are certain features of syntagmatic structure which appear to be general in human languages, and which we may thus take in this sense fundamental to their structure" (1970: 209).

The particular syntagm under study here is the syllable. Hooper (1973), citing previous work by Malmberg, has recently proposed a theory of syllable structure within the framework of "natural generative phonology" which makes use of the notions "consonantal strength" and "strength of syllable position."

A first premise in this approach to the syllable is that the syllable-initial position is "stronger" than the syllable final. "Strong" here means that segments in this position are more resistant to loss and thus, that more consonants can paradigmatically substitute here. Also, "strong" and "weak" refer to the ranking of consonants along a scale of sonority where the strongest consonant is the least vowel-like.

Hooper cites Jesperson and Saussure (from Malmberg 1963) as proposing that "sounds group themselves in a syllable according to their sonority or audibility" (p. 72). Both

of these linguists claimed that the most sonorous segments
occupied the nucleus of the syllable and working out from
this center, segments become less sonorant.

This leads Hooper to set up the following formula as
the inherent structure of the syllable (p. 73):

```
       MARGIN                  NUCLEUS               MARGIN
obst.   nasals liqds.   glides vowels glides liqds. nasals obst.
Least vowel-like          most vowel-like       Less vowel-
                                                      like
      STRONG                   WEAK              WEAK
```

Hooper gives a number of arguments as to why the syllable-initial position is stronger than the syllable final.
One explanation (Grammont, reported in Malmberg 1963) is
that the "beginning of the syllable is characterized by a
growing muscular tension in the voice-producing mechanism,
and after the nucleus, there is a decrease in tension"
(Hooper 1973: 73). Hooper reports that Malmberg sees a good
correlation with muscular tension and sonorous intensity.

Another argument that syllable-initial position is
stronger than syllable-final concerns the status of open
syllables. The argument can be summarized as follows:

> On a universal level, the CV syllable is the optimal
> syllable. There is no language which does not allow
> a type CV, and there are some languages which allow
> this type and no other. This means that a C in
> initial position is favored over a C in any other
> position, e.g., CCV or CVC, and that in initial posi-
> tion a C is favored over a V as in V or VC. It has
> also been observed that a CV syllable is the first

syllable type learned by children (Jakobson, 1968,
Jakobson and Halle 1956). (Hooper 1973: 75).

Still another reason for assuming this dichotomy of the syllable according to Hooper is the notion that phonological
processes known as "strengthening" occur only in syllable-
initial never in syllable second position. Thus, Hooper
points out that in English the aspirated [ph] occurs only
in syllable-initial position, e.g. [owphen] but never in second position after syllable initial /s/ as in [sp=in].

Furthermore, in English in syllable-final position
voiceless stops are optionally unreleased. Aspiration in
voiceless stops is obligatory only in syllable-initial position.

As additional proof of the strong-weak syllable distinction Hooper (p. 75), notes that it is more common for a
syllable final segment (presumably a consonant) to assimilate
to the following syllable's syllable-initial segment than
vice-versa. This unidirectional assimilation across syllable
boundaries can be seen as the strong position affecting the
preceding syllable's weak position.

The obvious diachronic evidence is that the same consonants are often lost in syllable final position but retained in syllable initial position. This can be seen as a corol-
lary of the more general diachronic process for languages to
favor open syllables (see Malmberg 1963, 1970). Thus, con-

sonants "weaken" and disappear in syllable-weak position.

Finally, Hooper stresses that the strong and weak consonantal positions are differentiated by the number of contrasts possible in each position. On this, Malmberg (1964 - a
source not cited by Hooper) is quite specific:

> In languages where closed syllables are possible it
> seems almost general that the number of oppositions is
> smaller and/or the number of combinations more reduced
> (the distribution more limited at the ends of the syl-
> lables). In any case, a system is never richer in
> syllable-final positions. I do not know of any lan-
> guage which admits more distinctive possibilities at
> the end of syllables than in initial position (Malm-
> berg 1964: 404)

There is another important factor of syllable final
weakening about which I can find no discussion in Hooper's
work. This concerns a type of "information theory" approach to
sequences of sounds. It is true that while this approach en-
joyed a period of popularity in linguistics it has now been
largely abandoned. Nevertheless in seeking to _explain_ why syllables have different properties with respect to their initial
and final positions, every possibility must be examined.

In speaking of "phonetic reductions" in Scandinavian
languages, German, and Spanish, Malmberg states:

> The stability of a phonetic - or more generally a lin-
> guistic unit - element is inversely proportional to its
> amount of information. The more predictable the less
> resistant. The least predictable of the elements in a
> chain is, of course, its first phoneme, since nothing
> can make us guess its character (unless the non-ling-
> uistic context strongly limits our choice). Already,

the second is to some extent signalled by the first, a vowel by the color of the preceding consonant, a consonant by different combinatory phenomena (forment transitions, etc.), by distributional rules, etc. (1964: 406).

Pulgram (1970) in the same vein has remarked:

In particular, it has repeatedly been suggested that the final phonemic portions of a morpheme carry less information than do its initial ones, and that they are therefore more subject to synchronic slurring and to diachronic change, especially loss. (Pulgram 1970: 72).

Scholes (1966) citing an earlier study on English which concluded that the redundancy is greatest in utterance final position, states:

In American English it is generally true that one can slur the ends of most words (and even sentences) without losing the message; whereas the articulation of the initial parts of words (and sentences) is not so easily thrown away and is thus apparently more crucial to the message identification. (Scholes 1966: 71).

Obviously, since words and morphemes in many languages can also be syllables, this information-theory approach has some application to the structure of the syllable. And, indeed, it is possible that even in polysyllabic utterances, the syllable-initial "carries more information" than the syllable-final.

I will not pursue this information-theory approach in this essay; however I believe that it should be considered at some point in a complete theory of the structural syllable.

In addition to the notions of strong and weak syllable position, Hooper's formulations rely on the notion "con-

sonantal strength." Hooper attempts to set this up as a
scalar feature. By giving acoustic and articulatory phonetic
evidence and by examining synchronic and diachronic phonological evidence, she arrives at the following universal strength
hierarchy of consonants where 6 is the strongest (Hooper 1973:
81):

			voiced	vl. continuant	
glides	liquids	nasals	continuant	voiced stop	vl. stop
1	2	3	4	5	6

Hooper admits that this formulation is very tentative since
voiceless continuants and voiced stops cannot be ranked with
respect to one another and since affricates are not ranked.
Later she encounters more problems in trying to place s in
the scheme.

My own feeling is that there is indeed some sort of
phenomenon at work here - perhaps "strength" will ultimately
not be the proper term or even the proper conceptual category
for describing it. Furthermore, it is quite obvious that
strength hierarchies are still fraught with problems and probably will remain so until the concept has undergone a great
deal of refinement. I agree with Hooper, however, in viewing
strength as a theoretical construct connected with physical
reality but abstract nevertheless (Hooper 1973: 73).

Given Hooper's rather convincing arguments about the
universal nature of some facets of syllable structure, it
would seem clear that the peculiarities of the syllable-

initial and syllable-final consonants of the Chinese syllable are characteristic of the syllable in all languages.
We can thus formulate the generalization on Chinese syllable
structure as a universal requirement on phonological structure.   Let us term this the Inherent Structure Requirement
on syntagmatic structure.[3]

3.5   The Constituent Structure Requirement

3.5.1   Constituent Structure of the Chinese Syllable

The final generalization postulated in the preceding
chapter was that the syllables in all Chinese languages
have a hierarchical constituent structure characterized by
the bonding of subsyllabic segments into various configurations.

Light (1974) drawing on Pike and Pike (1947) and Hockett (1955) has recently argued for treating the Chinese syllable in terms of constituent structure.   Light was concerned
with treating various subsyllabic portions as coherent units.
In particular, Light seems concerned with taking the traditional Chinese syllable division notions Initial, Medial,

----

3.   This requirement is worded so that it could be refined
to apply to other syntagms such as words or morphemes (if
these can be considered syntagms).   That is, for example,
"words" may also have an inherent structure, especially in
that they are made up of syllables which do seem to have an
inherent structure.

Final, Rime and giving them a phonological status other than
simply "phonemes."

Moreover, Light, in line with Hockett (1955) has suggested that the notion "constituent structure of syllable"
applies to all languages, not simply Chinese.

Light (1974) has presented the cogent arguments for
analyzing the Chinese syllable in terms of constituent structure. In the present essay, I should like to explore Hockett's notion of constituent structure in more detail than
Light and ultimately to propose that this notion be incorporated within phonological theory in a way different than
that proposed by Light.

3.5.2 Hockett's Conception of Syllable Structure

Hockett never "defines" the syllable other than as a
structural unit:

> In every known language, a macrosegment consists of
> one or more smaller structural units to which, by
> a generalization of its meaning, we shall assign
> the term syllable. It is not to be assumed that
> "syllables" in all languages are comparable to those
> of English - or to what are usually interpreted as
> syllables in English. In our generalized sense of
> the term, it will turn out that the so-called syl-
> lables of English indeed conform to the broader
> definition, but in other languages, we will find
> strikingly different units which also conform to
> the definition (Hockett 1955: 51).

The key concept in Hockett's structural syllable is "consti-

tuent costructure." Indeed, this is the entire approach to
phonology in Hockett's Manual of Phonology. The smallest
units in any language are ultimate phonologic constituents
"...each one a 'target-area' of articulatory motion, such
that any utterance in the language, long or short, consists
of some arrangement of elements selected from the stock"
(p. 43). This stock of units, claims Hockett, will be found
as a result of phonologic analysis and will be small (p.
42-43). However, it is the arrangement of these units that
is important.

> Ultimate phonologic constituents do not occur in
> an utterance as the individual bricks occur in
> a row of bricks. Rather, they occur in clusterings,
> these occur in still larger clusterings, and so
> on, up to the level of the whole utterance. That
> is, the phonologic structure of an utterance
> shows a hierarchic organization, involving units
> of various relative size-levels: the units at any
> size-level save the smallest consist of arrangements
> of units of the next smaller size-level. (1955: 43).

A syllable, then, consists of three constituents: an onset,
a peak and a coda.[4] However, these notions themselves do not

----

4. Another critical notion introduced by Hockett is the
"interlude." An interlude is a structure belonging to two
syllables simultaneously; it is coda-like and onset-like
at the same time. The notion interlude goes beyond the monosyllable which is the structure under analysis in this essay.
Also, interlude is tied to the larger problem of syllable division in polysyllabic languages. Chinese offers an opportunity to examine the structure of monosyllables without having to enter into intricate accounts of syllable division.
Ultimately, the notion interlude offers a real challenge to
phonological theory, though I shall not be discussing it

directly define constituent structure. Indeed, these are
the same positional, linear notions discussed earlier and are
a part of the modern linguistic approach to syntagmatic
patterning (c.f. Bloomfield, Trubetskoy, Pike as cited in
3.3 above). Constituent structure, then, involves much more
than simply these notions, and is, in fact, based on two
types of relationships, coordinate and subordinate. Here,
Hockett introduces the very important terms nucleus and
satellite. If some syllable element is subordinate to another, then the subordinate element is said to be a satellite, and the superordinate is the nucleus. The fact that
a syllable can be divided into onset, peak and coda tells
us only about its linear "surface structure". However, the
way these units (and lower level subsyllabic units) bond
into subordinate and coordinate "clusterings" reveals the
"deep" hierarchical structure of the syllable.

Let us examine Hockett's analysis of the English syllable "scrimp." This consists phonetically, says Hockett,
of an onset /skr/, a peak /i/ and a coda /mp/. However,
this division simply rests on phonetic common sense - it
says nothing of the actual IC structure of the syllable:

----

here since my focus is on the monosyllable. Professor J.
Bowers of Cornell has formulated some proposals to handle
interludes in English (personal communication). . "Bowers"
approach will be discussed in Chapter 6.

"The IC's of the syllable may be these three smaller units;
but it may also be that two of them belong together as the
two IC's of the whole." (p. 150). According to Hockett, if
we examine English syllables as a whole, it will become
apparent that there are a great number of syllables which
begin with no onset. At the same time, it will be seen that
"only certain special types of microsegment-final syllables
have a peak not followed by a coda" (p. 150). This leads
Hockett to conclude that "the bondage of peak and coda seems
to be slightly stronger than between onset and peak" (p. 43).
Given these observations of syllable structure in English,
the IC's of /skrimp/ are the onset /skr/ and the peak-coda
/imp/. Furthermore, since peaks (or peak-codas) can occur
with onsets but not vice-versa, than the peak-coda constituent is considered the <u>nucleus</u> and the onset is considered
the <u>satellite</u>. That is, a subordinate relationship exists
between the two IC's. However, /imp/ is also a syllable and
can be further divided into /i/ and /mp/. Furthermore, since
syllables can consist of a peak and no coda in English, the
/mp/ is considered satellite to the nucleus /i/. Again,
the rationale for cutting /imp/ as /i/ and /mp/ rather than
/im/ and /p/ is arrived at by comparing other forms, e.g.
"ramp", "romp", etc.

Hockett does not treat the onset /skr/ in this example. However, in his analysis of Fox, for example, he demonstrates that onset clusters are also to be broken into IC's.

(see p. 162-163). The constituent structure of the syllable
/skrimp/ than could be diagrammed as follows:

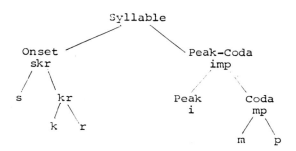

This diagram then reveals that an English syllable can be
analyzed as hierarchical much as the traditional Chinese
syllable was diagrammed earlier and much as the Shanghai
syllable /liaŋ/ was diagrammed in Chapter 2:

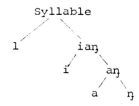

This is exactly the thesis of Hockett's Manual, syllables
in all languages have constituent structure.

Let us then propose the final requirement on a phonological theory as the Constituent Structure Requirement on

syntagmatic structure.[5] In this case, the syntagm is the syllable and the requirement states simply that syllables are to be assigned constituent structure.

3.6 Conclusion

In Chapter 2, four generalizations on syntagmatic structure were postulated first for Shanghai, then for all Chinese languages. In the present chapter, I have argued that these four generalizations can be seen as four deeper requirements on an adequate phonological theory. These four requirements are:

(I)   The Global Constraint Requirement

(II) The Local Constraints Requirement

(III) The Inherent Structure Requirement

(IV) The Constituent Structure Requirement

The following chapter is concerned with how standard generative theory has attempted to satisfy these requirements.

----

5. Again, the wording of this requirement allows for structures other than syllables to be characterized in terms of constituent structure. The notion "syntagm" serves well for just such reasons as this. "Words" also conceivably have constituent structure in terms of syllables (which have constituent structure) but the notion "word" covers a variety of structures depending on the language under study. "Syntagm" as it has been characterized in this essay can cover both the constituent structure of "words" and syllables within the same language - that is smaller syntagms can underlie larger syntagms, etc. As long as syntagmatic patterning can be demonstrated, we are dealing with syntagms.

Chapter Four

SYNTAGMATIC CONSTRAINTS IN GENERATIVE PHONOLOGY

4.1 Introduction

In the preceding chapter four constraints on phonological syntagmatic structure were formulated. Such constraints, more specifically, are said to apply to phonological syntagms - structures of various "sizes" within which
there is systematic syntagmatic patterning. The particular
syntagm under. examination has been a structural unit generally termed the "syllable", but the constraints so formulated are to apply to any phonological syntagm. For example,
the word and the morpheme have both been suggested in traditional as well as in current literature as phonological syntagms.

In addition, the constraints so formulated apply to
the syntagmatic dimension at the phonological (underlying)
level rather than at the surface phonetic level. This last
condition is in keeping with both modern structuralist
("sequences of phonemes") theories and with the standard
theory of generative phonology ("sequences of systematic
phonemes").

In the present chapter, I wish to explore the manner in which standard generative theory has approached these constraints on syntagmatic patterning. Specifically, I am concerned with the Local Constraints Requirement, the Global Constraint Requirement and the Constituent Structure requirement (in that order) with regard to the standard theory. To my knowledge, the Inherent Structure Requirement (dealing with strong and weak syllable positions) has never been a part of the standard theory. This seems quite natural since this requirement, as it is formulated, applies to a syntagm never explicitly recognized in the standard theory - the syllable. Therefore, this requirement will not be mentioned in the discussion which follows.

4.2 The Syntagm of the Standard Theory

As noted earlier, Trubetskoy (1971) has stated that syntagmatic patterning be stated in terms of "frame units", namely the word and the morpheme. His case for the morpheme is interesting:

> First, combinatory rules always presuppose a higher phonological unit within the framework of which they are valid. But this higher phonological unit need not always be the word. In many languages not the word, but the morpheme, which is a complex of phonemes present in several words and always associated with the same (material or formal) meaning, must be regarded as such a unit. (1971: 249)

Trubetskoy's argument for the morpheme rather than the word
as the proper syntagm in some languages is based on German.
In German, if syntagmatic constraints are stated in terms of
the word, there will be in word medial position an "almost
unlimited" number of consonantal combinations (1971: 249).
Examples of word medial clusters are: /kstst/ ("axtstiel" -
"handle of an axe"), /kssv/ ("Fuchsschwanz" - "foxtail"), and
/pstb/ ("Osbaum" - "fruit tree"). This leads Trubetskoy to
conclude:

> Combinatory rules of any kind can be formulated only
> with great difficulty. The phonemic structure of
> morphemes that make up German words, on the other
> hand, is rather clear. It is governed by quite
> specific combinatory rules. It is therefore exped-
> ient to study combinatory rules within the frame-
> work of morphemes and not within the frame of words.
> The first task of any investigation of combinations
> is merely to determine the phonological unit within
> which combinatory rules can be studied most appro-
> priately. (1971: 249).

Within standard generative theory the unit for stating
"combinatory rules," that is, the syntagm - has always been
the morpheme. This was first formulated, if I am not mis-
taken, by Halle (1959) in The Sound Pattern of Russian.
Halle never explicitly discusses just why the morpheme rather
than the syllable or the word was chosen as the appropriate
syntagm, though it seems likely his reasons may have been in
line with those proposed for German by Trubetskoy. In any
case, the morpheme has remained the syntagm within the stan-

dard theory.

4.3 Local Constraints on Syntagmatic Structure

Halle, in The Sound Pattern of Russian proposed that
constraints of the sequences of morphophonemes within morphemes be stated in terms of Morpheme Structure Rules (MS
Rules). It is quite obvious that such rules are the context-
sensitive, positionally-defined rules which were termed Local
Constraints in the preceding chapter. Just as suggested by
Bloomfield, Pike, Trubetskoy and indeed probably a great many
earlier linguists, constraints on segmental positions were
to be stated with respect to three positions: initial, medial, and final. Thus, Halle broke the main body of MS rules
into three groups: those constraints which immediately follow
the morpheme initial boundary marker (rules 1-4), those immediately preceding the final boundary (rules 5-8) and those
applying to medial clusters (rules 9 and 10). Furthermore,
the rules for medial clusters could only be applied after the
initial and final MS rules.

Stanley (1967) suggested that the notion Morpheme Structure Rules be replaced by the notion Morpheme Structure Conditions. The reason for this revision is in some respects
rather complex. In Walton (1971) I discussed Stanley's reformulation in some detail and will not repeat the discussion
here. Suffice to say that rules (phonological rules) change

feature values and map one level of representation onto another, whereas conditions neither change feature values nor map levels one onto another but rather state constraints at only one level, the systematic phonemic level. Thus MS conventions are not ordered like rules but rather apply simultaneously.

Of interest to the present essay is the manner in which local constraints are handled within Stanley's reformulation of MS rules. In Stanley's framework, Local Constraints, as I have termed them, are to be expressed as Sequence Structure Conditions of which there are two types: If-Then Sequence Structure Conditions and Negative Sequence Structure Conditions. If-Then Conditions are context sensitive conditions on morpheme structure. An example for English (from Stanley 1967) is:

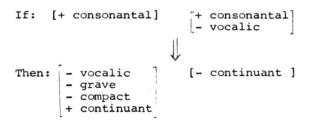

This Sequence Structure Condition states that if two consonantal segments occur morpheme-initially and if the second is a true consonant, then the first segment must be /s/ and the second must be an obstruent.

The Negative Condition simply states that a particular combination of segments is not allowed within the morphemes of the language. The status and utility of this latter type of condition has remained ambiguous (see Walton: 86) but the former notion of Sequence Structure Condition has been widely accepted within generative theory.

Given, then, the second requirement on a theory of phonology, the Local Constraints Requirement, it is clear that the Sequence Structure Conditions are specifically designed for and seemingly adequate for expressing the context-sensitive restrictions on sequences of segments within the syntagm.

4.4 The Global Constraint on Syntagmatic Structure

There is little difference in essence between Halle's sequence structure MS rules and Stanley's MS conditions - both types of devices are designed to capture context-sensitive cooccurrence restrictions of segments in morphemes. However, in Halle (1959) there was no proposal for handling the Global Constraint on syntagmatic structure. In fact, throughout the recent history of phonology it seems that no truly formal device has ever been proposed to capture the informal notion "canonical shape of syntagm (morpheme, syllable, word, etc.)".

However, one of the real contributions of Stanley's

work was to propose just such a device, which he termed the
"Positive Condition on Morpheme Structure." It is rather
obvious that Sequence Structure Conditions cannot express
the overall constraints on the structure of a syntagm since
they are context-sensitive and since, by virtue of being "If-
Then" conditions only one segment can be treated per convention. That is, a Sequence Structure Condition states that
if a segment (one segment) in a string within a syntagm has
certain properties in such and such an environment (context-
sensitive), then it also has other properties. But such a
device cannot express the notion "the syntagm in this language consists of the following various strings of segments."
This is simply another way of saying that Sequence Structure
Conditions are designed for Local Constraints only; they are
inadequate for expressing Global Constraints. This is in the
nature of Stanley's own remarks concerning the proper way to
account for the fact that a certain language has (C)V(C)
morphemes:

> The problem is that MS rules express 'if-then' con-
> ditions on morphemes, and what we have here is a
> 'positive' condition on morphemes, a condition that
> might be paraphrased as - every morpheme meets the
> condition (C)V(C)' (1968: S21)

In justifying the positive condition Stanley stated:

> This argument seems to be substantiated by the fact
> that the 'syllable structure' of many languages can
> only be described by a relatively complex set of

MS rules which not only miss generalizations, but which cannot capture restrictions on the length of morphemes which may exist. Positive MS conditions on the other hand seems ideally suited to describing such structure (1967: 432)

A Positive Condition on morphemes for a language whose morphemes have the shape #CV(V)# would be formulated as follows:

$$P(C)\# \begin{bmatrix} + \text{ consonantal} \\ - \text{ vocalic} \end{bmatrix} \begin{bmatrix} -\text{consonantal} \\ +\text{vocalic} \end{bmatrix} \left(\begin{bmatrix} -\text{consonantal} \\ +\text{vocalic} \end{bmatrix} \right)\#$$

That is, only morphemes having this shape and these possible lengths are admitted in the language.

Obviously, then, a Positive Condition is global - it expresses not cooccurrence restrictions among segments but rather all the possible arrays of C's and V's which the morphemes of the language manifest. The particular syntagm in Stanley's work is the morpheme but it should be clear that the framework would be suitable for stating global constraints on any syntagm. Thus, it would seem that within the standard theory, the Global Constraint Requirement on the structure of syntagms is met by the Positive Condition.

4.5   The Constituent Structure Requirement

4.5.1   The Nature of Constituent Structure

In 3.5, it was argued following Hockett (1955) that

the structure of the syllable was hierarchical rather than simply linear and that such a conception revealed subordinate and coordinate relationships among the subsyllabic elements of the syllable. In other words, it was argued that a syllable is made up of immediate constituents of various levels.

To get a clear understanding of how the notion "constituent structure" is to be treated in phonology, it is helpful to see how this notion has been characterized in syntax. Consider the following statement by Postal:

> Given any sentence in a natural language represented as a string of discrete entities, say morphemes or words, certainly almost all linguists are agreed that at least part of the structure of such a sentence can be represented in the form of a hierarchical categorization of these discrete elements (1964: 6)

Thus, Postal contends, the sentence "the man will eat the meat" consists of two parts, "the man" and "will eat the meat". The constituent "the man" consists of two parts "the" and "man"; "will eat the meat" consists of the parts "will eat" and "the meat" and so on.

More importantly, as Postal notes, most linguists would agree the "parts" of such a sentence belong to categories, and that these categories have labels. Thus, following Postal, the above sentence can be diagrammed as follows (1968: 6):

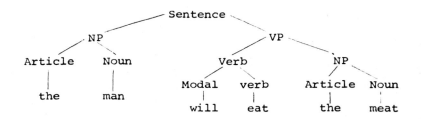

Postal goes on to state that the labeling of the categories (NP, Article, etc.) is necessary to represent the similarities and differences of elements in different sentences in different parts of sentences.

Such diagrams as the one above are commonly termed Phrase Markers (P-markers). Postal describes them as follows:

> The fundamental notion of a P-marker is that certain
> strings of elements are related to certain other
> single elements by the relation 'is a (member of the
> category).' This relation is represented by the
> fact that some strings of elements are traceable
> back to a single node. Elements traceable back to
> a single node A are said to be an A, or to be con-
> stituents of A. A is said to dominate such strings
> of elements... Thus P-markers appear to represent
> a straightforward characterization of the ideas
> involved in linguistic notions of hierarchical cate-
> gorization or constituency. (1964: 7).

Within generative theory, the type of hierarchical categorization described above is characterized in terms of a Phrase Structure Grammar - a system of rewriting rules. That is, a Phrase Structure Grammar (PSG) generates phrase-markers.

4.5.2 Constituent Structure and Generative Phonology

While the constituent structure approach outlined above was developed with respect to grammar, there have been suggestions that such notions could also be applied to phonological structure in the form of "phonological grammars." At least three proposals have been forwarded along these lines: Saporta and Contreras A Phonological Grammar of Spanish, Romeo's "Toward a Phonological Grammar of Modern Spoken Greek" and Cheng's "Mandarin Phonological Structure." The second of these is based directly on the first and will not be discussed further. Furthermore, there are very basic differences between the first work and the third.

The maximum syntagm in the Spanish phonological grammar is the Phonological Word (PW) which is made up of one or more minimum syntagms - syllables. Syllables are characterized in terms of the now familiar positional notions "onset", "nucleus" and "coda." The phrase-structure rules for a one or two syllable word is given as (Saporta and Contreras 1962: 20):

$$PW \longrightarrow \langle S \rangle \, \hat{} \, S$$
$$S \longrightarrow \langle O \rangle \, \hat{} \, N \, \hat{} \, \langle C \rangle$$

That is a phonological word (of up to two syllables) consists of one or more syllables, the first being optional. The syllable consists of an optional onset, an obligatory

nucleus, and an optional coda. These categories are then
expanded into specific segments and then, later, transforma-
tional rules are added to reorder some segments.

While it is obvious that a PSG can be applied to phonology, it is not at all clear that Saporta and Contreras
were concerned with capturing the hierarchical notions discussed above with respect to such grammars. In fact, it is
abundantly clear that they were not at all concerned with
hierarchical structure. Rather, these linguists were solely
concerned with using the notion of a "phonological grammar"
simply to generate phonologically grammatical linear strings
of phonemes, such that, for example, the sequence [fet]
though not occurring in English is an acceptable syllable,
whereas the syllable [fte] is not (and is therefore not
"grammatical"). The system of rewriting rules they propose
are simply a step by step expansion of each linear, positional category. The syllable consists of three linear positions.
Initial is expanded into all phonemes that can occur in initial position, etc. But nowhere is there any notion such as
those suggested by Postal above or by Hockett, that various
hierarchical relationships hold between say, the nucleus and
the final or that there exists bonding among various subsyllabic units. The only sort of relations expressed are
strictly linear. As such, the notion of PSG as employed by
these linguists is inadequate to meet the Constituent Struc-

ture Requirement.

The approach of Cheng (1966) who also proposed a PSG to generate syntagms is quite different from that proposed by Saporta and Contreras. Interestingly, and I believe significantly Cheng was working with a Chinese language - Mandarin - and the syntagm was definitely the syllable. The PSG in Cheng's view also generates syllables:

> A generative grammar will be given which generates all (but not necessarily the only) basic syllables in Mandarin. But as a part of the whole grammar this syllable grammar (SG) merely assigns 'structure' to the morphophonemic transcription of the morphemes given by some syntactic grammar. By structure of the syllable we mean the intraphonemic properties as well as the interphonemic organization of the syllable. In assigning structural relationships among phonemes we shall take into consideration the notion of rhyming which has been the central motif of traditional Chinese phonology (Cheng 1966: 136).

I believe it is obvious from this statement that Cheng is approaching the syllable in the hierarchical manner discussed by Postal and Hockett. This seems implicit in his concern with "interphonemic organization in the syllable" and in his comment on "assigning structural relationships among phonemes." The fact that Cheng does see the syllable this way is obvious from the following PSG rules and P-marker which Cheng formulates for Mandarin (I present here only fragments) where ⟨ ⟩ = optional and Ter = Terminal:

1. Syl ⟶ Seg + ⟨ T ⟩
2. Seg ⟶ ⟨ Init ⟩ + Final
3. Final ⟶ ⟨ Med ⟩ + Rime
4. Rime ⟶ Nuc + ⟨ Ter ⟩

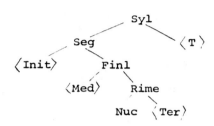

Cheng's approach then is quite in accord with the Constituent Structure Requirement. The structure of the Mandarin syllable is not simply portrayed as a linear string of optional and obligatory segments. Rather, certain relationships hold between the various segments within the syllable. Notice that a strictly linear notion of positions such as onset, peak, and coda cannot even capture the notions "final," "medial" and "rime."

Thus, there does exist within the standard theory a device to express the Constituent Structure Requirement.

4.6 Conclusion

With regard to the Global Constraint Requirement, the Local Constraints Requirement and the Constituent Structure Requirement, it would seem that the standard theory has, in fact, provided an array of formal devices to express just these generalizations.

Yet it is becoming increasingly obvious that the above
formulations are inadequate. On the one hand, it has been
recently suggested in some circles that the Global Constraint
and Local Constraints requirements on syntagmatic patterning
-- as stated in Chapter 3, represent an incorrect view of
the nature of syntagmatic patterning. Thus, it is suggested
that these constraints be reformulated. This has, in part,
resulted in the Inherent Structure Requirement. These proposals will be discussed in the following chapter. Moreover it can be shown that Cheng's application of the notion
Phrase Structure Grammar to phonological structure, while
properly oriented, is formally inadequate. This will be
discussed in Chapter 6.

Chapter Five

THE ROLE OF SYNTAGMATIC PATTERNING
AT THE SURFACE PHONETIC LEVEL

5.1 Introduction

In Chapter 2 it was suggested that in phonological
theory the syntagmatic dimension exists on two planes - the
phonological and the phonetic. It was further proposed that
the four requirements on phonological theory were to apply
to syntagms at the phonological, underlying level not the
surface phonetic level. This condition was attached in
keeping with the canons of both structuralist and generative
theories. In the structuralist approach, the sound pattern
or constraints on sequences of sounds were stated in terms
of sequences of phonemes, not phones. Thus, for example,
in discussing possible consonant clusters in initial position the structuralist would refer to possible phonemic
clusters. In generative theory, the possible concatenations
of sounds have always been stated in terms of the sequences
of morphophonemes within the morpheme.

Yet, in recent work (to be discussed below), it has
been suggested that syntagmatic constraints should not apply

to underlying representation but rather to surface phonetic representation. If these claims are valid, then the four requirements proposed earlier would have to be reformulated such that they did not apply to the underlying structure of syntagms but rather to the surface phonetic structure of syntagms. Moreover, the devices proposed in the preceding chapter for capturing the phonological structure of syntagms would have to be revised such that they could capture the phonetic structure of syntagms.

5.2   The Status of the Systematic Phonetic Level

       The question as to whether phonotactic patterning is to be stated at the underlying level or surface level (or both) centers on the linguistic status of the surface phonetic level. Therefore let us examine the status of this level in generative theory. The standard theory can be diagrammed as follows:

```
 ┌────────────────────────────────┐
 │ Lexical Representation          │
 ├────────────────────────────────┤
 │ MS Conditions                   │
 ├────────────────────────────────┤
 │ Underlying Representation        │
 ├────────────────────────────────┤
 │ Phonological Rules               │
 ├────────────────────────────────┤
 │ Surface Representations          │
 └────────────────────────────────┘
```

The surface representation is characterized as the "output" of the phonological rules which have applied to readjusted lexical forms and as the "input" to articulatory commands to the speech organs. Indeed, there seems to be no other status to this level other than the termination of one set of processes and the initiation of another set. In particular, there are no generalizations regarding phonological structure that are directly applicable at this level.

There is a critical distinction between the _existence_ of a level as opposed to the _independence_ of a level. I would mention that within the standard theory a level of surface phonetic representation does, of course, exist but this level is in no sense independent. It is, rather, "derived" from generalizations on morpheme structure plus the effects of phonological rules.

The effect of the phonological component in generative theory, then, is to deny to this level any structural characteristics independent of the effects of higher level constraints and processes. One way to check this claim is to ask if the constraints on the combinations of sounds in a language could possibly be directly stated with respect to the surface phonetic level. That is, could such constraints apply to the output of the phonological component? To this question, Postal has stated (1968: 213): "...an independent phonotactics is necessarily and in all cases useless and re-

dundant in its entirety." By "independent," Postal means
a phonotactics stated at the autonomous phonemic level of
modern structural linguistics but the effect of the statement
is that any phonotactics at the surface level is undesirable.
This can be seen by the following statement:

> In short, if a description which contains restric-
> tions on the combinations of morphophonemics in
> morphemes plus the morphophonemic rules is em-
> bedded in a grammar which defines combinations
> of morphemes into words, all possible combina-
> tions of phonetic elements in words are necessarily
> predicted. (Postal 1968: 213)

The thrust of Postal's view is then, that there is no need
to directly account for the "combinations of phonetic elements" at the surface level -- they are already indirectly
accounted for.

Such a view of phonology makes explicit claims about
the role of the surface phonetic level with respect to a
great many phonological processes. Consider such processes
as sound change, first-language acquisition, second-language
acquisition, borrowing, and native speaker judgements on
acceptable and non-acceptable forms. According to the standard theory, the surface phonetic level plays no direct role
in any of these processes since such a level does not exist
independently but only derivatively. Thus, for a phonetic
segment to undergo change, this change must come either from
a change in morpheme structure or from the addition or dele-

tion of some phonological rule. Likewise, for first-language acquisition, this claim would be that children are not sensitive to the direct effects of the surface phonetic level in formulating hypotheses about the language but rather to the effects of the underlying morpheme structure rules and the P-rules. Second-language acquisition would also involve the learner "by-passing" as it were, the surface phonetic level of the language to be learned and learning instead the underlying structure of morphemes and the P-rules. Borrowing, within such a framework, would not involve adapting the borrowed form directly to the surface phonetic level; rather, forms could only be borrowed by adapting them to the underlying morpheme structure and P-rules. Likewise, a native apeaker could not make an acceptability judgement directly on a surface phonetic form; he would instead have to consult the form's underlying composition and check to see which P-rules applied to it, for indeed, the only accessability to surface forms is through their derivation.

Suppose, however, that the surface phonetic level was not simply a derived level, having no organization of its own, but rather an independent level having its own organizational structure. The implications of such an independent leve would be that sound change could be initiated by factors in the surface structure, not in the underlying structure. The child would formulate hypotheses directly about the surface

structure rather than about the phonological structure underlying it. The same would be true for second-language acquisition. Borrowing would involve adapting forms directly to
the surface phonetic structure -- not to any underlying
factors. Native speakers of English would reject the form
*/bnik/ not because of any underlying morpheme structure con-
straint but simply because it "does not sound like" an English word -- i.e. it is rejected on straight-forward surface
phonetic grounds.

There is growing evidence that this second conception
of the nature of the surface phonetic level is the correct
one and that the notion of this level as "derived" in the
sense of the standard theory is incorrect. The remainder of
this chapter is devoted to an examination of this issue.

5.3 Phonetic Redundancy Rules

Stanley's MS conditions were strictly limited to expressing phonotactic constraints at the morphophonemic level.
One would assume that, much like Postal (1968), Stanley would
have not seen any reason for stating phonotactic constraints
at the phonetic level. This would seem apparent since he
was working within the standard theory where the phonetic
level is purely derived. Yet, it is rather clear that Stanley was concerned that another set of constraints might be
necessary at the phonetic level:

> It is possible that just as the MS Rules state redundancies at the systematic phonemic level, there are rules which state redundancies at the systematic phonetic level. (Stanley 1967: 397)

In arguing for the benefits of such phonetic redundancy rules Stanley (1968: 397) makes the following interesting statement: "Furthermore, they would provide a framework for making generalizations about the phonetic pattern of a language, a framework which is, at present, conspicuously lacking" (emphasis mine). I take the underlined portion as an admission on Stanley's part that the combined effect of MS Conditions which he was proposing plus the phonological rules are not adequate to express the "phonetic pattern" of a language. This is, then, an implicit admission that the phonetic level has an organization at least partially independent of the operation of MS conventions and P-rules. Other comments by Stanley support this implicit admission:

> In fact, the theory has no redundancy rules at the systematic phonetic level, rules which correspond to the MS rules at the systematic phonemic level... Moreover, the complexity and depth of ordering which in general exists in the P-rules show that it may be difficult to construct any natural set of phonetic redundancy rules, even in principle. This is because phonetic representations are only obtained as the output of this highly structured set of rules (the P-rules) so that in general a relationship among the elements of these representations cannot be simply stated in terms of these elements alone, but must be referred back to the systematic phonemic representations which underlie them. (p. 405)

This ultimately leads Stanley to conclude: "... any direct statements of the distribution of elements at the systematic phonetic level are likely to be complex and to involve the loss of generalization." (p. 406). Again, I believe these remarks indicate that Stanley felt the need for phonetic redundancy rules but was simply thwarted from stating them by the inherent nature of the theory.

5.4   The Theory of Markedness

The theory of marking conventions was proposed in large part as an alternative to Morpheme Structure rules and conditions. This theory has been discussed and outlined in various works (Chomsky and Halle (1968: Chapter 9); Postal (1968); Cairns (1969)) and I will not discuss it here. Rather, I should like to examine the theory only as it pertains to stating sequential constraints. Markedness theory was an attempt, in part, to characterize the notion "lexical redundancy," that is, it was concerned with formulating constraints on the sequences of morphophonemes in the lexicon. Yet, by virtue of the fact that the invariance condition (see Chomsky and Halle 1968: 166-168) does not apply between phonetic and lexical forms of morphemes, the underlying representation of morphemes can be quite abstract. Thus, there is no guarantee that the sequences of morpho-

phonemes have any necessary connection with the sequences
of phones. Nevertheless, the entire discussion of marking
conventions in Chomsky and Halle (1968) centers around the
notion of "natural rules" and natural configurations of segments where "natural" seems always to mean <u>phonetically</u>
natural not "morphophonemically" natural (see Chomsky and
Halle 1968, especially pp. 416-419). This is even more
evident in Cairn's work (1969). After discussing the universal constraints on stem initial consonant clusters at the
<u>lexical level</u> of representation, Cairns then suggests the
physical (p. 878) and perceptual (p. 879) origins of such
universals. Such origins are obviously phonetic in nature
(acoustic, motor, articulatory, auditory, etc.) yet they
are said to apply to what can be quite abstract lexical representations.

Cairns all but admits the problems inherent in using
phonetic detail to support lexical representations:

> There are, of course, many languages which notorious-
> ly violate the universal constraints established at
> the level of lexical representation. The Semitic
> languages, for example, have lexical representations
> which do not contain any vowels, but do contain
> two or three consonants. These languages appear to
> violate the theory described in this paper in fun-
> damental ways. (1969: 882-883).

To solve this problem, at least for Semitic languages,
Cairns proposes that perhaps his universal constraints apply

at the level of systematic phonemics but admits that this
would cause a radical revision of the theory of phonological
redundancy. He concludes the discussion of his dilemna by
the very interesting following statement:

> In any case, I can hardly imagine a language in which
> there were no constraints on the distribution of M's
> in the lexicon; <u>these constraints may always turn out
> to be a subset of those applying at other phono-
> logical levels</u> (Cairns 1969: 883)(Emphasis mine)

Now, if Cairns statement is true, then this could be taken
as an implicit admission that the <u>real</u> constraints in a language are at lower levels and <u>some</u> of these may also apply at
the lexical level. But this is just the opposite of the
view that the only kind of redundancy phonological theory is
to consider is lexical redundancy and Cairn's article is an
attempt to formulate a set of universal <u>lexical</u> redundancy
rules.

Furthermore, his statement, particularly the phrase
"other phonological levels," leaves the way for one to postulate that constraints exist at the surface phonetic level --
and that the constraints in the lexical representation are
possibly, as Cairns suggests, subsets of these surface phonetic constraints. If that is the case, then Cairns is making a case for some sort of independence of the surface phonetic level.

In sum, markedness theory seems to suffer from an

implicit recognition that certain phenomena on the phonetic
level are natural while maintaining that statements of
these phenomena are to be manifested in the lexicon -- the
very place of greatest abstractness of phonetic phenomena,
and therefore the place most removed from "natural" phenomena.
Shibatani makes the same point:

> As has been noted by many, Chomsky and Halle's attempt
> (Ch. 9) has some inherent inconsistencies. E.g.,
> the marking conventions which they posit (or restate)
> are mostly phonetically motivated and deal with pho-
> netic details; yet they are used primarily to eval-
> uate abstract non-phonetic entities, namely lexical
> representations (Shibatani 1973: 104-105)

Throughout the theory of markedness then, phenomena at the
surface phonetic level are taken as primary, implying the
notion that the surface phonetic level is primary rather
than derived.

5.5 Conspiracies

The now well known pheneomena of "conspiracies" or
rules which "look forward" provide more evidence of an implicit recognition of some independent phonetic organization at
the surface phonetic level in generative phonology. Kisseberth (1970) in first discussing the functional unities of
phonological rules gives the following example:

There are rather heavy constraints in Yawelmani phonetic representations on the clustering of consonants and vowels. No vowel-vowel sequences are
permitted. Words may neither end nor begin with
consonant clusters. Nowhere in a word may more than
two consonants occur in a sequence. The main focus
of this paper will be on the lack of word-final
consonant clusters and the lack of triliteral
clusters (p. 5)

Kisseberth then notes that no single phonological rule

accounts for such constraints but rather that "there are a

variety of phonological processes, which, it might be said

"conspire" to yield phonetic representations which contain

no word-final clusters and no triliteral clusters." (1970: 5).

The problem is, how do we know that there are "heavy

constraints in Yawelmani phonetic representations"? Genera-

tive theory specifically refuses to recognize phonetic con-

straints as such. There can be morpheme structure constraints

and P-rules and a derived phonetic structure but as Stanley

noted with respect to this very same level of phonetic repre-

sentation:

...a relationship among the surface phonetic elements
of these representations cannot simply be stated in
terms of these elements alone, but must be referred
back to the systematic phonemic representations
which underlie them (1967: 405)

Thus, Kisseberth is implicitly assuming phonetic con-

straints but there is no way that they can formally exist in

the theory.

Kiparsky (1973) recognized this. He classifies such

conspiracies as the one above as rules which 'look forward' to their phonetic output:

> They are sets of formally distinct rules which share a functional teleology, usually characterizable in terms of target configurations in the output of the phonological component. For example, a number of rules might work together to eliminate and prevent the introduction of clusters of three consonants (p. 3).

But, of course, to recognize "target configurations" at the surface or to recognize that three clusters cannot occur on the surface is to admit that the surface level actually has its own structure and that the phonological rules "conspire" to preserve it or reach it (as a target). That is, such an approach on the one hand says that the surface phonetic level does not exist with any independent structure, yet on the other hand recognizes conspiracies as working towards pre-existing structure. This is tantamount to admitting that there exist phonotactic constraints at the phonetic level -- the very claim which Postal, for example, argued against.

Kiparsky, more so that Kisseberth apparently, recognized that the notion of "conspiracies" implicitly recognizes surface phonotactics:

> Kisseberth noted that the output of the phonological component of a language often shows clearcut irregularities which do not necessarily have a simple source in any particular rule of the system, but are the result of complex interaction among several seem-

> ingly distinct processes or limitations on processes.
> <u>It was presumably the existance of such regularities
> in the output which gave structuralists the idea of
> a separate set of phonotactic statements distinct
> from the morphophonemic rules</u>... (p. 18-19) Emphasis
> mine.

Kiparsky never explicitly states that he recognizes such a
set of "phonotactic statements" as valid in generative theory.
Yet, in citing Kisseberth's evidence from Yawelmani he seems
to implicitly accept such a notion:

> Their functional relationship is that each of the
> five rules plays a part in <u>preserving the overall
> property of Yawelmani phonotactics</u> that there are no
> clusters of the form $\left\{ {C \atop \#} \right\} C \left\{ {C \atop \#} \right\}$, i.e., no medial
> clusters, no word initial #CC clusters and no word
> final CC# clusters (p. 19). Emphasis mine.

The problem, again, is that within t' e standard theory there
are no "regularities in the output" (see above), no "phonotactic statements" so there can be no "overall property of
Yawelmani phonotactics." Surface phonotactics do not exist independently in the manner in which Kisseberth and Kiparsky
are hinting; surface representations are simply the derived
output of "underlying phonotactics" and phonological rules.
Thus, there are no formal "target" generalizations such as
"no word initial clusters can occur at the surface phonetic
level", etc.

5.6 Surface Phonetic Constraints

With respect to phonetic redundancy rules (Stanley 1967), marking conventions and 'conspiracies' or rules which "look forward," I have argued that in each case there is an implicit recognition that the surface phonetic level is not simply derived but rather has some independent organization. However, explicit claims that this is the case have also been made.

Shibatani (1973), it seems, was the first to follow up Stanley's suggestion of accounting for phonetic as well as systematic phonemic patterning. Shibatani pointed out that certain constraints which hold at the morphophonemic level do not hold at the phonetic level and vice-versa. For example, in Russian, lexical sequence structure constraints allow only /iu/ and /au/ but at the phonetic level, after affixation processes, many types of vowel sequences are allowed (Shibatani 1973: 90). Likewise, morpheme-final voiced obstruents must be posited for the lexical level in German to cover alternatives such as [rat], [radəs] "wheel (gen.)", etc., whereas such utterance final voiced consonants are never permitted at the surface.

One of Shibatani's chief arguments for an independent set of rules to cover surface phonetic constraints was that the combination of MS rules and P-rules need not necessarily ever make, even indirectly, certain phonotactic statements.

For example, if morphemes were joined together during a derivation such that clusters were created, there would never be
a set of rules capturing the constraints on these cluster
patterns. The MS rules could not do this since they cover
morpheme-internal constraints only.

More interesting are Shibatani's arguments for treating the surface phonetic level as having some independent
characteristics. Only a few of his arguments will be summarized here. Referring to a study by Moskowitz (1971),
Shibatani notes that in child language acquisition constraints
on phonetic representation come first and morphophonemic alternations come later. He uses this evidence to support the
claim that there is "an independent mechanism that represents
phonetic constraints" (p. 94). Thus, any theory that sees
phonetic constraints as the indirect result of MS rules and
P-rules is inadequate -- phonetic constraints are "independent" of this higher level.

Native speaker judgments provide more evidence. The
approach to admissible and inadmissible forms in the standard
theory is that such constraints are expressed in the lexicon. That is, lexical redundancy rules account for /brIk/
(occurring), /blIk/ (admissible; not occurring) and */bnIk/
(inadmissible). However, Shibatani claims that such constraints should be expressed in terms of surface phonetic
representations. In German there is a phonetic constraint

that all word final obstruents must be unvoiced but there
is no such constraint at the underlying level. Therefore,
since there is no morpheme-structure rule preventing nonsense forms like [bund], [rad], and [lib], the claim would
be that native speakers of German would accept these as
"accidental gaps." But, according to Shibatani (p. 95):
"... it is easy to show that a native speaker of German
rejects these forms on the GROUND THAT THEY END IN VOICED
OBSTRUENTS, about which the German MSC's say nothing."

   After giving another example, Shibatani argues that
Chomsky and Halle should revise their claim that morpheme
structure conditions alone account for the native speaker's
intuition about nonsense forms by saying that MSC's plus
phonological rules capture these intuitions. But this would
mean that no single structure would express a native speaker's
intuition about nonsense forms. Thus, for a native speaker
to check a form as to its admissibility, he would have to
assign the form some underlying structure and then run it
through all the relevant P-rules. But there is no way to
directly posit the underlying form -- the native speaker
would have to hypothesize the underlying form and if his
hypothesis were wrong, he would simply have to hypothesize
another and another until he exhausted all possibilities.
Shibatani rejects this as an unlikely procedure in making
native-speaker judgments on admissibility:

> My claim is that there is a single structure and that
> it is the SPC's [surface phonetic constraints] of
> a language upon which a native speaker bases his
> judgment when confronted with a nonsense form.
> (1973: 96).

Historical change gives some impetus for the argument that the surface phonetic level has some constraints independent of underlying structure. In the standard theory, sound change is accounted for largely in terms of the addition and loss of phonological rules but not in terms of direct surface phonetic alternations -- this latter would be impossible since the surface structure is totally derived. Shibatani challenges this conception:

> But since SPC's [surface phonetic constraints] exist
> at the phonetic level, they are the most susceptible
> to phonological change. Addition or loss of rules
> may easily sway the status of some SPC's but SPC's
> do not play a totally passive role in phonological
> change. In some instances, SPC's actively interact
> with change. (1973: 102).

In this sense, Shibatani is following the notion first proposed by Chafe (1968) as "persistent rules." These are rules which affect sound change over long periods of time and work on low, _phonetic_ level forms rather than on underlying forms.

Upon examination of the roles the surface phonetic structure plays in sound change, Shibatani concludes:

> Many phonological rules have the function of recon-
> ciling a phonetically unpermitted sequence of seg-
> ments, created by affixation, etc., with what is
> compatible with SPC's. Thus change in SPC's opens
> up a new avenue in dealing with a phonetically un-
> permitted underlying representation, by allowing
> the creation of new phonological rules (1973: 104).

As one final example of the role of surface phonetic organi-

zation, Shibatani claims that it is problems in surface pho-

netics, not underlying processes which give the adult pro-

nunciation problems in learning a second language:

> The SPC's [surface phonetic constraints] are acquired
> in an early stage of mother-tongue acquisition, and
> they are deeply rooted in the competence of the
> native speaker.

Shibatani also gives other convincing arguments --

including, for example, arguments based on borrowing which

I shall not recount here. The essence of Shibatani's posi-

tion is that there exist phonotactic constraints at the

surface level which can only be captured by statements per-

taining directly to that level. Such constraints are termed

Surface Phonetic Constraints. However, he does not seek to

eliminate Morpheme Structure Conditions. Rather, he allows

that some syntagmatic constraints hold only at the lexical

level (MSC's), some only at the phonetic level (SPC's) and

some at both (M/SPC's). Surface Phonetic Constraints, ac-

cording to Shibatani can be If-Then Conditions, Negative

Conditions and Positive Conditions just as Stanley proposed

in order to account for constraints at the lexical level.
Positive Conditions are specifically constraints on "syllable
structure" but it is never clear if there will be lexical
"syllable structure" as well as surface "syllable structure."

The syntagm for SPC's is to be the word but he does
mention that it would sometimes be convenient to make reference to word-internal boundaries -- namely formative boundaries, in stating SPC's. But the word would quite clearly
be the maximum syntagm since he has already pointed out that
SPC's will be necessary to capture constraints across morpheme boundaries.

5.7   Syllable Structure Conditions

Hooper's (1973) approach differs from Shibatani's in
two important ways. First, she goes much further than Shibatani and rejects the notion of lexical level syntagmatic
constraints altogether -- that is, she rejects entirely the
notion Morpheme Structure Condition. The only relevant level
of syntagmatic patterning is the surface phonetic level.
Secondly, the syllable and not the word or the formative, is
to be the syntagm for these phonetic constraints.

Hooper's objections to stating phonotactic constraints
on MSC's can be briefly outlined. First, the morpheme is a
"syntactic-semantic unit" (1974: 1) or a unit of meaning, but
it is not a phonological unit. Grammatical morphemes present

a real problem. Some morphemes such as the past tense of
"hit" simply have no phonetic manifestation at all. How is
one to write an MSC for this morpheme? The past tense morpheme in "sang" and "brought" cannot be segmented phonologically so it would be impossible to characterize their morpheme structures. Other grammatical morphemes such as English past tense [t] and [d] and the plural [s] and [z] cannot occur in isolation. Thus again, writing morpheme structure conditions for such cases is impossible.

But there are problems other than grammatical morphemes.
Problems also arise with regard to lexical morphemes. For
instance, according to Hooper, in inflectional languages the
lexical morpheme-initial constraints are probably sufficient
to describe phonetic constraints also. However, stem final
morpheme constraints do not necessarily reflect word final
or syllable final constraints. Hooper (1974) presents the
following example from Spanish:

	Stem	Theme V	Progressive
'speak'	abl	a	ndo
'buy'	kompr	a	ndo
'sit'	sent	a	ndo

Hooper (1974: 2) notes that such stem-final clusters as /bl/,
/mpr/ and /nt/ are representative of a large number of stem
final consonant clusters. However, none of these three clusters may occur syllable finally in Spanish. Moreover, there

are only two syllable final clusters /ns/ and /rs/. Obviously, then, all these facts about syllable structure would be
missed if one attempted to account for them by MSC's.

In addition, as Hooper notes, since morphemes may consist of a number of syllables, the statement of segment combination restrictions grows increasingly complex while statements about syllable structure remain more simple. This is,
in effect, the same view I took in Walton (1971: 76, fn. 1),
in suggesting that syntagmatic patterning be stated in terms
of syllables and not morphemes.

Like Shibatani, Hooper also argues that Morpheme
Structure Conditions have no psychological reality. One of
the functions of MSC's was to capture the notion "possible
morpheme" in a language -- that is, to capture accidental
gaps. Hooper argues that the often cited example of */bnIk/
as an impossible English morpheme is actually an example of
an impossible English syllable since a form like "stabnik"
(based on "sputnik" and "beatnik") could conceivably be an
English word. That is, the restriction is not on a possible morpheme but rather on a syllable- (or possible word)
initial cluster */bn-/.

Hooper's argument against stating syntagmatic constraints in terms of morphemes can be summarized as follows:

> It is clear then, that constraints on sequence struc-
> ture that are stated in terms of the morpheme cannot
> make the strongest possible and most explanatory

generalizations about phonotactic structure. Instead
of using a unit of meaning, the morpheme, as a basic
unit for expressing constraints on phonological
structure, we should use a unit that is purely
phonological. The smallest unit that may be multi-
segmental (i.e. the smallest pronounceable unit)
is the syllable. If the constraints on sequence
structure are to represent what is pronounceable
in a specific language, then they should be stated
in terms of the smallest pronounceable unit. (Hooper
1973: 63).

The last statement in this quotation is extremely significant.
Although the notion of "pronounceability" has always been
behind phonotactic statements, Hooper, I believe, is the
first to give this notion explicit, formal import in generative theory. Pronounceability is ultimately behind Shibatani's arguments in the preceding section dealing with
native speaker judgments, first and second language acquisition, etc. In other words, his Surface Phonetic Constraints
can be seen as constraints to insure well-formedness in terms
of pronounceability -- a form is well-formed if it is pronounceable as an English syllable or word.

Much more important, however, is the fact that while
the morpheme is a unit with no phonological import -- i.e.
it is a morpho-syntactic unit, the syllable is a unit of pronunciation, of pure sound structure, and has no morpho-syntactic properties. By insisting on the syllable as the syntagm for stating syntagmatic constraints Hooper is paving
the way for what I shall call (in the following chapter) a

"totally independent level" of phonological organization.

Hooper proposes that the phonotactic constraints pertaining to the syllable be stated as syllable structure conditions and that these conditions take the form of positive
conditions (Hooper 1973: 67). Hooper's Positive Condition
has three characteristics which differentiate it in a significant way from Stanley's original Positive Condition on
Morpheme Structure: (1) it applies only to the syllable, not
morphemes; (2) it makes use of the notion "consonantal
strength;" (3) it makes use of the notions syllable-weak and
syllable-strong syllable positions. Obviously, each language would have one or a set of positive conditions to capture all facets of syllable structure. However, as Hooper
has argued, the notions "consonantal strength" and the notion of strong and weak syllable positions are universal.
She thus proposes the following universal condition on the
form of language specific syllable structure conditions:

$$P(C): \quad \$C_m C_n C_p C_q V C_r C_s C_t \$$$

Conditions: (1) $m > n > p > q$
(2) $r < s < t$
(3) $m > t$
(4) $m \neq 0$

The basic configuration places consonants as margins

with an obligatory vowel as the nucleus. Conditions (1) and
(2) indicate that consonants descend in strength from the
margins to the nucleus. Condition (3) means that in any
language the strongest consonant in syllable-initial position is always stronger than the strongest consonant permitted in syllable final position. One implication of (3) is
that syllable-final allophones will always be weaker than
syllable-initial allophones.

Finally, condition (4) is to guarantee that every language has at least CV syllables.

The Universal Syllable Structure Condition is tied
to a universal strength hierarchy. It should be emphasized
that the above condition is a condition on language specific
syllable structure conditions.

5.8 Surface Phonetics and Autonomous Phonemics

The arguments presented in this chapter center on the
notion that surface phonetic structure has some characteristics which are independent of underlying phonological factors
-- this is implicit in Stanley's "phonetic redundancy rules,"
in marking conventions, and in 'conspiracies' or rules which
'look forward,' and it is explicit in such notions as Shibatani's Surface Phonetic Constraints and in Hooper's Positive
Condition on Syllable Structure discussed just above. Before examining the overall effect on the standard theory of

such assumptions and proposals, one remaining problem must
first be dispensed with -- namely the relationship between
surface phonetic representation and autonomous (modern
structuralist) phonemic representation.

The thrust of the approach to syntagmatic phonology
in this chapter has been to deny the validity of stating
phonotactic constraints in terms of underlying structure.
Recall that the original four generalizations on Shanghai
syllable structure were stated in terms of "phonemes" --
that is, such statements were based on the "phonemic syllabary" of Shanghai (Chapter 2, Table 2) rather than the "phonetic syllabary" (Chapter 2, Table 1). In the light of the
present chapter, since surface <u>phonetic</u> constraints are to
be accounted for, the phonetic rather than the phonemic syllabary must provide the basis for such constraints.

However, it might be argued that since there is no
(segmental) morphophonemic alternation in Shanghai, there is
actually very little difference between the underlying level
and the surface phonetic level. If so, then it should make
little difference if constraints are stated in terms of phonemes or surface phones. In essence, this is simply an instance of the argument that phonotactics can be stated at the
structuralist "autonomous phonemic" level -- i.e. phonotactic
statements confine themselves to sequences of phonemes.

But such a claim is only valid depending on which te-

nets the analyst follows in establishing the autonomous phonemes. In modern structuralist phonemic theory the final
phonemic analysis often resulted from establishing a balance
between notions such as complimentary distribution, phonetic
similarity, pattern congruity and economy. Depending on
which principles were stressed and which were deemphasized,
the number, and therefore, of course, the sequential arrangements of the phonemes could vary significantly.

Consider, for instance, the structuralist phonemic
treatment of the palatal series in Mandarin. In Mandarin
there are four series of initial consonants which seem to
be structurally related: the dental series [ts, ts' s],
the retroflex series [tʂ, tʂ', ʂ, r̩], the palatal series
[tɕ, tɕ',] and the velar series [k, k', x]. The palatal
series occurs only before [i] and [ü] whereas the other
three series never occur in this position. In phonemicizing
these series Chao (1934) favors identifying the palatal
series with the velar series (based on native speaker intuition), Hockett (1947) and Hartman (1944) favor identifying
the palatal series with the dental series. But suppose
either of these approaches is followed. We then have sequences such as */kian/, */kiŋ/, */k'iŋ/, etc. by Chao's
analysis or */tsian/, */tsiŋ/, */ts'iŋ/ by Hartman's and
Hockett's analysis. If we are concerned with formulating
constraints on surface phonetic representations and we base

them on sequences of phonemes, then we have to say that in Mandarin, sequences such as */kiaŋ/ or *tsiaŋ/ are allowed as possible forms. Yet Mandarin speakers will reject these forms since they obviously violate surface phonetic constraints -- constraints which disallow, say, [k] followed by [i] or [ü]. One could argue that it is possible to account for phonotactic constraints by formulating statements in terms of phonemes and a set of rules which convert these into phones. But this is just the same position taken in the standard generative theory -- a position which has been argued against above. First, there is no direct way of accounting for surface phonetic structure and secondly, such an approach assumes native speakers borrow, learn language, make acceptability judgements, etc. in terms of underlying forms plus rules. Arguments were presented above that such approaches are untenable.

Thus, a taxonomic phonemic analysis need not directly reflect the syntagmatic surface phonetic structure. That is not to say that such an approach could not directly reflect surface structure -- it could indeed. But the problem is that modern structuralist theory is not constrained in its application of the principles of phonetic similarity, pattern congruity, economy, etc. so that analyses of varying abstractness -- with reference to the surface phonetic level -- are possible.

5.9   Conclusion

The overall conclusion of the examination of surface phonetic structure discussed in this chapter is that the characterization of syntagmatic patterning should not be approached in terms of underlying structure but rather surface structure. If we accept the arguments above, which I believe to be well founded, then it is clear that we must re-examine our conception of syntagmatic structure as outlined in Chapter 2. Given the arguments of the present chapter, the generalizations on Chinese syllable structure in Chapter 2 and the syntagmatic constraints formulated in Chapter 3 must be reformulated so that all generalizations and constraints involve surface phonetic generalizations and constraints. In essence, this means the notion "syntagm" as borrowed from Malmberg and as used in previous chapters must now be redefined as a unit of surface phonetic syntagmatic patterning. Henceforth, the four requirements on syntagmatic structure and the notion "syntagm" deal exclusively with surface as opposed to deep, syntagmatic structure.

The arguments outlined in this chapter then, involve a radical revision of standard generative theory. Such a theory requires that all syntagmatic patterning be stated as the result of an underlying representation and phonological rules. Nevertheless, Stanley notes the need for some device to capture surface phonetic patterning and he hints at "phonetic redundancy rules." Chomsky and Halle (1968) express dissatisfaction with morpheme structure rules and conditions but it is apparent that phonetic, not morphophonemic factors are at the bottom of the "natural" configurations which they propose in their marking conventions.

The notions of "conspiracies" and rules which "look forward" depend critically on a preexisting, independent set of surface phonetic constraints -- that is, there must be independent structure to "look forward" to -- yet these notions are formulated within a theory which explicitly denies that any such set of constraints can exist.

While Shibatani argues for independent surface phonetic constraints, he still allows for some syntagmatic constraints at the underlying level. Hooper rejects the notion of underlying syntagmatic patterning altogether. Her arguments center on the unsuitability of stating phonotactic constraints in terms of a morpho-syntactic unit like the morpheme, rather than in terms of a phonological, pronounceable unit, like the syllable.

In sum, the surface phonetic level must be granted a new status within generative theory. The next chapter is concerned with exploring what the ultimate status of such a level would be.

Chapter Six

THE SURFACE PHONETIC COMPONENT

6.1 Introduction

Following recent proposals in generative theory the
Global Constraint and Local Constraints Requirements on underlying syntagms formulated in Chapter 3 were reformulated in
the preceding chapter to apply to surface syntagms. In addition, the Inherent Structure Requirement which by its very
nature also applies only to the surface phonetic level was
formulated into a Positive Condition on surface syllable
structure.

In one sense, all these revisions are aimed at capturing surface phonetic rather than underlying phenomena.
As such, one could say that such revisions assume that the
organization at the surface phonetic level is semi-independent. This is so because all the revisions assume that certain phenomena are characterized only at the surface level
with no reference to underlying representation or phonological rules.

I use the term "semi-independent" because in a significant sense the surface phonetic level characterized in
these revisions is still largely "derived" in the sense dis-

cussed earlier. The basic structure of surface phonetic representations is in fact still determined by the underlying lexical and systematic phonemic representations plus the phonological rules. The purpose of Shibatani's "surface phonetic constraints" and Hooper's Positive Condition on syllable structure is not to assign structure but rather to interpret it. Both of the formal notions which Shibatani and Hooper utilize -- Sequence Structure Conditions and Positive Conditions -- as formulated by Stanley are actually types of filters. Using Stanley's (1967) terminology, such conditions apply to matrices - if a matrix is "accepted" then we have a unit in the language but if the matric is "rejected" then the unit is ill formed. The interesting question is: where do the matrices come from? The obvious answer is "the lexicon." Generative phonology assumes a "top-to-bottom" organization in which phonological phenomena are originally expressed as features of morphemes. Thus, it naturally follows that the basic phonological structure of a language is formulated in morphophonemic terms. The rest of the phonological component (P-rules, readjustment rules, surface phonetic constraints, syllable structure rules, etc.) takes the "given" structure and operates on it to arrive at a well-formed phonetic representation. Surface phonetic constraints and Positive Conditions then play only an ancillary role.

6.2 The Constituent Structure Requirement

In Chapter 4 it was proposed that the usual and probably most natural way to meet the Constituent Structure
Requirement was to make use of a phrase structure grammar.
Note, however, that a PSG -- as discussed by Postal --
assigns structure. Thus, the formal nature of the PSG is
quite different from the formal nature of the Sequence Structure Conditions and the Positive Condition: the former device assigns phonological structure, the latter devices interpret it. More importantly, it would seem that the PSG
is formally more powerful than the two interpretive conventions. The Sequence Structure Conditions and Positive Conditions are essentially sequential notions but constrained
to one plane, i.e. they are linear. They describe possible
linear sequences of C's and V's and surface phonetic elements -- and express the linear notions "comes before" and
"comes after." However, the structure generated by a PSG
is likewise sequential -- i.e. strings of elements. But,
the output of the PSG is not constrained to one plane, rather,
it is hierarchical. It not only expresses the notions
"comes before" and "comes after" but also "is dominated by,"
"dominates," "is subordinate to," etc. If this is so, then
any constraint expressed by one of the linear interpretative
conditions could also be expressed by the PSG.

It was noted above that the PSG is a more powerful

device than Sequence Structure Conditions and Positive Conditions. However, in an adequate theory, the power of a formal device must be understood and statable -- if a device
is too powerful, then it is not clear just how to constrain
it. Without constraint, such a device can be used to explain much more than it is appropriate for explaining. By
Stanley's own admission (1967) the Positive Condition is
extremely powerful and, in fact, it seems safe to say that
as a formal device its power is still not fully understood.
The formal nature of the PSG is, however, much better understood. Furthermore, the constraints on such a device are
statable in terms of a set of restrictions on PS rules, such
as, for example, only one symbol is rewritten per rule or
elements may not be deleted or permuted, etc. Thus, while
the PSG may be more powerful then the interpretative conditions it is also appropriately constrained.

Let us re-examine the Global Constraint and the Inherent Structure Constraint in light of this discussion. Both
are "global" -- they express structural information about
the entire syntagm. Both are linear rather than hierarchical and both make use of the sequential notions "comes before,"
"comes after." More significantly, both are simply Positive
Conditions. Thus, the functions which both perform can conceivably be expressed by a PSG since it has been argued that
PSG can subsume the device Positive Condition.

6.3 The Phonological Base

6.3.1 Two Views of Phonology

By subsuming the interpretative devices such as Surface Phonetic Constraints and Positive Conditions under a
PSG, it turns out that the surface phonetic level is no
longer semi-independent -- it is now totally independent.
The surface phonetic structure is not derived from the action of P-rules on underlying structures, the output of
which is subject to interpretative constraints. Rather, the
surface phonetic structure is generated and well-formedness
notions are built into the PSG rather than expressed as ancillary filters.

However, such a view of phonology is in direct con-
frontation with the standard theory of generative phonology
as outlined in the section 6.1 above. Is there any precedence for such a radical revision of the standard theory
along these lines? There have been at least two such proposals that I know of in the literature. Both concern a
type of "phonological base."

6.3.2 Sampson's Phonological Base Component

Sampson is concerned with capturing the notion of
"symmetry" in the distribution of phonemes in underlying
structures. Thus, his motivation for the phonological base

component is quite different than the motivations underlying
the present essay. Nevertheless, he does propose a PSG to
account for phonological structure:

> A natural way to formalize an evaluation criterion
> would be to incorporate a "phonological base
> component" into transformational-generative (TG)
> grammars -- i.e. a set of rules for generating
> all and only the phonologically acceptable structures
> in the language, in terms of underlying phonology
> (just as the standard syntactic base generates all
> and only the syntactically acceptable structures
> in terms of deep syntax.) (Sampson 1970: 590)

While he does propose a PSG to generate phonological structure, note that his proposal is to generate underlying structure. This is just the approach that the present work is
trying to avoid. Presumably such a device would generate
well-formed strings of morphophonemes or even autonomous
phonemes. But the revisions proposed in the preceding chapter were based on the idea that well-formedness could not
be treated in terms of underlying structure but rather surface phonetic structure.

Nevertheless, the spirit of Sampson's proposal is in
line with the one here with regard to "derived" versus "independent" phonological structure. In describing the function of a phonological base Sampson uses an analogy with the
syntactic base:

> A base component ... does not accept input, but
> generates output from an arbitrarily designated
> initial symbol; rather than processing sentence-
> representations from one level to another, the
> base defines a range of sentence-representations
> at some particular level. (1970: 591)

For instance, in the present essay, such an arbitrarily
designated initial symbol might be S for syntagm.

Sampson, however, still falls short of actually proposing a phonological component which is directly concerned
with the characterization of surface phonetic representation.
Let us now examine Cheng's proposal.

6.3.3 Cheng's Syllable Grammar Proposal

Above it was argued that an approach to phonology
which made use of a PSG to generate surface level structure would be at odds with the standard theory. In the
standard theory, it was argued, the basic structure is layed
out in the lexicon -- other components convert this basic
representation into a surface output. Another way of characterizing the standard theory is to say that the basic phonological structure is largely determined by the syntactic
component. For instance, morphemes are syntactic units --
that is, they are characterized in the lexicon by syntactic
function. However, as syntactic units, they are also given
a phonological representation. The point here is that the
units are morphologically or syntactically based -- they

are then given phonological interpretations.

Cheng (1966) proposes a rather different conception

of phonology:

> This paper attempts to present the Mandarin phono-
> logical system after the generative fashion. We
> find it convenient to treat this part of the
> grammar in two components: namely a syllable
> grammar and morphophonemics. The former attempts
> to designate the structure of the basic syllables
> independently of the syntactic component of the
> grammar. It consists of a set of P-rules to
> generate strings of phonemes for the basic sylla-
> bles. The latter operates on sequences of these
> syllables with intrasyllabic information designated
> by the syllable grammar, and with category and
> intersyllabic information which can be given by the
> syntactic component. It consists of T-rules and
> gives phonetic representation of sentences as its
> output. (Cheng 1966: 135)

According to Cheng, in this scheme a morphophonemic repre-

sentation of a sentence is assigned both syntactical and

syllable structures (p. 136). At another point he says that

the morphophonemic component "is likely to operate upon the

outputs of both the SG (syllable grammar) and syntactic

components" (p. 152).

However, he does maintain that at least part of pho-

nology can be independent:

> ... we do not deny the possibility of treating phono-
> logy entirely independent of syntax (cf. Martin 1957;
> Hockett 1947, 1950). But it seems to us that to
> make our analysis simple and meaningful some part
> of phonology must be stated in accordance with
> syntax.

> On the other hand we cannot agree to the contention
> that no part of phonology can be treated indepen-
> dently of the syntax of the language. We have shown
> in Section 2 that a grammar can be written so that
> it prescribes all possible phonemic (actually
> morphophonemic) shapes of morphemes that the syn-
> tax may have as its fundamental units. This SG
> accounts for the fact that a native speaker of
> Mandarin can tell that a sequence like stei or ist
> is not a 'word' in his language, while kai or iau
> may be something in his language no matter whether
> he knows its meaning or not, or whether it appears
> in the syntactic context or not. (Cheng 1966:
> (Emphasis mine).

I am a bit puzzled by the first statement but quite in agreement with the second. I assume that the ultimate purpose of th
phonological component is to connect sound with meaning --
this hardly seems possible if one is to treat phonology entirely independently of syntax. Thus, by rejecting this
idea Cheng is not making his analysis more "meaningful" or
"simple" but is rather making language description possible.

The second statement is in agreement with this essay
and presumably with the arguments proposed in the preceding
chapter. Shibatani, Stanley, Hooper and others referred to
there have put a great deal of emphasis on surface phonetic
structure. Likewise Hooper has put a great deal of emphasis
on the syllable as a "unit of pronunciation." Underlying
claims about borrowing, first and second language acquisition and native speaker judgements on admissible and inadmissible forms, is the implicit assumption that surface
phonetic forms may be syntactically and lexically undefined,

just as Cheng is claiming above. That is, whether a form
is "pronounceable" (in Hooper's terms) is directly related
to borrowing, acquisition, etc. and the "pronounceability"
of a form may have nothing to do with its meaning or its syntactic function. For instance, a native speaker can make
judgements about such forms given a list of nonsense words --
none of which is lexically or syntactically defined. Likewise, it is conceivable that a speaker could attempt to
borrow a foreign form and make changes in its pronunciation
without reference to syntax or meaning. In the same vein,
a child may "rehearse" a new form solely to master its pronunciation, i.e. surface phonetic structure, without knowing
its meaning and function. Likewise, a second-language learner
constantly grapples with surface forms, the meanings and
usages of which he is quite unclear. All these examples
make use of the notion "pronounceability" and this notion
need not be defined in terms other than purely phonological.

Thus, if I understand Cheng's proposal, a syllable
grammar is separate from the morphophonemic component for
just this reason -- syllable structure has its own independent organization.

This approach is essentially supportive of Hockett's
conception of constituent structure of the syllable. Furthermore, as we have seen, to characterize constituent structure we must assume independent phonological organization

at the surface phonetic level. Yet, Cheng's proposal suffers
from his use of phonemes -- which he actually equates with
morphophonemes. By following a phonemic approach he is dealing with underlying structure and therefore not surface phonetic forms. Thus, his syllable grammar more resembles the
base component proposed by Sampson. For instance, when Cheng
says, as quoted above, that native speakers of Mandarin can
tell that _stei_ and _ist_ are not 'words' in Mandarin while _kai_
and _iau_ may "be something in his language whether he knows
its meaning or not, or whether it appears in syntactic context or not" -- he is making a claim about surface phonetic
forms and not syllables specified in terms of underlying
phonemes or morphophonemes. Of course, if the phonemic
analysis is done so that the underlying and surface levels
are biunique then this is no problem. But generative theory
does not adhere to this constraint and as I argued in Chapter 5, autonomous phonemics need not necessarily adhere to
this condition either.

6.4 The Surface Phonetic Component

6.4.1 The Independence of the Surface Phonetic Component

Although Cheng's syllable grammar is not exactly adequate for expressing constituent structure at the surface,
it does offer some idea of how an independently generated

surface structure might interact with syntactically motivated
phonological structure. Cheng assumes three components: a
syllable-grammar, a morphophonemic component and a syntactic
component. Suppose we revise his syllable grammar so that
it does not generate phonemes or morphophonemes, but rather
surface phonetic elements. Moreover, suppose that instead
of a "syllable" grammar we speak of a "syntagm" grammar.
In addition, let this syntagm grammar be a part of a larger
component, the Surface Phonetic Component. In this conception of phonology there are still three components which interact. The syntactic component supplies morphemes in a
lexicon. Lexical items receive a morphophonemic, abstract,
characterization. The morphophonemic component is concerned
with the phonological processes which act on morphophonemic
representations to arrive at the surface phonetic representation. The surface phonetic representation, however, is
independently generated by the Surface Phonetic Component
which assigns structure by a PSG. Obviously, since both the
Surface Phonetic Component and the Morphophonemic Component
are concerned with the proper surface phonetic representation, one component cannot completely dominate the other.
This sort of domination has been the case in standard theory.
Phonetic structure has been interpretive. The lexicon and
phonological rules have dominated. This approach can be
seen as phonology from the top down. We begin with abstract

forms stated in terms of morphophonemes, apply phonological rules and get a derived surface structure. A Surface Phonetic Component represents an approach of phonology from the bottom up. We begin with a PSG which generates pronounceable, well-formed utterances without reference to any other component. Obviously, there must be an interface between the two. The morphophonemic model of generative theory cannot adequately account for surface phonetic structure -- a great deal of which seems to have no connection with morphophonemic processes. A Surface Phonetic Component only generates endless well-formed syntagms with no syntactic or lexical categorization -- much like turning out well-formed, pronounceable, nonsense forms.

The interface of these two components is a complex issue and well beyond the scope of this essay. The main point is that there must be some sort of constant reference between the two components. The Surface Phonetic Component must account for syntagms which will be derived from morphophonemic processes. Cheng distinguishes between basic syllables and non-basic syllables. I prefer to call the latter derived syllables. Basic syllables are generated by the PSG. Derived syllables are the results of morphophonemic processes on basic syllables. For example, in Mandarin, according to Cheng, shen (Tone 2) is a basic syllable as is me (toneless). However, the effect of mor-

phophonemics is to produced <u>shem</u> (Tone 2). <u>Shem</u> is a derived syllable -- the PSG does not produce Mandarin syllables
ending in <u>m</u> -- nevertheless this is still a syllable. An
analogous problem is mentioned by Hooper (1973). In English,
in monomorphemic monosyllables there is no syllable final
<u>bd</u> cluster. But as a result of morphophonemics we get
"rubbed" (rubd) etc. as a syllable having this cluster.
Hooper claims such forms are perhaps somewhat deviant.

There seem to be two ways of handling this. One is
to make sure that the PSG generates <u>all</u> surface syllables
regardless of whether they are monomorphemic or polymor-
phemic. Thus a syllable grammar of Mandarin must generate
syllables which can end in <u>m</u> and an English syllable grammar
must generate syllables which can end in <u>bd</u>. Another solution is to have a base PSG but also a separate device to
cover the phonetic shapes of derived as opposed to basic
syllables.

At the same time, the phonological rules of the Morphophonemic Component must have access to surface phonetic
information -- "looking forward" -- so that no P-rule is
allowed which violates surface phonetic structure. Likewise, P-rules may need access to syllable divisions in order
to be properly formulated.

I will discuss the interface no further in this essay.
I am mainly interested in demonstrating that an independent

surface phonetic structure exists and in discovering how
that independent structure is to be characterized.

6.4.2 Functional Notions in a PSG[1]

Above, it was suggested that the constituent structure of a syntagm can be assigned by a PSG and that such a
PSG is a part of the Surface Phonetic Component.

Cheng formulated a set of PS rules but these rules
(and thus Cheng's PSG) are misconceived. Consider the
following phrase structure marker from Chomsky (1965):

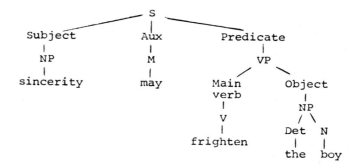

----

1. A theory of the role of functional relationships in
phonology is being developed by Professor John Bowers. The
ideas and formulations in this and the following sections
stem directly from my work with Professor Bowers both in
his Spring 1975 phonology seminar at Cornell and in a number
of stimulating conversations. I am deeply indebted to him
for leading me to understand the notion of "function" as
applied to phonology and to his insistence that I explore
Hockett's Manual of Phonology in the light of such "functional phonology."

In a phrase structure grammar relational notions are inherent in the rules of the grammar; categories, on the other
hand, are drawn from a set of substantive universals.
According to Chomsky, in such a P-marker as the one above
the categorical and functional notions have been confused -
namely functional notions have been assigned categorial
status. The notions "subject-of" and "predicate of" are
relational or functional notions. The notions NP and VP,
are not relational notions; they simply characterize certain categories. Consider then, the following P-marker:

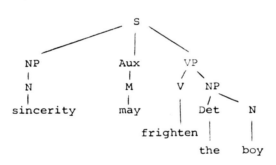

In this sentence, the relational or functional notions
"Subject" and "Predicate" are not to be seen. This is because relational notions are inherent in the structure of
the marker: that NP which occurs before VP expresses the
relation "subject of" sentence; that VP which occurs after
NP and Aux expresses the relational notion "Predicate-of"
sentence. Thus, the NP "functions" as subject and the VP

"functions" as predicate but these notions "subject" and
"predicate" are not categories.

Now consider Cheng's (1966: 146) P-marker (only a
fragment is given here):

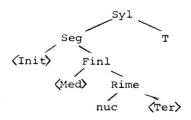

The problem here is that the notions Initial, Final, Rime,
Nucleus and Terminal are functional or relational notions,
yet they are being treated -- just as in Chomsky's first
example above -- as categorial notions. What is necessary
is a phrase structure model that captures the relational
notions "initial-of" (syntagm), "final of," "rime of," etc.

6.4.3 Bowers' PSG[2]

Bowers has proposed a PSG for syntagmatic phonetic

----

2. The PSG notions as well as the formalism utilized here
have been proposed by Professor John Bowers in his Spring
1975 phonology seminar and in conversations. Bowers' model
is much more elaborate and comprehensive than the fragment
which I am utilizing here. Specifically, Bowers' model goes
well beyond the Chinese data I am concerned with since he
also attempts to account for the very complex problem of
"interludes" (see Hockett (1955)). The analysis in this
essay is restricted to the monosyllable.

structure which can be described by the following PS rules
and phrase-marker:

$$S \longrightarrow (\overline{\overline{C}})\overline{V}$$
$$\overline{V} \longrightarrow V(\overline{\overline{C}})$$
$$\overline{\overline{C}} \longrightarrow (C)\overline{C}$$
$$\overline{C} \longrightarrow C(C)$$

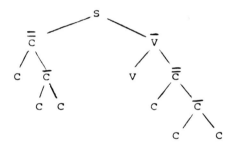

The above formulation was intended specifically to characterize English but, of course, a PSG base could be formulated
as a universal base.[3] The bar notation allows one expansion
of the symbol per bar. In this framework the substantive
universals are the categories S, Consonant and Vowel. Some
relational notions are:

----

3. Bowers' own model would include a recursive S to take
care of interludes and larger units which I have been calling "syntagms."

"Initial of"

"Final of"

"Nucleus of"

"Coda of"

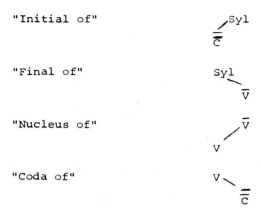

Of course, other relations exist among consonant clusters, glides, etc.

Thus, Bowers' model avoids the problems of category-function confusion. Applying this formulation to the English word "strange" we get the following P-marker:

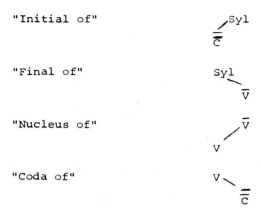

Since Bowers has proposed this formulation for structures beyond the syllable, in keeping with the terminology adopted earlier, such a device could be termed a Syntagm Grammar. However, for purposes of the following discussion, I will use the term PSG in this new, revised sense as proposed by Bowers.

6.5   The Implications of the PSG Base

6.5.1   The PSG and Syntagmatic Structure

The PSG has been proposed to express the constituent structure of syntagms -- in this essay -- syllables. It was argued earlier that the Global Constraint Requirement on syntagmatic structure (canonical form) and the Inherent Structure Requirement (syllable structure) were both characterized by Positive Conditions and as such, could be expressed by a PSG.

This is obviously true given the above formulation: canonical shape is now given by the various possible C's and V's which are generated by the PSG. Such a formulation is certainly superior to the linear Positive Condition which was proposed by Stanley to account for canonical shape. Stanley's formulation would inadequately characterize a maximum Chinese syllable as CVVC whereas the actual structure, functionally speaking is always:

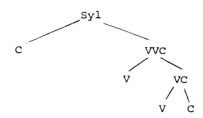

Moreover, Hooper's notions syllable-strong and syllable-weak position are likewise easily captured by such a framework. The Initial "functions as" a strong position, the Coda "functions as" a weak position. As noted earlier, since all of Hooper's strong-weak notions are sequential, all can be captured by the PSG. But now, notions like syllable-initial and syllable-final are not simply linear positional notions but structural, functional notions.

As a result, three of the requirements on phonology theory with respect to syntagmatic structure can now be expressed by one device, the PSG, thereby greatly simplifying the overall grammar.

6.5.2 The PSG and the Features Consonantal and Vocalic

The traditional practice of stating canonic form statements in terms of C's and V's implies that these categories have always been seen as somehow basic. Likewise, Stanley saw these features as somehow different from the others when he formulated the Positive Condition on canonic shape:

> ... in the theory of MS conditions, we require
> that positive conditions be used in stating re-
> strictions on syllable structure, that is in stating
> restrictions involving the features consonantal,
> vocalic and perhaps obstruent. This requirement is
> motivated by the fact that these features are
> typically interrelated in different ways than other
> features, a fact that implies that they should be
> treated formally in different ways. (Stanley 1967:
> 432).

Chomsky and Halle (1968) also based their first four marking
conventions on syllable structure and noted that these conventions differed from the other conventions "not only in
their content but also in the principles governing their
applications." (p. 408)

In the PSG proposed above, these categories again
receive special treatment. Here, they are characterized in
terms of their functions -- consonants function as initials
and codas, vowels function as the nucleus etc. Such a functional approach gives structural meaning to such units rather
than simply characterizing them in terms of inherent phonetic
terms. In fact, it may be possible to eliminate distinctive
features such as consonantal and vocalic since they are now
substantive categories in a relational network.

6.5.3   The PSG and the Feature Syllabic

The feature syllabic has sometimes been proposed for

several purposes. One claim proposed by Milner and Baily
(cited in Chomsky and Halle 1968) is that <u>syllabic</u> characterize all segments constituting a syllabic peak. Anderson
(1974: 297) uses the feature somewhat differently:

> ... this feature serves to organize the syllable
> into an initial ([-syllabic]) margin, a ([+syllabic])
> peak and perhaps a final ([-syllabic]) margin.
> (p. 297)

But Anderson does not see this feature as necessarily a
feature of segments:

> The feature [+syllabic] , then, would correspond not
> directly to a property of individual segments, but
> rather to the location of the peak/margin boundaries
> or the distribution of syllabic energy across the
> syllable. (1974: 267)

In the PSG approach such notions as "initial margin," "final
margin," and "peak" are structural notions of the syllable
-- they are built in. Thus, the feature, in the sense Anderson is using it would not be necessary. Anderson's approach
is to try to characterize the syllable in terms of sequential,
linear, positional notions by a sequence of linear features.
The PSG approach need not always capture functional notions
by features.

Likewise, the notion $\bar{V}$ in the PSG is not meant to be
taken necessarily as a vowel. This category is meant to
capture the notion "syllabicity." The symbol $\bar{V}$ could stand
for, any ayllabic segment, consonantal or vocalic. Thus,

here again, there is no need for the feature syllabic.

Incidentally, this formulation solves a problem common in Chinese language descriptions. As I pointed out in Walton (1971) past investigators have often ignored syllabic nasal and lateral syllables in canonic form statements since they often foul up Morpheme Structure statements. This often results in setting up an underlying ad hoc vowel so that the canonical shape #C# is avoided and we get #CV# but delete the vowel on the surface. I argued against such an approach in Walton (1971) and posited the syllable type #C#. However, this led to an awkward syllable formula and ultimately an awkward Positive Condition. This canonic shape for Shanghai was given in Chapter 2:

$$\#C((V)V\left(\begin{matrix}V\\C\end{matrix}\right))\#$$

Thus, the minimal syllable is #C#, but notice that the C is a margin unit and not in the nucleus position. However, this is just one of the defects of a Positive Condition: it does not provide for notions like nucleus, only notions such as C and V.

In the present framework, this could be handled quite naturally since $\bar{V}$ could simply represent the syllabic consonant.

6.6   Phonetic Representation and the PSG

6.6.1   Units at the Surface Phonetic Level

The PSG generates surface phonetic level representations and characterizes surface phonetic organization -- yet
what are the units at this level? I have argued elsewhere
in this work that such units cannot be autonomous phonemes
and, of course, they are not systematic phonemes. Therefore, it would seem that the units involved are simply
"phones." But "phones" can have a range of detail from
minute to quite broad. Obviously, it is not necessary for
characterizing surface phonetic structure in terms of the
constituent structure of a syllable that all low level phonetic information (e.g. degree of aspiration) be present.
Such detail can be given by "detail rules" as proposed by
Postal (1968). The single strong requirement on such surface units is that they provide surface contrasts between
forms -- degrees of aspiration of English do not do this
so this need not be dealt with in the PSG. We could simply
term these units "surface phonetic phonemes," though perhaps no special term is required as long as it is understood that additional "detail rules" will apply.

6.6.2   Phonetic Representation and the Notion "Function"

Consider the surface phonetic representation of the

Shanghai syllable #liaŋ# in the standard theory (only a
fragment is given):

	l	i	a	ŋ
Syllabic	-	+	+	-
Sonorant	+	+	+	+
Consonantal	+	-	-	+
Continuant	-	+	+	-
Coronal	+	-	-	-

Note that this conception of the syllable /liaŋ/ is
linear and sequential and that each segment is differentiated
from the other. Furthermore, each segment is characterized
by a universal set of features. These features may be ranked
in some hierarchy -- this is presumably one of the goals of
markedness theory. But in the characterization above,
each segment is basically independent -- the only relationships involved among segments are "comes before," "comes
after."

Now consider the following formulation:[4]

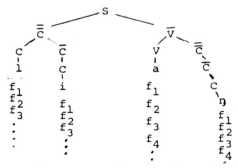

---
4. This particular interpretation of the syllable #lian#
will be discussed in the following chapter.

In this formulation each segment enters into relationships
with the other segments. That is, each segment is <u>function-</u>
<u>ally</u> characterized.

The consequences of looking at phonological structure
in this sense is that some features can probably be ranked
in a hierarchy universally <u>but</u> <u>with</u> <u>respect</u> <u>to</u> <u>how</u> <u>they</u> <u>func-</u>
<u>tion</u> <u>in</u> <u>phonological</u> <u>structures</u>, not simply in terms of
their inherent qualities. Obviously the inherent qualities
and the structural functions must be related but in order
to understand this relationship we must find out how units
function structurally. It may well be that such a conception of surface phonetic structure will have ramifications
in determining feature hierarchies, in slips of the tongue,
in sound change, in rime and a good deal other areas. I
shall not explore these notions here but see Bowers (forth-
coming).[5]

6.7 The Design of the Surface Phonetic Components

The PSG outlined in this chapter has provided a device for satisfying the Global Constraint Requirement, the
Inherent Structure Requirement and the Constituent Structure
Requirement. This leaves one requirement yet to be treated,
the Local Constraints Requirement.

----
5. Bowers has presented cogent arguments based on slips of
the tongue to justify particular functional analyses of word
initial consonant clusters in English.

In Chapter 4, it was demonstrated that such constraints
can be adequately expressed by Sequence Structure Conditions.
Indeed, such conditions will still be necessary even with a
PSG base. The PSG generates structure in terms of the structure of the syllable. The terminal symbols of the PSG outlined above could presumably be filled by all C's and V's
in the language. However, this will never be the case.
The PSG itself will constrain the occurrence of many consonants structurally. For instance in English we find the
maximum Initial expressed as:

$$\begin{array}{c}
\overset{=}{C} \diagup \text{Syl} \\
C_1 \quad \overset{=}{C} \\
C_2 \quad C_3
\end{array}$$

Structurally, C_1 can only be s̲ and C_3 can only be a liquid
or a glide.

However, even though a great many facts are captured
functionally, there will still be some sequences which are
not captured in this way, e.g. s̲r̲. Such cases simply represent local (context sensitive) co-occurrence constraints
which can be quite adequately accounted for by sequence
structure conditions.

Moreover, as discussed earlier, the Surface Phonetic

Component may also require a set of Detail Rules to handle low level phonetic phenomena not relevant to constituent structure.

Thus the Surface Phonetic Component might be represented as this:

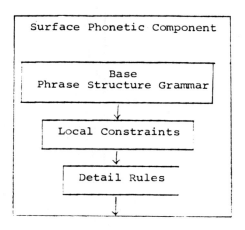

Of course, I have not attempted here to indicate the interface of the various outputs of the sub-components with the morphophonemic component.

6.8 Summary and Conclusion

This essay began with the claim that certain features of Chinese phonological structure could not be adequately characterized within the present framework of generative theory. Specifically, the problem was seen to lie in cer-

tain facets of Chinese syllable structure. In Chapter 2
a number of observations were made about the structure of
the syllable in a specific Chinese language, the Shanghai
dialect of Wu. These observations were formulated as a
set of valid linguistic generalizations about Chinese which,
as it turned out, were all concerned with syntagmatic phonological structure. Following both traditional and generative theories, these syntagmatic generalizations were
formulated in terms of underlying structure.

These generalizations on syntagmatic patterning were
seen to apply to all Chinese languages and in Chapter 3, it
was argued that, in fact, such generalizations could be reformulated as a set of constraints on phonological theory
and thus as a set of constraints on all languages. In
Chapter 4 it was revealed that three of the four requirements on syntagmatic structure could seemingly be met by
utilizing and synthezizing certain notions which have been
proposed at various times within the standard theory.

However, in Chapter 5, various inadequacies of the
standard theory were brought to light. These inadequacies
were not so much concerned with the formal devices proposed in Chapter 4 as they were with the conception of syntagmatic phonology inherent in the standard theory. The
crux of the issue was that the standard theory attempted to
account for the syntagmatic nature of surface phonetic or-

ganization in terms of underlying structure and rules and
that such an approach could be shown to be inadequate. The
proposed revisions sought to treat syntagmatic patterning
as a surface phonetic phenomenon. Accepting these proposed
revisions as valid, it then became necessary to reformulate
the four requirements on syntagmatic patterning (and thus
the original generalizations on Shanghai and Chinese syllable structure) such that they applied to the surface phonetic
level of phonological organization rather than the underlying level. In addition, a formal device for capturing
the notion "syllable strength" was adopted from Hooper (1973),
thus satisfying the Inherent Structure Requirement.

In Chapter 4, it had been proposed that some version
of a Phrase Structure Grammar could be utilized to satisfy
the Constituent Structure Requirement. Given the revisions
in generative theory proposed in Chapter 5, however, it became clear that such a PSG would have to generate surface
phonetic elements. It has been argued in the present chapter that such a notion that surface phonetic elements can
be directly generated rather than derived from underlying
phonological structure and rules is presently untenable in
generative theory. Moreover, such a claim is much stronger
than any revision proposed in Chapter 5. Nevertheless,
Sampson (1970) has hinted at such an approach and Cheng
(1966) has suggested and defended this approach within the

early framework of generative phonology. In addition, as it turns out, a surface structure PSG can adequately capture the notions Positive Condition on Syntagm (canonical shape) and Positive Condition on Syllable Structure. Thus the Global Constraint, the Inherent Structure Requirement and the Constituent Structure Requirement are satisfied by such a PSG.

In conclusion, it seems that the most adequate way to express the four requirements on syntagmatic phonological structure - thereby accounting for the character of Chinese syntagmatic structure -- is in terms of a <u>Surface Phonetic Component</u> which consists of a PSG base, a Local Constraints sub-component and perhaps a Detail Rule sub-component.

Such an approach represents a radical departure from the standard theory in that the primacy of morphophonemic processes is no longer an inherent feature of phonological theory. Surface phonetic structure is in a sense independent of morphophonemic patterning -- a point which linguists working on Chinese have been trying to make for some time (c.f. Wang's proposal for a "new phonemic" level cited in Chapter 1). The Surface Phonetic Component and the Morphophonemic Component share the burden of connecting sound with meaning but the interface is not conceived as it would be in standard theory where the Morphophonemic Component would provide phonological structure and the Surface Phonetic Component would interpret, constrain, filter, and readjust this structure. While it is not at all clear just how the two components would interface, it must be the case that neither dominates the other; each can serve as input to the other, rather than as in the standard framework where only one -- the morphophonemic -- is input to the other -- the surface phonetic.

Such an approach to phonology, then, allows for a realistic and certainly more adequate characterization of Chinese phonological structure. The following chapter is concerned with briefly reexamining the Shanghai data presented in Chapter 2 in light of the proposed Surface Phonetic Component.

Chapter Seven

THE SURFACE PHONETIC COMPONENT IN SHANGHAINESE

7.1 Introduction

In the preceding chapter it was argued that there
exists a level of phonetic organization which is independent of higher level, morphophonemic patterns. The primary
unit of this level of phonetic organization is the syntagm.
Furthermore, it has been suggested that four requirements
must be met in an adequate characterization of the syntagmatic phonetic structure of a given language. First, the
canonical shape of the syntagms of a language must be accounted for -- hence, the Global Constraint Requirement.
Furthermore, specific cooccurrence restrictions which ob-
tain between the segments of a syntagm must likewise be
accounted for - hence the Local Constraints Requirement. In
addition, it seems plausible to assume that the syntagms of
a language are subject to certain inherent structural tendencies such as "strengthening" of segments in syllable or
word final position. This assumption is incorporated into
the Inherent Structure Requirement. Finally, it has been

argued that the elements of a syntagm enter into certain
functional relationships with one another in such a way that
the syntagms manifest an internal hierarchical organizational
structure. This led to the postulation of the Constituent
Structure Requirement. Given these requirements, it has
been proposed that the phonetic organization of the syntagm
is most adequately characterized in terms of a type of
Phrase Structure model of phonological structure.

The present chapter is concerned with briefly reexamining the Shanghai data presented in Chapter 2 in terms
of the framework outlined directly above.

7.2 The Base Component

In meeting the four requirements discussed above, it
is obvious that the Constituent Structure Requirement presents the most significant problems. The Local Constraints
Requirement is satisfied by a set of Sequence Structure Conditions identical in form to those proposed in Walton (1971)
for Shanghai. Recall that these conditions are not a part
of the base Phrase Structure component. Recall further that
the Global Constraint Requirement on canonical shape and
the Inherent Structure Requirement can both be subsumed under
the Constituent Structure Requirement.

In approaching the data, then, the goal is to account
for the syntagmatic structure of Shanghai surface phonetic

syllables in terms of constituent structure. An examination
of the Phonetic Syllabary (Chapter 2) reveals that there are
five types of surface phonetic syllables (just as there were
five types of phonological syllables):

1.	C	$ŋ$	(Tone 3)	"fish"
2.	CV	mi	(Tone 3)	"uncooked rice"
3.	CVC	$lo?$	(Tone 5)	"sex"
4.	CVV	hue	(Tone 3)	"great, heroic"
5.	$CVVC$	$huaŋ$	(Tone 1)	"marriage"

In Chapter 2 the traditional analysis of the Chinese syllable was given as below.

Tone			
Initial	Final		
	Medial	Rime	
		Nucleus	Ending

Furthermore, in Chapter 2 arguments were presented in
justification of an identical analysis of the modern Shanghai
syllable. Such arguments were based chiefly on the privilege
of paradigmatic substitution of certain units in certain positions. For instance, the fillers of the Initial position
are entirely different from those of the Final position and
if one were to make a break in the syllable it is obvious
that the least amount of bonding obtains between the Initial
and the Final. Likewise, the Rime is a coherent unit since

it can occur in some cases with a medial and in other cases
without the medial. Furthermore, the nucleus functions as
a coherent unit since it can occur in some cases without
the medial or the ending. Thus, various units are seen as
coherent at various levels.

In terms of the present framework, these relationships are to be expressed in terms of a set of Phrase Structure rules. Given the above discussion, such a base component for Shanghai might be formulated along the following
lines:

$$\text{Syllable} \longrightarrow (C)\overline{\overline{V}}$$
$$\overline{\overline{V}} \longrightarrow (V)\overline{V}$$
$$\overline{V} \longrightarrow V(C)$$

Let us consider how such a base would characterize the basic
syllable types listed earlier. Type 1, consisting of a sin-
gle syllabic consonant would result from the expansion of $\overline{\overline{V}}$
to obligatory $\underline{V}$. However, it is important to note that the
symbol $\underline{V}$ is _functionally_ a syllable nucleus and not necessarily a vowel. That is, by definition every syllable must
have a nucleus and such a nucleus may be either vowel or
consonant. If it is a consonant, it must be syllabic in
nature. Thus $ŋ$ "fish" would be derived as follows:

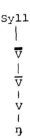

Obviously, these rules can also account for Type 2 syllables - CV - in a straightforward manner. The form mi "uncooked rice" would be represented as:

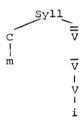

Likewise, there is no problem in accounting for Type 3 syllables - CVC - under the base component proposed above. Consider, for instance, the derivation of $lo?$ - "sex":

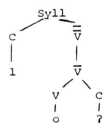

If we follow the interpretation of the Shanghai syllable along the lines of the traditional analysis of the Chinese syllable then Type 4 - CVV - and Type 5 - CVVC - syllables would be characterized as follows for the forms hue
"great, heroic" and $huaŋ$ "marriage":

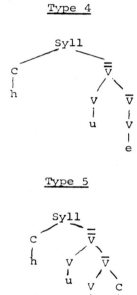

Type 4

Type 5

Such a base component, then, adequately characterizes the
constituent structure of Shanghai syllables as long as the
standard interpretation of Chinese syllable structure is
followed. However, the traditional Chinese analysis of the
syllable with respect to the status of medials has often

been ignored by modern linguists. A revision of the status
of the medial would necessitate a revision of the base component formulated above. Thus, some discussion of the status
of the syllable medial is necessary.

7.3 The Status of the Medial

Both modern structuralist and generative analyses of
various Chinese languages have often approached the analysis
of the medial with considerations that go beyond those of
the traditional Chinese phonologist. Depending on the theory
employed,various possibilities exist for the structural interpretation of medials. In structuralist approaches, one
of the chief considerations in interpreting medials is the
interplay of pattern pressure or pattern congruity with
phoneme inventory. For instance, in Shanghai, the medial u̲
occurs only after velars and post-velars. In a structuralist analysis where one is concerned with proper phonemiciza--
tion, two possibilities exist in such a case. One is to set
up a series of labio-velar (etc.) phonemes such as /k^w/
thereby increasing phoneme inventory but simplifying pattern
congruity (CVC vs. CVVC). The other possibility is to set
up an underlying sequence of consonant plus vowel, such as
/ku/ thereby reducing phoneme inventory (no labio-velars)
but complicating pattern congruity (e.g. CVVC vs. CVC). As
noted in Walton (1971) both McCoy and T. Cheng have discussed

just this problem in Cantonese. McCoy (1966: Fn. 22, 188-9)
noted that whereas earlier linguists had analyzed Cantonese
labio-velar initials as, for example, $/k^w/$ such sounds could
have been interpreted as /k/ plus medial /u/ without any
increase in phoneme inventory but with some pattern imbalance
in syllable types.

In a generative analysis of Cantonese, T. Cheng (1968:
C24) discussed the interpretation of labio-velars in much
the same fashion. She concluded that $\underline{k}^w$ and $\underline{k'}^w$ should not
be set up on the systematic phonemic level for the following
reasons:

(1) KUX and K'UX are not distinct from K^wUX and K'^wUX
respectively.

(2) The rounding need not be a part of the initial
consonant, but can be represented by a following
$\underline{u}$.

(3) Secondary rounding can then be predicted by the
following segment.

(4) Secondary rounding is not common for Chinese
initials and therefore is best considered as
assimilation to the following rounded vowel.

Discussions on this problem abound in the literature concerned with Cantonese. Here, I have simply chosen several
representative examples. The point is that the interpretation of a $\underline{u}$ medial in these cases is not so clear-cut as the
traditional analysis would lead us to believe. That is, it
is possible to consider the medial as being a feature of the

initial (i.e., /k^w/ + /x/ vs. /k/ + /u/ + /x/).

If we were following either a structuralist or standard generative approach such conditions as those just mentioned would be of some value in determining the analysis
of the medials in Shanghainese. However, the approaches
just discussed differ in a significant way from the present
approach. Note that these are attempts to account for surface phonetic structure in terms of underlying (phonemic or
systematic phonemic) structure. In the present framework
however, we are interested not in the underlying interpretation of a segment or segments but in the surface "function"
of a segment. That is, in surface phonetic organization is
the medial <u>structurally</u> a part of the Initial or <u>structurally</u>
a part of the Final? Questions of inventory or of pattern
congruity must be rephrased at the surface phonetic level
into functional terms.

Thus, the problem, is terms of the present framework
can be summarized as follows. If the medial in Shanghai is
to be analyzed as a part of the <u>Final</u>, then the base component and structural description provided in the previous section is appropriate. If the medial is to be considered a
part of the <u>Initial</u>, then a different set of base rules would
have to be formulated:

$$\text{Syll} \longrightarrow (\bar{C})\bar{V}$$
$$\bar{C} \longrightarrow C(C)$$
$$\bar{V} \longrightarrow V(C)$$

Using this base, the syllable $huaŋ$ would not be characterized as:

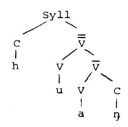

but rather as:

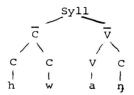

Given the second alternative, the structural convention would
be that the right branching consonant directly dominated by
C̄ will always be a semi-consonant or will always be restricted to either w or y.

Unfortunately, there is no available data on Shanghai
which can directly resolve this problem. The sort of data
required would have to go beyond what Zwicky (1973) has
termed the "orthodox list" of sources for resolving analyti-
cal problems in phonology. The orthodox sources of data for
resolving such a problem would be (1) variant shapes of mor-

phemes and (2) distributional restrictions on phonological
elements. Source (1) does not exist in most Chinese languages, including Shanghai. Source (2) relies on "linear"
distribution rather than on hierarchical distribution as
is required in a constituent structure analysis.

Zwicky lists twenty-two other, supposedly "unorthodox"
sources of data for resolving problems in phonological analysis. I list a number of these here:

(1) speech errors
(2) misperceptions
(3) aphasia
(4) borrowing
(5) linguistic games
(6) productivity of processes
(7) poetic requirements
(8) historical change
(9) acquisition
(10) stylistic variation
(11) patterns of exceptions
(12) informant judgements on novel forms
(13) distorted speech

If, for instance, there was data available that demonstrated
that in speech errors (e.g. spoonerisms) the h of $huaŋ$ was
transposed or that hu was transposed then one could make
arguments for the interpretation of u as either a member of
the final (-uan) or as a semi-consonant member of the initial (hw-).

While data such as this is not available, it would seem
that future research might uncover just the necessary data.
A promising area, for instance, would be Chinese secret languages. Chao (1931) discusses just such data in an arti-

cle on secret languages (Shanghai not included). At one
point, he specifically refers to the use of secret languages
as a way of resolving whether a medial "belongs to" the
Initial or the Final. His examples are quite interesting
and are presented below (Chao 1931: 317):

Peking	kwa :拐-囗 kwai-lwa	(considered as: kw + wa
Gwangzhou	kwa :橄 囗 lɒ-kwi	(considered as: kw + a
Fuzhou	kwa :囗-囗 lwa - ki	(considered as: k + wa)

That is, the word for "melon" when pronounced in standard
Peking Mandarin is <u>kwa</u> but when the word is respelled in
secret language by splitting up the Initial from the Final
(and adding other elements) the <u>w</u> is assigned to both the
Initial and the Final. On the other hand, in Cantonese
when the word <u>kwa</u> is divided in secret language, the <u>w</u>
remains with the initial implying that the medial structurally goes with the Initial. In the Min language of Fuzhou,
however, the word <u>kwa</u> is divided such that the medial is
assigned to the Final. Chao's examples demonstrate two important points. One is that knowledge of the structure of
secret languages may provide valuable psycholinguistic information. The other is that the proper interpretation of
medials as structurally aligning with the Initial or with
the Final may vary from Chinese language to language and

-157-

possibly even from dialect to dialect.

In sum, it would appear from a functional point of view
that there is not sufficient information to vigorously defend either possibility with regard to Shanghai medials.
Given this situation, I prefer the base component presented
in the previous section if only for the reason that it seems
more in accord with the traditional conception of the medial
as belonging to the Final.

7.4 Conclusion

A more standard treatment of the Shanghai data would
be that proposed by Walton (1971). In such a treatment
two facets of the present framework would be conspicuously
absent. First, no attempt would be made to account explicitly for inherent syllable structure, though, of course, the
investigator might implicitly be aware of such structure.
In the present treatment, inherent structure is captured in
terms of constituent structure. That is, the notions of
"strong" position and "weak" position in the syllable are
defined as structural relations defined by the base component. For example

defines initial position and thus "strong" position, whereas
the derivation

$$
\begin{array}{l}
\text{Syll} \\
\quad \searrow \\
\quad\ \overline{\overline{V}} \\
\quad \swarrow\ \searrow \\
V\quad \overline{V} \\
\qquad\ \searrow \\
\qquad\quad C
\end{array}
$$

indicates that the right-most and lowest C must occupy syllable "weak" position.

Furthermore, the standard model would make no attempt
to capture surface phonetic relationships in terms of hierarchical or constituent structure. That is, notions such as
"initial of" and "final of" would not be characterized in
any explicit way.

In the standard approach, there are, in fact, only two
conventions available for characterizing syntagmatic structure: Sequence Structure Conditions and the Positive Condition. The former convention has been preserved in the present approach but the latter has been shown to be inadequate
in at least three specifics. First, such a condition applies
to underlying structure rather than to surface phonetic
structure. Secondly, such a device as the Positive Condition is formally incapable of expressing functional (hierar-

chical) relationships. Finally, with a reformulation such as that proposed by Hooper (1973) such a device is incapable of expressing syllable "strength" relationships.

Thus, the phrase structure approach outlined in the preceding section presents a rather significant change in the treatment of the Shanghai data as it was characterized in Walton (1971). However, the framework formulated in the preceding chapter and applied in the present chapter to Shanghainese is still inadequate in its present form since no provision has been made for the characterization of tone in Chinese languages. The remaining chapters of this essay are devoted to an investigation of this problem.

Chapter Eight

THE REPRESENTATION OF TONE

8.1 Introduction

The phonological base outlined in the preceding two
chapters is inadequate in its present form since it does
not account for yet another component of the syllable in
Chinese - tone. Chinese is normally classified as a "lexical tone" language where each morpheme - normally each syllable in Chinese - is assigned a tone in the lexical representation.

Cheng's formulation of the syllable grammar can hardly be said to provide an adequate characterization of tone.
In his framework, the syllable has an optimal ⟨T⟩ which is
expanded into 1, 2, 3, and 4 which stand for the four tones
of Mandarin. But this can hardly count as a "representation."
For instance Cheng does not expand ⟨Init⟩ into a number of
alphabetic symbols. Rather, he attempts to characterize
these elements first in terms of point of articulation and
manner of articulation, and finally in terms of retroflexion,
africation, aspiration, nasalization, liquidization, and
friction. Likewise, a truly adequate characterization of
tone cannot just stop with 1, 2, 3 and 4 -- we must know

what the "commands to the vocal tract" at the phonetic level
are supposed to say vis-a-vis tone and its relationship to
the segmental portion of the syllable.

The present chapter is concerned with an outline of
the basic problems of tone representation, most of which
came to light after Cheng's syllable-grammar formulation.

8.2   The Theoretical Status of "Representation"

The present concern with tone in generative theory
has recently been succintly summarized by Hyman and Schuh
(1974):

> In recent years the subject of tone has become one
> of the major objects of discussion in phonological
> circles. Generative phonologists have particularly
> concentrated their efforts on the underlying repre-
> sentation of tone. For example, they have primarily
> been interested in the following questions: (1) how
> many underlying (i.e., phonological) levels of
> tone are possible in a given language (2) How are
> these tones represented in distinctive features
> (3) Should contour tones be analyzed as single
> phonological units or as sequences of level tones?
> (4) Is tone segmental or suprasegmental?

The observation by Hyman and Schuh that generative
phonologists have concentrated their efforts on the representation of tone warrants some discussion. The notion of
"representation" is sometimes considered a "non-issue."
In fact, there has been, it seems to me, a feeling among
many linguists that generative phonology (and perhaps

generative linguistics in general) has been overconcerned
with representations and formalism. I would agree that the
value of formal simplicity as some sort of evaluation measure has from time to time been exaggerated in generative
studies. On the other hand it must be argued that formalism
is critical to scientific inquiry. Leben (in Hyman 1973)
has advanced the argument for formalizing tone representation in generative phonology:

> In the study of tone, as in any other study of
> linguistic structure, we have every reason to
> expect that concern with the formal aspects of
> representation, far from resulting in what some
> have called a "pseudo-algebra" or a "sterile game,"
> will produce a real algebra which is subject to
> empirical disconfirmation when applied to language
> which will, in the end, shed light on the behavior
> of tone (p. 122-123).

Indeed, part of the present concern with the representation
of tone stems from the fact that simply calling tone "suprasegmental" has not produced enlightening insights into the
nature of tone. For example, consider Maran's (1971: 9)
comment on "suprasegmental features":

> Frequently, tonal phenomena are simple given a
> separate category called 'suprasegmental features.'
> It is quite obvious that this treatment has not
> brought about any understanding of the articulatory
> correlates of tone.

Finally, we can take the following statement by Fromkin (1974:
5) as a summary of the whole issue of tone representation:

Historically, tone like other prosodic phenomena has been considered 'suprasegmental' but formally treated segmentally, as a feature of vowels. How tone is represented is not merely a matter of taste; there should be different consequences dependent on the different representations.

Given these arguments, I believe we must conclude that the quest for proper representation of tone is not a pseudo-problem but a legitimate requirement of phonological theory.

8.3   Tone and Distinctive Features

Prior to generative studies on Chinese, tone was considered a suprasegmental and descriptions were generally restricted to describing the relative pitch levels and contours of the tones. These were often represented by number systems (e.g. rising tone could be 35) or by diacritics. I believe it is safe to assume that most investigators treated the tone, phonetically, as restricted to the vowel (and remaining voiced segments).

However, with the advent of generative phonology and the concomitant use of Praguian distinctive features the domain of tone within the syllable became a problem which remains unsolved to the present. That this problem should arise is quite natural. Distinctive features were formulated to characterize segments. Phonological and phonetic representations were to be characterized as matrices in which the

rows corresponded to the features and the columns corresponded
to segments. Tone, however, has traditionally been considered "suprasegmental" and thus could not fit neatly into
segmental matrices.

In Walton (1971) I traced the history of this problem
in Chinese language description by choosing several representative works from different periods. What follows is
basically a summary of that earlier discussion.

Yen (1965) in describing Amoy tones, considered tone
to be a feature of the syllable boundary (following Halle
(1959:19)) rather than of a particular segment or string of
segments within the syllable. In fact, Yen argued against
considering tone to be a part of a segment since (1) additional distinctive features such as High, Low, Rising would
have to be added (2) it would be difficult to decide just
which voiced segment should carry the tone (3) if the tone
was assigned to one segment phonologically there would have
to be an interpretive convention to "spread" it phonetically
over other voiced segments in the output and (4) tone was
obviously a property of the whole syllable, not some one
segment. In effect, since there was no place to put tone
within the segmental syllable, it had to go to the only
place left - the boundary. Thus tone was a boundary feature.

Ballard (1966) unlike Yen, proposed to make use of
distinctive features for characterizing tone but unlike Yen,

did not want to create new features specifically for tone.
Thus, he introduced the feature prosodic and then suggested
a reinterpretation of the segmental distinctive features
such that whenever they were used in conjunction with the
feature Prosodic they would be describing harmonics and not
formants. Therefore [+compact] in conjunction with [+Pro-
sodic] would characterize falling tone, etc. However,
Ballard never actually formalized this notion in terms of
a phonemic or lexical matrix so it is not clear just where
the tone features go (i.e., in which segment(s)).

Wang (1967) like Yen also argued that tone was a
feature of the whole syllable. However, unlike the previous
investigators he explicitly rejected the notion that the
same set of features used for the characterization of segmentals be also used for tones. Wang's arguments are extremely convincing and worth quoting in full:

> In languages like Chinese the tone features are
> sometimes relevant for the initial consonant,
> sometimes for the nuclear vowel, and sometimes
> for the final consonant in various phonological
> rules. If we were to add a column of tone
> features to a phonological matrix of segmental
> features, then it becomes arbitrary where pre-
> cisely to insert this column. Furthermore, seg-
> mental features are usually not relevant to the
> various types of tone sandhi; that is to say, the
> interaction of tones in a sequence is independent
> of the nature of the segments which occur with the
> tones. Phonetically, of course, the domain of
> the tone is over the entire voiced portion of the

syllable. From these considerations, it is preferable to formalize the tone features differently
from the segmental features and regard them as
features of individual syllables. (1967: 95)

After arguing that tone features were indeed different from
segmental features, Wang went on to propose a set of binary-
valued distinctive features for tone. These are <u>Contour</u>,
<u>High</u>, <u>Central</u>, <u>Mid</u>, <u>Rising</u>, <u>Falling</u> and <u>Convex</u> (for details
see Wang 1967: 96-99).

3.4 <u>Tone: Segmental or Suprasegmental?</u>

One of the goals in formulating any theory is simplicity. Another goal is constraint: a theory should be general enough to explain the phenomena at hand, but if it is
too general it ceases to explain and begins to list. Wang's
proposal creates more complexity in several senses. First,
there are now two sets of features and these are quite
different in nature from one another. Moreover, the domain
of features is now more complex - covering both segment sized
units and larger units as well. Also, a new notion "syllable" must somehow be integrated into the segmental dis-
tinctive-feature framework.

There are various ways to remedy this complexity.
One way is to "constrain" the theory so that phenomena can
be characterized by one explanation rather than, say, by
two. For example, one way to constrain the theory would

be to treat tone as segmental. If such an approach could account for tone, then it would be simpler and more highly valued.

Two different kinds of proposals (at least) have been put forward in recent years that suggest that tone in language families such as Chinese should be considered a feature of segments. I term these the Sonorant Feature approach and the Feature Assimilation approach.

The Sonorant Feature approach, put forward by Woo (1972) maintains that tones are to be represented as level pitch heights on sequences of sonorants. She proposes to replace Wang's Contour, Rise, Fall, etc. with three features which for the time being, we can call High, Mid, and Low. Thus, a low rising tone is a sequence of Low followed by High, each feature assigned to successive sonorant segments.

The Feature Assimilation approach as put forward by Maran (1969, 1971), Halle and Stevens (1971) among others is based on the oft-noted influence of segmentals on tone. For instance, low tones often occur in conjunction with syllable initial voiced segments. Most cases of this segment-tone association can be seen to involve glottic features such as Voice, Aspiration, Breathiness, etc. One way to account for this tone-segment relationship would be to use the same set of features to account both for the glottic features of segments (e.g. voicing) and for tone.

In such a case, then, tone would be a segmental feature on sonorant segments, subject to the influence of contiguous segments. For example, suppose that there was a glottic feature Low, which when applied to consonants was to characterize voicing and when applied to vowels was to characterize low pitch. Then, in a CV sequence where the C is voiced, the low pitch on the vowel can be seen as the very natural process of assimilation - the lowness of the consonant affects the pitch height of the following vowel. Thus, one set of features takes care of both segments and tones and provides a natural way to interrelate the two.

The two approaches differ mainly in that Woo's Sonorant Feature conception still recognizes tone features which are distinct from segmental features. But while tone features are different from segmental features, such tone features are assigned to segments. The Feature Assimilation approach utilizes one set of features - glottic features - there are no separate tone features. Nevertheless both approaches are in agreement that tone is best represented as a feature of segments. Furthermore, the Feature Assimilation approach must, by its nature, treat contour tones as sequences of level tones just as proposed by Woo. This is true since the proposed glottic features refer to discrete states of the glottis such as Low, Mid, and High on separate segments.

8.5 Conclusion

These attempts to constrain and simplify the theory
by treating tone as segmental rather than suprasegmental
are admirable in their intent. Yet, I shall argue that they
must ultimately fail.

I, too, wish to constrain the characterization of
tone within generative theory, but I disagree strongly with
the tack which the preceding approaches take in achieving
this goal. Such approaches are not so much attempts to constrain the characterization of tone as they are to reduce
tone to the familiar. Let the "familiar" be the only kind
of phonology discussed in the standard works on generative
phonology (e.g., Sound Pattern of English, Aspects of
Phonological Theory, etc.), namely segmental phonology
(including stress).

My own approach to constraining the theory with regard to tone is rather different. I suggest that tone be
first characterized quite explicitly in phonetic terms -
that is at the surface level. Then, the phonological representation of tone is constrained in the same way the
phonological representation of segmentals is constrained.
For example, the same set of features must be used at both
levels.

Secondly, rather than trying to merge two dimensions --
to constrain tonal representation by reducing it to segmental

representation -- I suggest that we first examine the inherent properties of each dimension and the relationship among the various phenomena within each dimension and then, and only then, examine the relationship which exists between the two dimensions.

In the following two chapters I will argue against the Sonorant Feature approach and the Feature Assimilation approach (respectively). Then I shall suggest the direction which I believe investigation into tonal representation should take.

Chapter Nine

TONE AS A FEATURE OF SONORANT SEGMENTS

9.1 Introduction

Woo's essay on the nature of tone is quite complex
involving many details of stress, acoustic findings, proposed marking conventions and the like. Here, I am simply
concerned with her very basic arguments of why tone should
be considered a feature of sonorant segments. Since the
bulk of her argument centers on the analysis of tone in
Mandarin, the discussion here will be chiefly restricted to
this language.

9.2 Summary of Woo's Argument

Woo begins by observing that for purposes of tone description there are two systems -- the Orientalist system
and the Africanist system (including some American Indian
languages) and that this distinction derives from "the way
dynamic or moving tones are described, and the assumptions
which each make about the nature of the segment or segments
to which the features are assigned" (1972: 24). Specifically, in the Orientalist system dynamic (contour) tones are

-171-

associated with the syllable (or syllabic vowel) whereas
in the Africanist system tones are said to be represented by
seuqences of pitch heights where each is associated with a
particular sonorant segment.

Woo then quite correctly reasons that an adequate set
of distinctive features should be able to account both for
the Orientalist and Africanist languages. Particularly,
she is concerned with whether Wang's (1967) features such as
Rise and Fall are the only way to account for dynamic tones
in the Orientalist languages. She presents the problem thusly:

> With these questions in mind, let us now look at an
> Orientalist language to see if, in fact, its tones
> cannot be described as simply sequences of pitch
> height features as the African languages are. (1972:
> 24).

The language which Woo chooses for examination of possible
tone reinterpretation is Mandarin Chinese. Mandarin canonical structure is normally described as:

$$(C)(G)V_1(\left\{ \begin{matrix} V2 \\ N \end{matrix} \right\})$$

where $V_1 \neq V_2$, G = glide and N = either n or ng. Initial
consonant and glide aside, syllables can include open syllables with only V_1, which is considered a pure vowel (as
opposed to a dipthong) and V_1, plus either n or ng in which

case V_1 is again considered pure.

Now, the condition that each pitch height be associated with a particular sonorant segment necessitates that every syllable consist of at least two sonorant segments. For Mandarin syllables having dipthongs and VN sonorant clusters this interpretation presents no problem; however, Mandarin syllables consisting of only one vowel segment (the pure vowel syllable) present a problem. Woo presents arguments based on acoustic evidence of duration to demonstrate that these Mandarin pure vowels can be interpreted as geminate clusters. However, to account for Mandarin Tone 3 a sequence of three sonorant segments would be necessary in the underlying representation since this tone is falling-rising and would be characterized as a sequence of say, [+ Mid][+ Low] [+ High]. However, this would cause a radical revision of Mandarin canonical shape, since now a pure vowel would have to be represented as VVV. The solution is to choose the prefinal form of Tone 3 (the form which occurs before another syllable) which is a rising tone and therefore consists of only two segments and then add a segment for the "long form" of Tone 3 when it occurs in isolation or phrase final position (i.e., as a falling-rising tone). Such an analysis then allows Woo to dispense with Wang's features such as <u>Rise</u> and <u>Fall</u>, etc. and use only three level-tone features.

9.3 <u>Critique of Woo's Approach</u>

9.3.1 <u>The Mandarin Data</u>

Woo states (p. 25) that "it is generally assumed that all pure vowels are normally long and that vocalic clusters which are dipthongs consist of two short members." However, she does note that long vowels have never been posited for Mandarin, since vowel-length is not distinctive. Indeed, I have never seen an analysis which even hinted that there were "long" or "short" vowels in Mandarin. Dipthongs are posited not because they have anything to do with length but simply because they involve two different places of articulation.

However, there is another reason why previous investigators never concerned themselves with the phonetic length of pure vowels. This reason is that duration in such cases is not regarded as a feature of the individual segment but rather of the entire syllable or final of the syllable. This in turn means that the tone of the syllable may also affect the phonetic length of the pure vowel. Mandarin tones are normally characterized as follows:

Tone 1	High, Level
Tone 2	Mid-rising
Tone 3	Low-rising in non-final position
	Falling-rising in isolation
	Mid-rising before another Tone 3
Tone 4	High-falling

Some tones, however, have rather characteristic durations and all tones can be described as having slightly different durations. For instance, Kratochvil, whom Woo cites a number of times, has characterized the duration of Mandarin tones as follows (1968: 37):

Tone 1	Slightly above average duration
Tone 2	Slightly below average duration
Tone 3	Well above average duration
Tone 4	Far below average duration

In fact, Woo's own acoustic investigation of voice prints on Mandarin monosyllables reveals this facet of tone duration: "one sees that within each tone group, there is a fixed duration for the entire syllable" (p. 27). If these observations are correct, then one begins to see why "long vowels" and "short vowels" of dipthongs are never discussed in analyses of Mandarin: a great deal of the phonetic length of such vowels is determined by the tone duration, not the intrinsic duration of the vowel or vowels. That is, tone class determines vowel length to some degree, incidentally.

In examining the duration of isolation syllables in each of the four tones of Mandarin, Woo states:

> The duration of syllables with different tones is not the same, but that is not relevant, for what is significant is the fact that syllables with the same pitch configuration also have the same duration for the syllabic nucleus. Thus, although the syllabic nucleus may consist of a pure vowel, a dipthong or a vowel and nasal cluster, there are no

acoustic properties of duration which distinguishes
any of the three. (Woo 1972: 27).

However, Woo's acoustic data leads me to just the
opposite conclusion: the fact that the duration of syllables
in different tones is not the same is quite relevant. The
fact that the syllabic nuclei in syllables with the same
pitch have the same duration is an incidental result of the
fact that the pitch largely determines the length of these
syllabic nuclei.

Woo examines a number of syllables in each tone but
she never gives the same segmental syllable in all four
tones. Thus, from her data we get:

Tone 1	Tone 2	Tone 3	Tone 4
ba	ma	jah	daa

Suppose, instead that just one segmental syllable is considered in each tone. I take her first example, and use Pin-
yin romanization:

Tone 1	Tone 2	Tone 3	Tone 4
slightly above average	slightly below average	well above average	far below average
ba	ba	ba	ba

The duration of the a in each tone will be different. For
example in Tone 3 it will be "long" and in Tone 4 it will be
"short" (as Woo herself admits). If this is the case, then

how can one argue that there is any kind of "vowel length"
here in a linguistically relevant sense? The vowel length
can change drastically depending on the tone.

I am not claiming that vowels do not have some "intrinsic duration." Indeed, they must have some duration to
be identifiable. Likewise, I would acknowledge that vowels
in dipthongs and vowel plus nasal clusters may "share" the
duration of the syllabic nucleus somewhat equally, but I
suspect that these factors are the ones which are less relevant than the fact that the total duration of such clusters
varies as the tone varies.

Consider Woo's second experiment involving A + B
(disyllabic) compounds. In those cases where the A member
is stressed, the duration of the vowel in the B member is
only one half the duration of the B member under stress.
Furthermore, if the B member is made up of a dipthong or VN
cluster, the last segment of the cluster or dipthong tends
to disappear when the B member is unstressed. The unstressed B member in such compounds is said to be in the "neutral
tone," i.e., it does not have a full lexical tone.

Again, we can look at the problem in a purely segmental way as Woo does or we can propose an alternative which is
motivated from tonal length considerations.

According to Woo, since the second segment drops off
in such cases and since pure vowels have only one half of

their stressed duration in such cases, then this is an argument for treating pure vowels as "long vowels" or as geminate vowels.

However, suppose one assumes the following: syllable (and therefore vocalic segmental) length is directly related to the tone length. Suppose, then, in an unstressed neutral tone syllable, since there is no "target" tone, there is no tone duration and therefore the duration of the vocalic (or VN) members automatically shorten. In either my approach or Woo's one recognizes that segments can be deleted and that the pure vowels are phonetically short - this is a function of stressed-unstressed combinations. But my interpretation says: no tone = no characteristic tone duration = short syllable. Woo's approach seems to say: no stress = segmental shortening but no mention of tone. I believe that my explanation is as adequate as Woo's but goes further since it recognizes that duration of the syllable is largely a function of tone -- in this particular case any tone -- and absence of tone implies loss of duration.

A much more important issue is the treatment of Mandarin Tone 3. In this case tonal duration is at the heart of the solution. Woo does not want to represent the isolation form of Tone 3 syllables consisting of say, a pure vowel, as a sequence of three tone features in sequence since this would necessitate three underlying vowels and thereby upset

the canonical shape configuration of Mandarin monosyllables.
Woo cites acoustic evidence yet again to show that if Tone
3 syllables occur first in a sequence of three syllables, the
duration of the sonorant portion of the Tone 3 syllable is
equivalent to the sonorant portions of Tone 1 and Tone 2
syllables in equivalent positions. Thus Woo chooses the prefinal form of Tone 3 as the underlying form since this only
necessitates two tone positions. Again, however, this ultimately makes counter-intuitive claims about how tone works.
For instance, in some environments, Tone 3 changes to Tone 2,
in other cases Tone 3 simply becomes low rising (i.e. prefinal) but in both these cases, it is indeed the tone which
is changing. For example, if a Tone 3 syllable "ba" occurring before another Tone 3 syllable "ma" changes to Tone 2,
we assume that the length of the vowel in "ba" will be automatically adjusted to conform to the duration of the a of an
original Tone 2 syllable.

Given these observations, I then consider Woo's rea-
soning highly questionable when she says:

> It therefore appears that the total duration of the
> sonorant cluster, beginning with the main vowel is
> determined by the number of sonorants in the syllable
> nucleus. (1972: 39)

It would seem, to the contrary, that if all Tone 3 syllables
have "a duration in isolation which is approximately 3/2

that of the other tones" (Woo 1972: 39) and that if such
syllables can have practically any segmental constituency,
then the number of sonorants in the syllabic nucleus is
totally irrelevant with regard to duration.

The thrust of my objection to Woo's analysis is that
the "vowel length" of pure vowels is redundantly predictable
in terms of the tone class and that dipthongs and VN clusters
likewise vary in length depending on the tone class. But
this redundancy is unidirectional: given the segmental syllable "ba" we cannot predict if the "syllabic nucleus" will
be short, as in Tone 4 or extra-long as in Tone 3. However,
if we have a CV syllable that is in Tone 4, we can predict
that the vowel will be "short" and given that it is in Tone
3, we can predict it will be "extra-long." Woo has taken
the redundant information and made it lexically significant
and has taken the lexically significant feature -- tone duration (e.g. Tone 3 = extra-long) and made it redundant in
terms of abstractly posited underlying segments.

9.3.2 Syllabic Consonants

In an earlier analysis of Northern Tepehuan (Woo
1970) Woo states the following:

> Is Northern Tepehuan unique in demanding that deflect-
> ed tones occur only over vowel sequences? I think
> not. Recent studies in other languages, namely

my own on Mandarin and Cantonese, and Abrahamson's
on Thai, demonstrate that this relationship of
length and deflected tone is also valid in these
languages.

Thus the fact that no rising or falling contours
are found on syllables containing a single sonorant
follows from the fact that there is no second sonorant to carry the pitch specification. (p. 29, ft.
18).

In Woo (1972) she states:

We have now seen that at least for one of the
Oriental languages, a segmental analysis of tone
is valid. It would then appear that unless the
structure of Mandarin is shown to be radically
different from all other languages in the Orient,
the segmental analysis should hold for these other
languages. We have done some spectrographic examination of Cantonese and find that the segmental
analysis certainly holds there. (p. 46)

As I pointed out in Walton (1971: 106) it is very

curious that Woo makes references to her work on Cantonese

only to leave such forms as these totally unmentioned:

#ŋ# Low-falling tone (common surname); #ŋ# Low-rising tone

("five"); #m# low-falling tone ("negative"). In Walton

(1971: 68) I also discussed such syllables in the Shanghai

dialect of Wu, for example: #m# low-rising tone ("acorn");

#ŋ# low-rising tone ("fish; five"). Other examples were

given from Yen's treatment of Amoy and Cheng's (1968) anal-

ysis of Cantonese. The facts are these: many Chinese lan-

guages have syllables consisting solely of a syllabic nasal

(or lateral) which bear contour tones, though the total

number of such forms in a given language is rather small.

Nevertheless, such forms are devastating to Woo's conception of segmental tone. In the first statement above Woo claims that contour tones cannot occur on syllables containing a single sonorant since "there is no second sonorant to carry the second pitch classification." Moreover, she twice refers to studies of Cantonese. The question is then, how will the Cantonese word for "five", a syllabic velar nasal with low rising tone, be represented? Would she set up an abstract #ŋŋ# and then eliminate one of the velar nasals at the surface? But even if one of the velar nasals is eliminated, how is the word to be represented at the surface? There will still be only one sonorant segment.

One could argue, as many investigators have, that monoconsonantal syllables consist of underlying consonant plus some vowel. In Walton (1971) I argued against such ad hoc solutions. However, we know that Woo would not take this approach since all of her underlying representations with respect to tone have been extremely phonetically motivated, chiefly with detailed acoustic evidence.

One could also argue that such syllable types are marginal or peripheral since there are never many of them. Thus, they are somehow exceptions, to be ignored (as Woo has done). But such syllable types are wide-spread in Chinese languages and dialects. Native speakers do not regard

them as anomalous but find them quite natural. In tone
sandhi processes they behave just as all other syllables
having the same tone.

To the contrary, monosegmental consonantal syllables
offer an excellent opportunity to study the relationship
between tone and segment. If one's approach to tone is via
the segment, then such syllable types are unusual. However,
if one's approach to tone is that it has certain non-segmental properties of its own -- such as pitch height and
duration, then there is absolutely nothing irregular about
such syllable types. In Shanghai or Cantonese, a low rising
tone is a feature of the syllable -- regardless of the segmental make-up of the syllable. The minimum requirement for
the realization of a recognizable syllable in non-whispered
speech would be some segmental (or segmental configuration)
and some tone. The tone requirement means that the segment
or segments involved must be voiced and must last long enough
for the tonal configuration -- pitch, amplitude and duration
-- to be realized. But as to which segments or how many
segments, this is a consideration largely independent of the
tone. Of course, syllabic nasals (and laterals) are unique
in that they are monosegmental and yet voiced and capable of
being prolonged long enough for the tone to be realized.

Earlier, it was pointed out that a representation of
tone should make empirical claims about how tone works.

Under Woo's approach to tone, since tone must always be
represented as a sequence of sonorant segments, then forms
such as syllabic nasals or syllables with contour tones
should never evolve in language change. Yet, most syllabic
nasals in Chinese can be shown to have developed from CV
syllables where the vowel dropped. Of course, this is not
extraordinary since nasals can bear tone as I have argued
above. Thus, Woo's approach to representation makes claims
about tone which are not borne out empirically.

9.3.4 Tone Sandhi

In 7.3 above Wang was quoted as saying that "segmental features are usually not relevant in the various types of
sandhi; that is to say, the interaction of tones in a sequence is independent of the nature of the segments which
occur with the tones." This is quite true, yet Woo never
seems to grasp it. Thus we find her giving a rule such as
this (1972: 76):

$$\begin{bmatrix} + \text{ son} \\ + \text{ Low T} \end{bmatrix} \rightarrow [+\text{High T}]/ \underset{[+\text{Low T}]}{V} \underline{\hspace{1cm}} \#\#C_0(G) \underset{[+\text{Low T}]}{V}$$

for converting the sequence of two low tones to rising tone
plus low tone. However, the fact that vowels are involved
in the notation or that the configuration $\#\#C_0(G) \underset{[+\text{Low T}]}{V}$
has to be stated has nothing to do with the actual process

of tone change. That is, the segments -- be they preceded
by this or that segment or followed by this or that segment
-- are totally irrelevant. What is relevant is a syllable
boundary and any stress or tempo information plus some syntactic information. The effect of Woo's interpretation is
to take a straightforward <u>tonal</u> process and turn it into a
complicated <u>tone and segment</u> process. Furthermore, after
the above rule has applied, a segment will have to be added
if the final part of the formulation is at the end of a
phonological phrase. That is, since Tone 3 has an underlying
representation of only two segments, when it occurs in phonological phrase final position (or in isolation) a segment
must be inserted to carry the third tone feature. Woo
gives the following rule (p. 77):

$$\emptyset \quad \begin{bmatrix} V \\ -syl \\ +Low\ T \\ \propto F \end{bmatrix} \quad / \quad \begin{bmatrix} V \\ +Low\ T \\ \propto F \\ +stress \end{bmatrix} \underline{\hspace{2cm}} \begin{bmatrix} +son \\ +Low\ T \end{bmatrix}$$

phon.phrase

If it is the case that in Mandarin and in many other
Chinese languages and dialects that tone changes totally
without regard to segmentals, isn't this a significant linguistic generalization? Moreover, it would seem that if a
theory of tone analysis not only ignores this fact but actually obscures it as some sort of tonal-segmental phenomena,
then such a theory is inadequate and even misleading.

9.3.5 Tone as a Syllable Feature

Wang also quite explicitly proposed that tones were
not the features of individual segments but rather of syllables (see 7.3 above). Again, however, Woo seems not to
understand the essence of this claim since she interprets
it to mean that tone is a feature of the sonorants of the
syllable:

> ...if it is true that in Oriental languages a rising
> pitch contour can occur on a <u>single sonorant</u>, and
> must be specified as such in the lexicon, whereas
> African languages require a rising pitch contour only
> if the syllable contains two sonorants, then cer-
> tain difficulties arise with the features [rise]
> and [fall] (Woo 1973: 25) Emphasis mine.

However, Wang never said that tone (including [rise] and
[fall]) was to be associated with a "single sonorant." In
fact, he explicitly said that tone features were different
from segmental features and had the syllable as their domain. Further, he directly stated that tone could <u>not</u> be
assigned to a single segment since it was arbitrary as to
which segment should carry the tone (c.f. Wang's statement
7.3 above).

Later Woo makes the following observation:

> What are the consequences of applying a system of
> features such as Wang's? Using these features one
> could capture the relationship between the dynamic
> tones and sonorant clusters by saying, for example,
> that if a syllable were marked with the feature

[+rise], then that feature is not just a feature
of one segment, but rather of the whole sonorant
cluster of the syllable. However, this interpretation necessitates defining a totally new kind of
feature, namely a cluster feature. (1973: 35)

Here we see that "syllable" is now to be reinterpreted as "sonorant cluster." Again, Wang never suggested that
tones be assigned to sonorant clusters within the syllable.
Woo's other alternative, that features like Wang's [rise]
be "distributed to all of the sonorants in a syllable so
that the sequence VV, would be marked $\underset{[+\text{ rise}]}{V} \quad \underset{[+\text{ rise}]}{V}$ "
has absolutely nothing to do with Wang's proposal. He spe-
cifically stated that tone was not to be assigned to segments
and V is definitely a segment. Thus, one can only conclude
that Woo takes "feature of the syllable" to mean "feature
of one or more segments within the syllable." I shall re-
turn to what I consider the source of this misinterpretation
in Chapter 12.

9.3.6 Conclusion

Woo has sought to formulate a thesis based on linking
tone directly to sonorant segments -- even to derive the duration of tones from the duration of accumulations of segments. Such an approach to segmentalizing tones assumes the
primacy of segments over tones, of segmental length over an
independent "tonal length." I have suggested that such an
approach is misguided.

First, it is phonetically unmotivated -- phonetic
length or duration is not simply a function of sequences of
sonorants. Indeed, the a of the Mandarin sequence "ba" can
have a variety of phonetic lengths depending on tone. Secondly, and more importantly, such an approach cannot handle
monosegmental syllables consisting of a single consonantal
sonorant -- a syllable type found quite commonly in Chinese.
In fact, such syllables seem to disprove Woo's restriction
that contour tones cannot occur with single sonorant segments
and therefore to disprove her entire approach to segmentalizing tone. Such syllable types are impossible to capture
within her framework since it explicitly denies their existence.

In addition, such a segment oriented approach unnec-
essarily complicates phonological processes such as tone
sandhi in Mandarin which have nothing to do with segmentals.
As it turns out, such an approach obscures the extremely
significant fact that tone changes operate totally within the
domain of tone, not segmentals, in a great many Chinese languages and dialects.

Finally, Woo continually maintains that the only alternative to her proposals is to assign Wang's tone features
like [rise] and [fall] either to one sonorant segment of a
group of sonorants or to a group of sonorants when Wang has
explicitly stated that the tonal features he proposes are

different from segmental features and are to be assigned to the whole syllable. Thus many of her arguments are simply pseudo-arguments. In sum, I conclude that the Sonorant Feature approach to tone representation is inadequate and untenable for characterizing tone in Chinese.

Chapter Ten

THE FEATURE ASSIMILATION APPROACH

10.1 Introduction

In the preceding chapter it was argued that the Sonorant Feature approach does not offer convincing reasons
for treating tone as a feature of segments in Chinese.
There is, however, another argument for treating tone as
a feature of segments which does not come up in the Mandarin material on which Woo relied in establishing her approach. This argument has here been termed the Feature
Assimilation approach.

10.2 Tone and Segment in Chinese

In dealing with the Mandarin material in the preceding chapter there was little reason to assume that segments affect pitch height and, as I argued, little reason
to assume that segments directly affect tone duration.

Yet, there is both historically and synchronically,
a great deal of evidence throughout the Sino-Tibetan family
that various relationships hold between segmentals and
tones. Let us begin by an examination of the relationship

between syllable-initial consonant and pitch height.

Traditionally Chinese phonologists have recognized four tone categories which can be labelled I, II, III, IV. There is no solid evidence for the historical phonetic values of these tones. However, it is generally recognized that in Middle Chinese (ca. 600 A.D.) there were eight pitches within these four categories. Lower pitched tones were associated with syllables having voiced initials, upper pitch syllables were associated with syllables having voiceless initials. Furthermore, category IV was distinguished from the other three in that all syllables ending in the voiceless stops *-p, *-t, *-k. That is, the presence of these final stops caused such syllables to be grouped together tonally. Letting a = syllables with voiceless initials and b = syllables with voiced initials, we can form a grid for looking at both Middle Chinese and modern tone systems:

	I	II	III	IV
a	Hi T	Hi T	Hi T	Hi T -p -t -k
b	Low T	Low T	Low T	Low T -p -t -k

Several examples from modern dialects would be use-

ful here. Consider first, the Wenzhou dialect of Wu.[1]
Here the voiced initials are still preserved, though category IV syllables have lost their final stops:

	I	II	III	IV
a	High-level ˧	Mid-rising ˧	High-falling ˥	Mid-fall-rise ˧
b	Mid-fall ˩	Low rise ˧	Low level ˩	Low fall-rise ˧

For another example, consider a Northern Wu dialect such
as Shanghai:[2]

	I	II III	IV
a	High-fall ˥	mid-rise ˧	High short ˧ʔ
b	Low rise ˧		Low short ˩ʔ

Here there have been various mergers but it is still the
case that syllables having low pitches are associated with
voiced initials. Moreover, category IV syllables still preserve their stop nature in the form of glottal stop.

----
1. The tonal data here is drawn from my own work on Wenzhou.

2. The data here is drawn from Kiangsu Sheng Ho Shanghai
Shih Fang Yen Kai Kuang.

It is generally assumed and indeed seems to be the case that in all Chinese languages, syllables ending in stops are somewhat shorter than open syllables or nasal final syllables.

10.3 The Physiological Explanation

A number of explanations or at least reasonable hypotheses have been advanced to account for the effect of a consonant on the pitch height of the following segment(s) (e.g. Ladefoged (1964) Ohala (1973), Matisoff (1973), Maran (1971), Halle and Stevens (1971)). The gist of these arguments is that the fundamental frequency of the consonant is due to such factors as vocal chord tension (e.g. lax or stiff), aerodynamic factors and perhaps larynx raising and lowering. These factors carry over to the following segment(s) which also are characterized by the continuation of the fundamental frequency. The general notion seems to be that voiced consonants, especially obstruents, tend to have a lowering effect on the fundamental frequency of the following vowel:

> Specifically, [ɦ], voiced or breathy-voiced ob-
> struents seem to depress tone on the vowel follow-
> ing, whereas voiceless, particularly voiceless
> aspirated obstruents, [h], and implosives seem to
> raise the tone on the following vowel. (Ohala
> 1973: 3)

Of course, this effect on the following vowel is not necessarily phonologically distinctive as, for example, in
English or say in Middle Chinese, where the voiced/voice-
less distinction in initial consonants carried the contrastive function.

As for the effect of final stops on the duration of
the preceding segment(s), Chen (1970) has argued that this
is probably a universal constraint. As such, since tone
is "carried" by voiced segments phonetically, it is quite
natural to expect syllables ending in stops to have "short"
tones.

It has also been argued that final consonants can
affect the pitch height of the preceding segment(s). This
does not seem to be the case in Chinese languages but has
been reported for other Sino-Tibetan languages. I will not
discuss this phenomenon here; the reader is referred to
Maran (1971) and Matisoff (1970).

10.4   The Feature Assimilation Approach

From the above discussion it is apparent that there
is often a relationship between certain features of tone
and certain features of segments. The first attempt to
characterize this relationship in terms of distinctive
features was Maran (1969) and later Maran (1971). Significantly, Maran sought to characterize tone as a feature

of segments:

> And thus, pitch variation for tonal purposes be-
> comes an issue which concerns the manner of voicing.
> By making this operational premise, we also place
> the phenomenon of tonal levels under the primacy
> of the vocal bands; furthermore, the tonal phenom-
> enon is no longer strictly suprasegmental in the
> traditional sense. What we have done now is to
> claim that articulatorily, tones are produced by
> the addition of manner-of-production features to
> the specification of segments where spontaneous
> voicing is possible. (Maran 1971: 12)

Maran presented an example of his new set of features as

follows (from Maran 1971: 14):

	v	v́	v̀	ʔ	ʔ̸	h	h̸	t	th	d
voiced	+	+	+	-	-	-	-	-	-	+
spread	-	-	-	-	-	+	+	-	+	-
constricted	-	-	-	+	+	-	-	+	-	-
raised	-	+	-	+	-	+	-	+	-	-
lowered	-	-	+	-	+	-	+	-	-	+

Raised and Lowered refer to pitch height; if both these

features have a minus value the tone is Mid. Spread indi-

cates that the vocal bands are apart such as for producing

h and the aspiration in aspirated stops. Sounds which are

[-spread] are either Constricted or Voiced. Constricted

indicates that the vocal bands are pulled together and the

airflow stopped as in glottalized stops and the glottal

stop. Voiced is seen as describing the state of the chords

between "open" as in Spread and "pulled together" as in

Constricted. Maran notes that Voiced could be expressed

as [-constricted, -spread] but he retains Voiced "to min-

imize the novelty effect of the feature system..." (1971:
13).

The effect of this feature revision (from say Chomsky and Halle (1968)) is that tone is expressed as a feature
of vowels. Moreover, for Maran's purposes, such a framework
allows high and low tones to be assimilated by the vowel
from the following consonant (or from the preceding consonant). For example, in Jinghpaw high tones occur only if
the final segment is <u>ʔ</u>, <u>h</u>, <u>p</u>, <u>t</u>, <u>k</u> (i.e. all voiceless)
and low tones only if the following segment is <u>ʔ</u>, <u>h</u>, <u>b</u>, <u>d</u>,
<u>g</u> (i.e. all voiced).

In summarizing the utility of the proposed features
<u>Raised</u> and <u>Lowered</u> Maran concluded:

> ...we make it possible for the description of
> phenomena such as tones to emanate from the same
> source of phonetic features as those which spe-
> cify nonvocalic segments. Thus, at the level of
> classificatory phonetic features we need not im-
> pose classificatory divisions such as segmental
> and suprasegmental. (1971: 18)

The next major proposal along this line was that
of Halle and Stevens (1971). They proposed that the four
features <u>Spread Glottis</u>, <u>Constricted Glottis</u>, <u>Stiff Vocal</u>
<u>Chords</u> and <u>Slack Vocal Chords</u> be included in the universal
phonetic feature framework "to replace such traditional
features as voicing, glottalization, vowel pitch and so
forth" (p. 201). The features <u>Stiff</u> and <u>Slack</u> are parti-

cularly important for tone-segment relationships. In obstruents, <u>Slack</u> vocal chords tend to facilitate voicing
whereas <u>Stiff</u> vocal chords tend to make such voicing impossible. Of particular interest here are Halle's comments
in a later article (Halle (1971)) on the relationship of
these features to tone characterization:

> It has long been known that the articulatory mech-
> anism of pitch distinction must involve the stiff-
> ness of the vocal chords. If one assumes that in
> the neutral position for speech (see Chomsky and
> Halle (1968: 300)) the vocal chords have the stiff-
> ness appropriate for the mid pitch level, then it
> follows that to produce a sound with high pitch the
> vocal chords must be stiffened beyond that of the
> neutral position, whereas to produce a sound with
> low pitch they must be slackened below the neutral
> stiffness. (1971: 182)

Noting the correlation in Far Eastern languages of the relationship between voicing and pitch level Halle states:
"In other words, the vocal chord configuration -- stiff or
slack -- in the consonant is assimilated by the following
vowel subsequent to which the contrast in consonants is
lost." (Halle 1971: 182)

However, perhaps the clearest and most explicit characterization of what I have been calling the Feature Assimilation approach is that short vowels -- generally shortened
by the presence of a following stop consonant -- cannot
manifest contour tones. Halle (1971) argues for the relevance of such a claim:

> If furthermore, the assumption is made that the
> domain of the feature is the segment, then the
> absence of non-stationary tones on short vowels
> is not just a curious fact, but rather a logical
> consequence of the theory; since the only way to
> represent non-stationary tone is as sequences of
> stationary tones, a short vowel which can only
> be represented by a single segment cannot have a
> non-stationary tone. (Halle 1971: 191)

Woo (1972) likewise advances this same argument.
In proposing her framework, quite early on she claims that
"so far as we know, no dynamic tone can occur with a short
vowel distinctively" (p. 30). Later she gives quite intricate phonetic-perception arguments that while dynamic tones
are sometimes "perceived" on short vowels, this is only the
result of stress and intonation factors (p. 126). This
leads her ultimately to claim that: "We feel that the
effect of consonants, particularly the final consonant,
and stress probably account for the majority of 'contour'
tones heard on short syllables" (p. 132).

10.5 Inadequacies of the Feature Assimilation Approach

Although the Feature Assimilation approach was formulated for quite different reasons, the result (and therefore the inadequacy) is identical to the result of the
Sonorant Feature approach: tone is to be characterized as
a feature of individual segments. Features such as Raised,
and Lowered, Stiff and Slack apply to segments (vowels).

If contour tones are to be characterized within such a
framework such tones must be split up into sequences of segments. The tone lowering effect of a preceding voiced consonant will assimilate to the vowel, but this only takes
care of the initial portion of the pitch contour. Other
segments will be necessary to "carry" the remainder of
the contour. For instance, how would the Shanghai syllable
/ba/ with a low rising tone be represented using the Maran-
Halle-Stevens framework? The initial consonant is truly
voiced and in this language low tones are associated with
voiced initial obstruents. The only representation that
seems possible would be:

	b	a	a
Raised	-	-	+
Lowered	+	+	-
Constricted	+	-	-
Spread	-	-	-

The system is particularly appealing in that low pitch can
be seen as a natural assimilation of the lowness of the preceding voiced consonant. However, an additional segment
is needed so that the feature [+ Raised] can follow [+Lowered]
thus giving a low-high sequence or in other words a rising
tone. In Wenzhou (see above) where low tone is likewise
associated with voiced initial obstruents, the syllable
/ba/ with low falling-rising tone would require three vowel
segments. Again the voicing assimilation would be accounted

for in a natural way but two additional segments would be
necessary.

Thus, following this framework we end up exactly with
the problems discussed in the preceding chapter. We would
have to show phonetically that "long vowels" exist in Shanghai and Wenzhou. Furthermore, the tone sandhi systems of
both these languages operate without direct reference to
segmentals. Thus, here again, a theory of tone representation is being put forward which obscures tonal processes
by confusing them with segmental notions.

Moreover, this system was put forward to handle assimilation between segment and tone but a great many Chinese
languages, perhaps most, do not have such relationships.
What such a theory does, then, is to complicate the characterization of such languages while bringing none of the
benefits of an "assimilation" approach.

The other argument, given by Halle and Woo, that dynamic tones cannot occur on short vowels, also bears examination. Woo's argument (see above) is quite interesting
and indicative of her entire approach to tone. In justifying treating tone as a segment, Woo takes extremely fine
phonetic detail -- in milliseconds -- to defend the point
that vowel length exists in Mandarin. Yet, when confronted
with what "appear" to be contour tones on short vowels, the
phonetics are to be explained away and perception becomes

the key.

Quite a number of Chinese languages and dialects have
been described as having short syllables with contour tones.
The <u>Han Yu Fang Yan Ci Hui</u> which Woo cites for other purposes lists five Chinese languages where contour tones are
reported on short syllables. These are: (1) Taiyuan 54;
(2) Suzhow 23; (3) Meixian (Hakka) 21; (4) Amoy 32; (5) Fu-
zhow 23. In each case, the syllable ends in a stop and is
presumably "short." Now it could be the case that all the
investigators "misperceived" stationary tones here but it
seems unlikely. McCoy (1966) reports contour tones on stopped
stopped syllables in various dialects of Cantonese and I
have collected data on such Wu dialects as Taishun and Li-
shui which definitely have <u>very</u> pronounced contour tones
on stopped syllables. Woo could still stand by her claim
since she stated that dynamic tones do not occur "with a
short vowel <u>distinctively</u>" (p. 30; emphasis mine). I am
not sure what this means, but I assume it means that contour tones <u>could</u> occur on short vowels phonetically and yet
not phonologically. But if this is so, then why the phonetic-perception arguments against phonetic contour tones
on short vowels? Even more puzzling is the rationale of
the argument. On the one hand, vowel length which is not
distinctive in Mandarin (as Woo acknowledges) is set up on
<u>phonetic</u> (acoustic) grounds, but contour tones which appar-

ently do exist at the phonetic level (if I understand her use of the word "distinctively") are to be reinterpreted on phonological grounds. In other words, how are phonetic, "non-distinctive" contour tones to be represented at the surface phonetic level? Obviously, an additional segment would have to be added. This must be so if Mandarin under-lying Tone 3 with two segments carrying the tone is to add an additional segment, by rule, to carry the additional phonetic-level pitch feature so that phrase final forms have a mid-low-high tone specification.

Actually, however, as I see it, the "short-vowel--level-tone" argument is simply one instance of the more im-portant "one-segment" -- "one-level-tone-feature" argument. Recall Halle's statement that the "absence of non-station-ary tones on short vowels is not just a curious fact." This is because the theory, as he and Woo see it, states that any non-stationary tone is a sequence of stationary tones. Therefore, since a short vowel can only be represented by a single segment, it can only have one tone feature, i.e., a stationary tone feature.

However, I have argued earlier that syllabic nasal and lateral syllables having contour tones must necessarily render such arguments invalid. Such a syllable is only one single segment, yet it does indeed have a non-stationary

tone. In fact, the short-vowel argument is totally eclipsed
by the syllabic consonant argument since the evidence is
not subject to the sort of acoustic-phonetic-perception
contortions necessary to argue that contour tones cannot
occur on short vowels.

10.6 Conclusion

The Feature Assimilation argument is based on a very
understandable desire to account for the quite natural process of assimilation. In some languages, there seem to be
rather clear cases of some segmental feature influencing
tone. However, in an attempt to give a more realistic account of assimilation we end up with a totally unrealistic,
unmotivated, and even misleading framework for characterizing tone. For it turns out that such a framework suffers
exactly those inadequacies of the Sonorant Feature framework rejected in the previous chapter. Once again, one is
forced to conclude that any framework which attempts to
characterize tone in Chinese totally as a feature of individual segments in inadequate.

Chapter Eleven

THE TONE PROGRAM

11.1 Introduction

In the preceding two chapters two proposals for characterizing tone have been examined and rejected. Interestingly, both approaches are extremely phonetically motivated.
Woo expends considerable effort amassing acoustic evidence
to back her interpretation of tone as a feature of segments.
Likewise, Maran and Halle are proposing new phonetic features such as Raised, Lowered, Slack, etc. Furthermore,
they approach the assimilation process on very low-level
phonetic grounds -- fundamental frequency carrying over
from consonants to vowels, etc. Yet each approach runs
into difficulty. I believe that this is because while both
approaches are indeed phonetically motivated, they are
segmentally oriented. Their phonetic arguments are not
couched solely or even primarily in terms of the surface
phonetic characteristics of tone but rather primarily in
terms of segments and secondarily in terms of how phonetic
tone is to fit in.

I propose an approach in which segmentals are initially ignored and tone is examined "in its own terms,"

at the surface phonetic level. Discussions and formulations involving tone have been far too concerned with the
proper set of underlying distinctive features. That is,
within generative theory tone has not been formulated with
respect to surface phonetic representation nearly as rigor-
ously as segmentals. Indeed, the surface phonetic representation of tone constrains the underlying representation
of tone:

> We think, then, that there may be good reason to
> limit the class of phonological matrices in terms
> of the set of universal phonetic features. For
> the linguist or the child learning the language,
> the set of phonetic representations of utterances
> is a given empirical fact. (Chomsky and Halle 1968:
> 170)

However, if there is no rigorous surface phonetic characterization of tone, then we are free, to some extent, to
make erroneous assumptions about how tone works. This
indeed is the problem, in my view, with both the Sonorant
Feature and Feature Assimilation approaches.

However, the problem is much deeper than this. The
surface phonetic level of representation is concerned with
more than just the proper set of pitch features. A surface
phonetic representation of tone is seen, in generative
theory, as a set of commands to the vocal tract. The symbol [p] is not simply a command -- "bilabial" -- rather

it is a bundle of commands involving place and manner of
articulation. Likewise, a surface phonetic characterization of Mandarin Tone 4 should be more than simply [+High],
[+Low] (Woo) or $\begin{bmatrix} +High \\ +Fall \end{bmatrix}$ or even just [+Fall]. A surface
representation which gives commands to the articulatory
organs must also be concerned with, for example, the duration of Tone 4, the amplitude (or loudness) of Tone 4 and
perhaps even the speed of pitch-change of Tone 4. If a
universal phonetic alphabet is indeed to characterize tone,
then there must be a specification that tells us that a
Cantonese high falling tone is identical to or different
from a Mandarin high falling tone.

This approach, then, treats the tone first and fore-
most as an entity distinct from segmentals and places constraints on underlying tonal representations in terms of
surface phonetic characteristics. In this chapter, then,
I should like to lead into the phonological representation
of tone in Chinese by beginning with its surface phonetic
characteristics.

11.2   The Separability of Tone and Segment

There is often an assumption that no matter how tone
is represented phonologically, i.e., in underlying represen-

tations, it must always be "mapped onto" segmentals at the phonetic level. This, I believe, is implicit in both Woo's approach and in Maran and Halle's approach.

However, I wish to argue that tone is not "mapped onto" segmentals in Chinese languages at the phonetic level but rather remains separate from segmentals in various and interesting ways. I begin with some observations from field work; these need not be taken as proof of my position but rather as evidence.

To begin, I suggest that native speakers of Chinese can quite easily "lift a tone off" of a syllable. With some coaching a native speaker can hum the tone of a syllable, or even whistle it. Moreover, when such tones are hummed, the tone not only has its characteristic pitch height but also its characteristic duration and amplitude. In doing field work on Southern Wu dialects, I was particularly interested in tone sandhi. After some time, and largely as an experiment, I began to ask native speakers not only to hum isolation syllables -- and therefore isolation tones -- but also tone combinations. To check my own record, I would often take a small set of syllables, all with different tones and hum them, asking the native speaker for correct identification of the syllable. After

some practice and "games" native speakers would quite easily hum full phrases. Whistling the tones was also revealing since again both loudness and duration were always preserved.

These observations are suggestive that native speakers can quite easily factor out tone from segmentals. Indeed, hummed tones are quite reminiscent of syllabic nasal
syllables discussed in Chapter 9. Recall that the tones
of such syllables have the same pitch contour, approximate
duration and amplitude of other, polysegmental syllables,
having the same tone.

Another observation on the separability of tone comes
from working with a native speaker of the Ruian dialect of
Southern Wu. In this case, the native speaker had no conscious knowledge of how many tones her dialect had nor the
nature of these tones. Of course, no alphabetic or roman-
ized system existed for writing her dialect. After some
time, however, she began to learn the "phonemic" transcrip-
tion system I was using and eventually began to write her
own language using it. This, of course, required that she
become conscious of the number (8) and nature of the tones
in her language. As a part of my analysis I wished to
check for "accidental gaps" in the syllabary. For instance,
if a syllable /ba/ existed in my corpus in say two tones,
I wished to know if it also occurred in the six other tones--

that is, I wished to know if there were morphemes corresponding to /ba/ in the six other tones. In such a case,
one procedure especially towards the end of the analysis,
is to go through the syllabary, taking a segmental syllable
(such as /ba/) and pronouncing it in all eight tones --
asking in each case if there is a word "X". The Ruian
informant, now familiar with her tone system, upon learning the order in which the tones were presented, insisted
on checking each possible form herself without waiting for
me to pronounce the form first. She would pronounce each
form several times -- and then say either "yes - it means..."
or "no, there is no such word." In a very real sense what
this exercise amounts to is taking a segmental syllable
(such as /ba/) and "plugging it in" to each of the eight
tones, one by one. In doing so, the native speaker is,
of course, pronouncing a great many forms for the first
time and then combing the lexicon to see if such a form
really means anything. Again, this seems to reflect a ready
separability of the tone from the segmental syllable --
the segmental syllable remains the same while different
tones are "put on it." This is not to say tone is completely separable from the segmental syllable. The native speaker does not start with an isolation, toneless syllable
(this is impossible) but rather somehow links a tone to the
segmental syllable and then checks the result as to occur-

ring or non-occurring.

In the case above, the native speaker had no prior
knowledge of her tone system. However, there are cases in
which native speakers have learned on their own or perhaps
have been taught in school the tones of their language in
terms of the traditional classificatory system (discussed
in Chapter 10 in terms of I, II, III, IV): Ping, Shang,
Chu, Ru, upper and lower series. Thus, I have met a number of Cantonese speakers from Hong Kong who have been
taught the tones of standard Cantonese in terms of this
system. Such speakers can quite easily take a segmental
syllable and "run it through" the system -- often in the
order Upper Ping, Upper Shang, Upper Chu, Upper Ru, Lower
Ping, etc. Again, what is interesting here is that native
speakers produce nonsense syllables with great ease by
simply "plugging in" each of the tones to the given segmental syllable.

Another good case for separability of tone from segments at the phonetic level is tone sandhi. In most (all?)
Chinese languages and dialects tones change only with regard
to other tones but not with regard to segmentals. For
example, the most commonly cited tone sandhi rule in Mandarin is that Tone 3 changes to Tone 2 when occurring before another Tone 3. It does not matter what segmentals
are involved -- they play no role in the tone-change. In

fact, whole chains (under some circumstances) of Tone 3 syllables will undergo this rule -- all but the last changing to Tone 2. In such cases, it is as though tone existed in its own domain and was subject only to influences within this domain (I do not mean to imply that syntactic and tempo factors are ignored -- only that segmental factors are).

There is also other evidence of a different nature that suggests that tone is phonetically separable from segments. Fromkin (1974: 8) cites evidence from aphasia that tends to reinforce this interpretation:

> Aphasic studies have also shown the separation of tonal phenomena from segmental phenomena. Tonal contours may be retained when other phonological features are lost. Lyman reports on a study conducted in Peiping that Chinese aphasics often retain tonal contours despite the loss of segmental information on words. It is also the case that loss of intonation is rare in aphasia. (emphasis mine)

Fromkin also cites the fact that child language acquisition studies have shown that children seem to imitate intonation patterns as well as respond to them even before the babbling period: (1974: 8)

> This has been shown to be true of children learning intonation (non-tonal) languages and tone languages. In one study, children learning Chinese, for example, could be distinguished by their tonal contours from other children. (emphasis mine)

These observations that tone is in some sense separable from the segmental syllable, when linked with the problems encountered when tone is considered segmental (i.e. the Sonorant Feature and Feature Assimilation approaches) suggest that the generative approach to tone is in need of revision.

11.3 The Tone Program

11.3.1 The Notion "Program"

It has frequently been suggested that sounds are produced in terms of some higher level neurological or motor pattern -- not simply one by one:

> It has been hypothesized that rapid sequences of movements, such as trains of CVCV articulations or the execution of complicated piano passages, consist of "ballistic" movements, i.e., that they have a predetermined time pattern and are triggered of as a whole... (Lehiste 1970: 8)

Lenneberg (1967) has noted that in speech so many muscular events occur so rapidly that there must be some higher level of organization:

> Lenneberg emphasizes that the activation of so many muscles in such a short time cannot depend on volition alone; there must be "preprogrammed" trains of events that run off automatically. These patterns are complex motor configurations that extend over periods whose duration may comprise that of a syllable or a word. (Lehiste 1970: 9)

The notion that the syllable is a unit of temporal and sequential organization of sounds is not new (e.g. Kozhevnikov
and Christovich (1965); Ladefoged (1967); Liberman,
Cooper, Shankweiler, and Studdert-Kennedy (1967)). This
leads Lehiste, in her work on suprasegmentals, to state:

> In summary, it appears highly likely that articu-
> latory movements are indeed programmed as sequences.
> It seems, further, that the time patterns of this
> articulatory sequences are correlated with lin-
> guistic units, and that there exists a basic unit,
> of the size of a syllable, within which time patterns
> are realized... (Lehiste 1970: 9)

From these comments, I should like to introduce the
notion of "program" with relation to tone and to the syllable in Chinese. However, I do not mean to use it in the
literal, neurological, motor-theory sense as used above.
Rather, I am suggesting the notion "program" as a heuristic
device to make clear certain facets of tone and syllable.
Using such a device allows us to look at tone in a rather
straightforward manner and provides a conception of tone
which can later be translated into the realm of linguistic
theory per se. As a part of this heuristic approach, we
can assume that tone is produced by a "unitary command"
which aims for a sequence or configuration of "targets".

Specifically, I propose that there are two programs
underlying the Chinese syllable: a segmental program and
a tone program. The segmental program is a command which

involves a sequence of target consonants and vowels. The
tone program can be thought of as consisting of a sequential series of target pitch-heights, a target duration, a
target amplitude and a target speed-of-pitch-change. The
two programs are in one sense separate: one is not mapped
onto another. Nevertheless, they must be coordinated to
occur simultaneously. There are several ways of conceiving
of the interface -- this is the topic of the following
chapter -- but we could postulate a third program which
coordinates the two or we could speak of the two as sub-
programs which are "matched" by the overall syllable program.

The components of such a tone program for Chinese
might be diagrammed as follows:

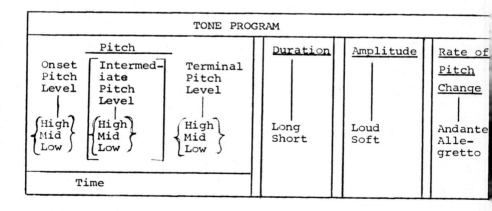

The terms <u>High</u>, <u>Mid</u>, <u>Low</u> for pitch, <u>Long</u> and <u>Short</u> for dura-

tion, <u>Loud</u> and <u>Soft</u> for amplitude and <u>Andante</u> and <u>Allegretto</u>
for rate of pitch change need not be considered features
so much as parameters which may underlie features. The
"Intermediate" pitch level specification is enclosed in
brackets to indicate that it is optional.

Before discussing the parameters of the tone program,
I should like first to justify the notion that it is possible to characterize the syllable in Chinese as consisting
of two independent programs.

11.3.2   The Tone Program vs. the Segmental Program

The dichotomy of the syllable into two programs presents a more realistic way to approach the interaction of
tones and segments. In the segmental program consonants
and vowels may have their own "intrinsic" pitches. Thus,
a voiced consonant may cause a lowering of the pitch of
the following vowel even though the language in question
is not a tonal language. For instance, Wang (1967) notes
that in English, the syllable "bin" has a lower pitch than
"pin." Moreover, vowels may also have an intrinsic pitch.
According to Lehiste "higher vowels have higher fundamental
frequency." (1970: 68) Duration is also a factor of the
segmental program -- consonants and vowels seem to have
intrinsic durations. For instance, according to Lehiste,

the intrinsic duration of consonants is influence by both
their place and manner of articulation. (1970: 27) As for
vowels, Lehiste notes that the intrinsic duration of vowels
appears to be correlated with tongue height -- other factors
held constant, high vowels are shorter than low vowels.
(1970: 18) Furthermore, vowel length is conditioned by
surrounding segmentals. Likewise, vowels are said to have
intrinsic intensity of amplitudes (see Lehiste: 1970: 120).
The point of this low-level phonetic discussion is to demonstrate that factors such as pitch and duration and loudness --
factors which are sometimes linked to tone -- are often simply the characteristics of segmentals or groups of segmentals (e.g. syllables). Naturally, the interaction of these
segmental features with each other will influence the overall phonetic character of the syllable.

On the other hand, a device such as the Tone Program
claims that tones, just like segmentals, have their own "in
trinsic" qualities. For instance, the pitch heights of Mandarin tones have nothing to do with segmentals (c.f. the
discussion of tone sandhi). Such tones can be hummed and
whistled in isolation with the characteristic pitch levels.
Likewise, a tone may have its own "intrinsic" duration --
which again has nothing to do with segmentals. Mandarin
Tone 3 is "extra-long" regardless of the segmentals involved.

Mandarin Tone 4 is "well below average duration" regardless
of the segmentals involved. Again, tones may have their
own characteristic amplitude. According to Krotochvill
(1968: 37), Mandarin Tone 1 has the same loudness throughout the vowel. In Mandarin Tone 2 the loudness rises toward
the end of the vowel. In Mandarin Tone 3 the loudness falls
slightly with a small rise at the end. Mandarin Tone 4 is
characterized by the loudness falling quite sharply toward
the end of the vowel. Tones may also have "intrinsic" rate-
of-pitch change characteristics. Mandarin Tone 2 is often
characterized as "rising quickly" or "rising sharply."
Of Mandarin Tone 3, Krotochvil states the tone contour is
"mildly" falling in the first two thirds of the vowel, and
"sharply" rising in the last third. Of Tone 4, he claims
that the "loudness" falls "sharply" toward the end but the
whole tone is often characterized as "fast" falling (rather
than just the loudness). Thus, the Tone Program like the
Segment Program can consist of a number of intrinsic variables.

11.3.3 The Tone Program and Distinctive Features

If the surface phonetic representation is indeed to
represent commands to the vocal tract, and if phonetic representation is to be characterized in terms of a set of

universal phonetic features, then it would seem likely that
a set of features for characterizing tone should be in the
universal set. Such features may well be n-ary but the
more basic question concerns which features are necessary.
I suggest that the Tone Program device offers some clues.

11.3.3.1 Pitch

For Chinese languages, no more than five pitch heights
are seen as necessary (see Wang 1967) for specifying tones
at the phonetic level. These could be characterized in an
n-ary system (values 1-5, 5 being the highest) or in terms
of a binary system using at least three pitch features.
Such systems have been proposed: High, Central, Mid (Wang
1967), High, Mid, Low (Sampson 1969), and High, Low, Modify
(Woo 1972). Of course, there will be redundancy in such
binary systems since not all combinations are possible.
For the Tone Program I have proposed three features since
they are adequate for surface representations and presumably
would be required for underlying representation.

As a part of the Tone Program, I have provided for
two obligatory and one optional specifications for the pitch
of any syllable. This assumes that one of the defining
characteristics of pitch in Chinese is that it has a beginning pitch "target" and an ending pitch "target." The op-

tional specification has two purposes. One is to express
the turning point in "complex" (rise-fall, fall-rise) tones
and the other is simply to provide more phonetic detail,
if necessary. As an instance of the first purpose, Mandarin
Tone 3 in isolation demands a three position specification
since it is falling-rising. In favor of the phonetic detail
argument are specifications such as <u>331</u> for Suzhou.[1] This
sort of phonetic detail is fairly common in Chinese tone
description. The second digit is not a reversal point as
in a complex tone. More likely, the investigator is trying
to note that phonetically the tone is rather sustained before it drops as opposed to an unsustained <u>31</u> drop.

One might argue that two pitch positions are not always necessary since stopped syllables often have such short
tones that there seems to be no reason to think of a starting and ending point. However, I have argued that phonetically, contour tones do occur with stopped syllables. Thus,
it would seem preferable to characterize tones on stopped
syllables in terms of two positions and make use of the
duration feature <u>Short</u> to characterize these tones.

Such a device makes certain claims about Chinese
tone. One is that while tone could phonetically be charac-

----
1. This particular example is taken from <u>Han Yu Fang Yan
Ci Hui</u>; such tonal descriptions are fairly common in
descriptions of tone systems in Chinese.

terized in terms of four or five or a great many positions
("digits") depending on the detail, three positions will be
sufficient. Another claim is that at least two positions
must be specified.

In conclusion, then, as Wang pointed out (1967: 93)
the five level system with a maximum of three positions to
be specified results in a possible 125 phonetic tone configurations. Chen reports 69 different "phonetic shapes" in
a study of 737 dialects of Chinese (1973: 93).

11.3.3.2 Duration

The notion of duration in the phonetic specification
of tone has been rather vague. Features such as Short have
been proposed for characterizing tones on stopped syllables,
but such syllables are only the most obvious case of phonetic duration playing a significant role. Since there
has never been any sort of standard scale, it has been left
up to each investigator to mention whether or not a tone
is particularly long or short.

Consider again Woo's claim that Mandarin Tone 3 is
1.5 times as long as the other tones and consider Kratochvil's claim that Tone 4 is shorter than average. The question is, at the phonetic level, how much duration information do we want to specify? In fact, one could argue that
it is not important to specify it at all. Yet, Woo consi-

dered phonetic duration information to be extremely important in supporting her thesis of long vowels in Mandarin.
Moreover, we do not yet understand the effect of duration
in historical change or in synchronic processes such as
tone sandhi. For instance, stress may influence duration
which may then influence pitch contour.

However, even if duration is to be specified, as I
believe it should, it is not at all clear how. Like pitch,
duration is a feature on a physical continuum. However,
unlike pitch, we have no five point scale. In the Tone
Program I have simply suggested two extremes. If these
were eventually to be formulated as features then there
is also the possibility of a mid-range (e.g. [-Long],
[-Short]). I will not pursue the matter further. I simply suggest that duration, as a parameter of tone, should
be expressed at the surface phonetic level.

11.3.3 Amplitude

Intensity likewise seems to vary from tone to tone.
Its role in perception, historical change, tone sandhi,
etc. has, to my knowledge, never been studied as distinct
from the other features of tone. There have been suggestions that amplitude plays a role in discriminating whis-
pered speech in Chinese (c.f. Kratochvil 1968). This alone
would suggest its potential in perception.

Like the other tone features, amplitude is also a
continuum feature and again I have only suggested some
extremes.

11.3.3.4 Rate of Pitch Change

I have suggested this as a separate component of the
tone program since it seems quite possible -- at least from
field work -- that while two tones may be identical in starting and ending pitches, one may rise or fall more "sharply"
than the other. Of course, this is intricately tied up
with the duration component of the tone program as well as
with the pitch component. However, it seems possible that
within a complex tone, at least, there exists the possibility
of a fixed overall duration and fixed pitch heights but
"sharp" or "mild" rises and falls within these limitations
-- much as Kratochvil proposed for Mandarin Tone 3.

Again, this is a continuum phenomenon and I have
only suggested some possible extremes.

11.3.3.5 The Interaction of Tone Program Components

The possible relations which hold between the four
components of the Tone Program will be quite important in
arriving at an adequate surface representation of tone.
This is so because there may be a great deal of redundancy

between the components or between the sub-parts of the components. For instance, in Mandarin, Tone 4 which is falling, is characterized by loudness rapidly falling off. Do all falling tones in all Chinese languages display some sort of similarity with respect to amplitude? Mandarin Tone 2 -- rising -- is marked by greater amplitude at the ending point -- again, is this characteristic in some intrinsic sense or rising tones -- or perhaps rising tones which end at a very high pitch? Or is rate-of-pitch-change responsible for the amplitude character of Mandarin Tone 2? Is it possible for tones to have the same overall durations and yet different rates of pitch change? Are there constraints on how quickly a tone can rise or fall?

It would seem that little is known about many of these interactions. Yet, knowledge of such factors should lead to a greater understanding of such processes as tone change, tone sandhi, tone acquisition and ultimately -- tone representation. Here, I am simply proposing that the Tone Program -- as a separate program from segmentals -- offers quite a number of its own problems. Perhaps these should be more thoroughly investigated before tone is relegated to the domain of the segment.

11.4   The Phonetic Representation of Tone

I believe most linguists working within the generative framework would agree that there are at least four
requirements or functions of the surface phonetic level of
representation. First, a surface phonetic representation
need not attempt to represent every physical detail of an
utterance (this would be impossible) but it should reveal
those facets of the utterance which are felt to be critical
in describing the language. Anderson has put it thusly:

> Of course, we want any proposed set of parameters
> for phonetic description to include every
> feature that can serve systematically to differ-
> entiate one utterance from another in any language.
> 1974: 7)

A second requirement is that surface forms be characterized in terms of a finite, universal set of features.
Again, Anderson states: "It is also necessary that the
set of parameters include every feature in terms of which
one language differs systematically from another, for
otherwise linguists would be unable to characterize this
distinction." (1974: 7)

A third requirement is that the surface level serve
as a representation of commands to the vocal tract (Chomsky and Halle (1968), Postal (1968)).

Finally, the surface level constrains the underly-

ing representation. This is in line with Postal's Naturalness Condition or with the notion of "concreteness" in
phonology. Underlying representations should correspond
as closely as possible to surface representation; devia-
tions have a "cost" in terms of rules added.

Applying these requirements to the characterization
of tone at the surface level, it is indeed difficult to
see how tone -- as conceived in terms of a Tone Program --
could be considered segmental or how one could propose that
tone is mapped onto segments. By the first requirement
just discussed, pitch height and duration at least would
be required at the phonetic level. By the second requirement, probably all the components of the tone program would
have to be specified. That is, a high-falling tone in
Mandarin must be characterized as the same as or different
from a high-falling tone in Cantonese. The difference may
turn out to be in amplitude, in duration, in rate-of-pitch-
change or in some combination of these components. A
high short tone on stopped syllables in Cantonese may be
qualitatively different from a high short tone on stopped
syllables in Shanghai. The universal set of features must
have the machinery to capture this difference -- thus it
must be prepared to deal with such notions as amplitude,
duration, etc.

By the third requirement, again, all the components

of the Tone Program must be included. If a Mandarin Tone
4 is to be a Mandarin Tone 4, it must have a particular
duration and a particular amplitude display and perhaps a
particular rate-of-pitch-change contour -- all in addition
to the pitch specifications.

Are all of these components to be represented as
features of segments? There seem to be enough problems
simply in attempting to characterize pitch as a segmental
feature. But pitch, as I am arguing here, is merely the
tip of an iceberg. Indeed, unless we drastically modify
our conception of surface phonetic representation, it
seems very unlikely that tone can be mapped onto segments
at the surface phonetic level. The Tone Program must be
realized phonetically -- the commands necessary to real-
ize this program physically must be sent to the vocal tract --
and there is no necessary reason to assume that these
commands are filtered through segments. In fact, there
is a good deal of evidence -- as I have tried to demonstrate
-- that such "commands" have nothing to do with segmentals
in a great many Chinese languages, such as Mandarin. In
any case, it would be interesting to see how duration,
for instance, or amplitude, or rate-of-pitch-change could
be seen as features of segments without radically alter-
ing the segmental representation or distorting the inherent

(intrinsic) features (duration, pitch, amplitude, etc.)
of the segments.

11.5 The Phonological Representation of Tone

The approach to the phonological representation of
tone taken in this essay has been via the surface phonetic
representation. I have mentioned that phonological representation is in large part constrained by the properties
of the surface phonetic representation. Within generative
theory the main justification for setting up underlying
representations which differ from surface representations
is to account for morphophonemic variation. Morphophonemic
variation aside for the moment, a relevant question would
be whether tone could be characterized at the underlying
level in some way radically different from the surface
level. For instance, it has been argued in this essay
that tone should not be represented as a feature of individual segments at the phonetic level. But could such an
argument be given for the phonological level? I do not
see how this could be done without greatly complicating
the mapping of underlying representation onto the surface.
If, in lexical entries, one wishes to characterize pitch
as, say a feature of two segments and then have rules which
"expand" pitch to cover the whole syllable, a number of prob-

lems will arise. Since it has been argued that tone is to
be characterized as distinct from segmentals at the phonetic
level, such rules will be quite unusual and therefore costly.
They would be quite unnatural since they would be converting segmental phenomena into tonal phenomena. Moreover, two
types of feature systems would have to be employed to handle
tones. At the underlying level, there would be a set of
tone features for characterizing tone as a feature of segments. But at the surface, no such features exist. The
only features for specifying tone at the surface level are
features which apply to the entire syllable via the Tone
Program. This would be a direct violation of the notion so
often stated (Chomsky and Halle 1968: 170) that the same
set of features, namely the ones characteristic of the surface phonetic level, are to be used at both surface and
underlying levels. Also, such a situation would be complicated by the fact that while the pitch features would be
sepcified as features of segments at the underlying level,
duration presumably would not. Such an approach would then
destroy the integrity of the Tone Program and therefore
of the tone by maintaining that some of its characteristics
are segmentally determined while others are not, which is
often not the case (e.g., Mandarin).

The argument here is essentially this: if tone is
truly to be characterized at the surface phonetic level as

distinct from segmental representation, then the same conditions must hold at the underlying level; thus, tone must
also be characterized as separate from segmentals in the
underlying representation.

The only escape from this "concrete phonology" approach
would be if morphophonemic alternation justified setting up
more abstract underlying forms. Yet, in Chinese, I believe
that only in rare cases can a morphophonemic argument be
formulated for treating tone as a feature of segments at the
underlying level. If anything, just the opposite normally
seems the case -- tonal morphophonemics generally have little
or nothing to do with segments.

Thus, the real issue in the underlying representation
of tone does not involve segmentals. In fact, since there
is so little information on the role of duration, intensity
and rate-of-pitch-change in morphophonemics in Chinese, the
central issue of the underlying representation ends up being
the underlying representation of pitch. Here the greatest
controversy seems to be whether or not contour tones are to
be treated as sequences of level tones or as unitary contour
tones.

The arguments pro and con have almost invariably been
couched with reference to segmentals and segmental representation (c.f. Chapters 9 and 10 above). However, the thesis
here is that tones have no necessary connection with seg-

mentals at either the surface or deep levels. Therefore,
the arguments for representing contour tones as sequences
of level tones or as unitary tones must take a somewhat
different turn. For instance, both Woo's Sonorant Feature
approach and Maran-Halle's Feature Assimilation approach
would specify Rise as a sequence of Low plus High, but these
latter features would have to each be attached to a particular segment. Here, such a segment-oriented approach has
been rejected but this does not mean that the notion of
sequences of level tones as representing contour tones must
be rejected.

Indeed, I believe Woo gives an excellent argument
for such an approach and the argument has nothing to do
with segments.

Consider the following two tone specifications using
Wang's (1967) tone features:

(a) $\nearrow$ high-rising $\begin{bmatrix} +contour \\ +high \\ -central \\ -mid \\ +rising \end{bmatrix}$ (b) $\searrow$ high-falling $\begin{bmatrix} +contour \\ +high \\ -central \\ -mid \\ +falling \end{bmatrix}$

Thus, (a) rises to high pitch while (b) falls from high pitch,
but as Woo notes (1973: 36) such representations make unusual claims. In (a) the feature High represents the end
of the tone, whereas in (b) High indicates the initial point

of the tone. This leads Woo to state:

The feature matrix $\begin{bmatrix} +\text{high} \\ -\text{mid} \\ -\text{central} \\ +\text{rise} \end{bmatrix}$ therefore does not

represent a set of physiological instructions which
are to be realized simultaneously, but sequentially,
as are the instructions for series of matrices
within boundaries. (1973: 36-37).

This is so, because the instructions actually assume that
the command is not rise from <u>High</u> but rather to <u>High</u> and
this involves knowing the correct sequence. Taken as presented by Wang, the representation as a command would either
be ambiguous or impossible.

Complex tones present even more serious problems in
Wang's framework. A high falling-rising tone in Wang's system would be classified as:

$$\begin{bmatrix} +\text{high} \\ -\text{mid} \\ -\text{central} \\ +\text{rise} \\ +\text{fall} \\ -\text{convex} \end{bmatrix}$$

The problem here, as Woo points out, is that without the
feature <u>Convex</u> it is not clear whether the tone first rises
from [-high] to [+high] and then falls from [+high] back to
[-high] or whether it behaves just the opposite falling from
high and then rising. The feature <u>Convex</u> then, is necessary
to determine the <u>order</u>: a [-convex] tone falls and then

rises, whereas a [+convex] tone rises and then falls. Thus, the feature Convex serves only to provide sequential order and is extremely restricted: it can only come into a play if a tone is specified [+rise, +fall]. Woo concludes:

> Thus we see that this system of features contains not just features determining the order in which pitch heights are realized but also a feature determining the order in which the ordering features are realized. (1973: 37)

Woo's criticism seems quite well founded. In the one case certain assumptions are made about how tone works but the representation obscures this. In the other case, a tone feature is actually used as a sequencing device.

I have proposed for the Tone Program that the tone could phonetically be characterized in terms of three pitch heights and three positions. There seems to be good evidence that a phonetic representation of tone would have to express these notions in terms of features such as those proposed for the Tone Program. Suppose then that the pitch component of the Tone Program is converted into a set of features, say, High, Mid and Low which must be specified with respect to at least two, possibly three positions. If such a phonetic representation were also postulated for the underlying level this would be an argument against features such as Rise and Fall and would accomplish not only surface-deep concreteness but also resolve the problem which Woo

has discovered in Wang's feature framework. If this procedure were followed, then tone at the underlying level,
and the surface level could be characterized as sequences
of level tones, though not, of course, related in any way
to segments.

There is, however, one serious problem with such an
approach. Tonal morphophonemics have not been taken into
account. Of course, using the underlying features High,
Mid and Low as level pitch heights presents no problem.
There might be valid morphophonemic reasons for characterizing for example, a phonetic low-high sequence as low-low
at the underlying level. The present framework actually
allows for this. The problem is whether underlying representations such as Rise or Fall should be allowed or whether
such tones should always be characterized as sequences of
level pitch features. Again -- this problem within the present framework has nothing to do with segments, only tonal
morphophonemics.

The preferred solution would be to constrain the
underlying representation in terms of the surface representation. We must characterize contour tones at the surface
in terms of a sequence of level pitch heights. A surface
feature Rise can hardly be assumed to be a command to the
vocal tract. That is, the beginning and ending pitches
must be specified. Moreover, a surface feature like Rise

is fraught with the problems which -- as Woo pointed out --
are inherent in Wang's use of such features. Thus, if no
feature <u>Rise</u> can be posited at the surface, then, following
the usual dictum that only one set of features, the same
set in fact, are to be used for both surface and underlying
representation, we must disallow underlying tones such as
<u>Rise</u>.

However, morphophonemic representations represent
an attempt to account for underlying regularities and natural
processes such as assimilation, dissimilation, etc. Suppose
it were the case that the most likely explanation for a
morphophonemic alternation involving two tones was that the
two tones agree or disagree in the <u>direction of the pitch</u>
<u>contour</u>, without regard to pitch heights. For example,
suppose it were the case that a tone sandhi rule seemed to
be aimed at changing the first of two rising tones into a
falling tone to create dissimilation. It could be the case
that the morphophonemic change is not concerned with pitch
heights at all -- simply direction of contour.

At the heart of the issue is this. The Tone Program
and indeed, all the features in generative phonology are
posited with respect to the speaker, not the hearer. That
is, a surface phonetic representation represents a series
of commands to the vocal organs. Such representations say
little about perception as distinct from production. The

Tone Program approaches tone from the production point of view: each tone must be characterized as a set of commands to articulatory organs, therefore the notion "Rise" must be broken down into "start at pitch height X and go to pitch height Y." However, a morphophonemic alternation may be conditioned by perception factors. In such a case the morphophonemic rule could be motivated by the need for preserving distinctions in, say, two tone combinations (compound words). In such a situation the hearer as opposed to the speaker, is not concerned with the beginning and ending pitches per se -- he is only listening for the direction of the tone - rising or falling. Thus, to the hearer, Rise (or Fall) may indeed be a unitary feature. If it turned out that in a language a great many tone sandhi rules were motivated simply by perception factors, such that the directions of tones were critical whereas the starting and ending points were not, then a theory of tonology that specified that all tones must be characterized as sequences of level tones would be misleading. It would be claiming that all tonal processes involve discrete pitch heights whereas it could be the case that some tonal processes involve only pitch direction (e.g., rise, fall) but not discrete pitch heights.

In sum, I believe that it would be premature to constrain the theory such that all underlying tones must be represented as series of discrete, level pitches. This would be preferred, especially from the production view point. But we know very little about the perception of tone and of what role purely perceptual factors play in tonal morphophonemics. Thus, it would seem to me, that we must also allow that underlying tones be characterized by unitary features such as Rise and Fall if there is morphophonemic justification for such representation and if the use of discrete, level pitch features only obscure such tonal morphophonemic processes.

11.6 Conclusion

Recent generative work on tone representation has often been characterized with representing tone as it relates to segments. In this chapter I have suggested that tone be examined on its own terms, so to speak, without reference to its relation to segments. In order to see tone as a phenomenon independent of segmental influence, I have argued that tone is, in fact, in some sense separable from the segmental syllable in Chinese. That is, native speakers can actually "plug-in" different tones to the same segmental syllable and can even plug in tones to segmental syllables which they have never said before (i.e., nonsense forms). If tone truly is separable, then how is it to be character-

ized? I have proposed a heuristic device, the Tone Program,
to demonstrate not only the separability of tone, but also
its "inherent" characteristics and ultimately (hopefully)
to demonstrate how these inherent features interact with
each other. If tone is separable, and if it does have inherent characteristics, then these must be represented in
the surface phonetic representation as commands to the vocal
tract. It seems quite unlikely that such commands are
directly related to the commands for producing the segmental
portion of the Chinese syllable. It seems even less likely,
then, that tone could ever be characterized as a feature
of segments at the surface phonetic level.

Such conclusions, reached with regard to the surface
phonetic level representation of tone have critical implications for the underlying representation of tone. Unless
quite valid morphophonemic reasons can be brought forward,
the theory demands that the underlying representation reflect
the surface representation as clearly as possible. With
regard to pitch features, therefore, I maintain that tone
can be represented in the underlying representation in
terms of the surface representation, that is, in terms of
three pitch heights, High, Mid and Low and three pitch
positions beginning, intermediate (turning point), and
ending. Such features are features of the syllable and

are not tied in any way to specific segments (but see
the next chapter). However, I maintain that the theory
should allow underlying representations making use of unitary features such as <u>Rise</u> and <u>Fall</u> if it can be shown that
they are morphophonemically motivated.

In this chapter, I have assumed that tone and segment
are totally unrelated but the Feature Assimilation approach
has made it quite clear that such relationships can occur
in some languages. The next chapter, then, is concerned
with tone-segment relationships.

Chapter Twelve

THE INTERFACE OF TONE AND SEGMENT

12.1 Introduction

With respect to the characterization of tone, much
recent generative work seems to have focused on the proper
underlying representation. Implicit in such an approach is
the belief that tone will ultimately be mapped onto segments
at the phonetic level. However, in this essay, it has been
argued that tone is not mapped onto segments at the surface
phonetic level but rather is "independently programmed."

The insistence of the mapping of tones onto segments
serves only to reveal that generative theory has a built-
in segmental bias. In Chapter 8 it was argued that the problem of tone representation in generative theory seems to
have originated in trying to fit tone into a matrix where
the columns stand for segments and rows are features. The
use of such a matrix then, claims that all sounds must eventually be represented in terms of discrete segments. Yet,
while tone can be broken into a series of discrete commands,
there seems to be no reason to assume that each of the discrete commands will match each segmental command, one for

one. It is true that tone can occur only in conjunction with voiced segments but this need not imply that each tone command can be reduced to a particular segment. It is for this reason that the notion Tone Program was introduced -- to stress the independent nature of tone.

One could say, then, that generative theory obscures the characterization of tone by the use of matrices designed to characterize segments. But obviously, this is not the true source of the problem of tone representation. Matrices were designed to characterize segments and thus the theory suffers from a bias in which segments are somehow "primary" and tones are "secondary". One could argue, as I suggested in Chapter 1, that this bias stems from an alphabetic tradition in which suprasegmentals are characterized not by segment size units, but by diacritics or perhaps by nothing, as, for example, English stress. Perhaps this in turn stems from the fact that suprasegmental factors in Western, alphabetic languages play a secondary role and are therefore to be treated as secondary phenomena. In the Chinese case, however, tone is just as primary in its role as any segment-sized, alphabetic-like unit. In China, entire dictionaries have, in the past, been organized first by tone, then by final, etc. The equivalent to such suprasegmental-dominated approach in the West would be to organize dictionaries by

the stress patterns of polysyllabic words -- not a very likely approach.

In sum, I believe one could make a good case that
since generative phonological theory is rooted so deeply in
an alphabetic tradition and in a tradition devoid of lexical
tone, its basic formulation -- i.e. phonology is primarily
though not solely the phonology of segments -- is inherently
biased toward the idea that tone can be reduced to segments.

In this chapter, I should like to explore the nature
of the interface between tone and segment when this bias is
removed.

12.2 Segments Mapped Onto Tones

Perhaps the most crucial argument against the mapping
of tones onto segments would be to maintain that segments
are mapped onto tones. Let us consider, again, Woo's treatment of tone and segment at the phonetic level with regard
to Mandarin Tone 3. Woo found that syllables having this
tone were one and a half times longer than the other syllables. Thus, if one measured the vowel in such syllables,
it would indeed be longer than vowels in the other tones.
But then again -- all finals whether consisting of pure vowel, dipthong or VN cluster would also be longer according to
her data. Now if the a of the syllable "ba" is going to

change its duration with each tone -- as Woo's own acoustic
findings indicate -- then it is obvious that in a very real
sense the a is being mapped onto the tone. The Tone Program determines the length of the final portion of the syllable, the Segment Program provides that the vowel be prolonged in accordance with the Tone Program. Woo's own acoustic findings clearly show that this is the case but Woo did
not look at tone from the perspective of tone dominating segment.

Another example, more controversial and less clear-
cut comes from the characterization of the so-called apical
vowels in many Chinese languages and dialects. In Walton
(1971) I discussed the characterization of such vowels in
Mandarin. Some of that discussion is relevant here.

Hartman (1944) in describing the Mandarin phonological system did not consider these vowels to be true vowels:

> They are homorganic with the preceding consonant
> and hence the point of articulation falls outside
> the standard vowel classification. This has led
> a number of observers to conclude that the con-
> sonants in question form syllables without vowels.
> (Hartman 1944: 31)

To Hartman, the chief characteristic of such sounds was their
"syllabicity" -- thus he termed them "syllabic continuants."
In his framework, "syllabic" indicates the potential for
carrying tone. In essence, "apical vowels" were simply

voiced, frictionless continuants of the preceding consonants.

Hockett (1947) treated apical vowels in Mandarin in much the same manner. Using a framework in which features were either "determining" or "determined" he maintained that the apical vowel consisted solely of determined features. It was characterized as an unrounded high back vowel but the tongue position and throat muscles were actually determined by the preceding consonant.

In another analysis, Chao (1934) characterized such apical vowels as being a "prolongation of the preceding consonant." In a more recent work (Chao 1968: 19) he termed the apical vowel a "syllable carrier" in which the last part of the consonant is "buzzed" so that this last part can "carry" the syllable.

Thus it is true that such sounds could be considered vowels since they have some sort of vowel quality. But this quality seems entirely determined, hence Hockett's "semiconsonant," Hartman's "syllabic continuant" and Chao's "syllable carrier." Hockett (1955) describes the nature of such a determined vowel (in a work not concerned specifically with Chinese) in discussing the lack of total distinction between vocoids and contoids:

> ...hold the tongue in the proper position for a
> prolonged buzzing z-z-z-z, and produce such a
> prolonged buzz. This sound is a contoid. Now

without moving any part of the speech tract north
of the lungs, a diminution of pressure from the
lungs can eliminate the "buzz" of this prolonged
z-z-z-z, whereupon the result sounds like an obscure vowel -- a vocoid. (p. 30)

In Walton (1971) I showed that the apical vowel in

Shanghai was quite similar to that of Mandarin. For example,

in both languages such vowels occur only after [ts, ts', s]

(though Shanghai can be interpreted as having a [z] initial

in addition). In both languages such vowels never occur

alone (the other vowels do), can never be preceded by a

glide, and can never be followed by another sound. Such

restrictions led me (p. 82, ft. 17) to suggest that perhaps

such sounds were not vowels in the normal sense and moreover

to suggest the possibility that psycholinguistic tests could

be carried out to demonstrate that native speakers do not

regard them as "vowels" in the same sense as other vowels.

More importantly for the present discussion, I argued that

perhaps such "vowels" were supplied simply to carry the tone

-- much in line with Hartman's and Chao's "syllable carrier"

notions. Using the notion of two different syllable pro-

grams one could argue that the Tone Program "demands" that

the Segmental Program provide voicing to carry the tone.

Since there is no "target" vowel in the usual sense, the

initial segment is simply prolonged -- much in the manner

that Hockett describes above -- so that the Segment Program

"obeys" the Tone Program. Such a treatment is admittedly
novel but I bring it up here to demonstrate that it is conceivable that tone dominates segment (in this case an apical vowel) perhaps to the degree that the segment has no
intrinsic qualities of its own at all. That is, tone causes
the consonant to be prolonged producing a "dummy" carrier.
Again, if this could indeed be defended as an adequate analysis, we would have an even more interesting case of a segment being mapped onto a tone rather than vice-versa. However, as will be discussed shortly, the most appealing
approach is to forget the whole notion of "mapping" in either
direction, and speak instead of an interface between two
dimensions.

12.3 Tone-Segment Relationships

The Feature Assimilation approach is based on the
relationship between voicing in consonants and pitch height,
and on the effect of final consonants -- usually stops --
on the duration of the tone. In every case cited by Maran,
Halle, and Halle-Stevens in Chapter 10, this influence is
always seen to be on the preceding or following vowel.
This is the consequence of assigning pitch phenomena to
segments.

There is no doubt that glottic features influence

tone but there seems to be no reason to assume that such influence is restricted solely to the preceding or following
vowel. In the present framework, where tone is not characterized as a feature of segments, such relationships hold
between the glottic features of initial and final segments
and various sub-components of the tone program. For instance, a voiced obstruent initial in, say Wenzhou does not
"lower the tone" but rather lowers the beginning pitch
height -- only one sub-component of the Tone Program. In
fact, it is common in Chinese languages for tones which begin
"low" -- that is at 1 or 2 on the pitch scale -- to go into
the mid and upper ranges -- 3, 4, 5 -- at the terminal position of the pitch specification.

Likewise, a final voiceless stop does not -- in Chinese languages in any case -- influence the tone so much as
one sub-component -- namely duration. As we have seen,
pitch height(s) are independent of the influence of the final stop. Rather than claiming that final stops shorten
the preceding vowel, which then shortens the duration of the
tone -- as is done in the Feature Assimilation approach --
it seems more natural to assume that such stops simply short-
en the whole syllable and since tone is a syllable feature
is is automatically shortened.

Thus, one can agree that glottic features influence
certain sub-components of the Tone Program without reducing

tone to a feature of specific segments.

12.4 Tone-Segment Features

The Feature Assimilation approach, as its name implies, seeks to capture tone-segment relationships such
that features assimilate from one segment to the next. Thus,
a voiced obstruent characterized as say, [+Low] influences
the following vowel so that it too becomes [+Low] thereby
resulting in a low tone.

But a rule such as $[\alpha Low] \longrightarrow [\alpha Low]/\_\_\_\_[\alpha Low]$ will
not be possible in an approach which makes use of two sets
of features -- one for tone and one for segments. However,
I have tried to demonstrate that such a two-program approach
is more in accord with the linguistic facts -- if such an
approach is more complex this is so because tone is more
complex than the Feature Assimilation approach allows. Moreover, the set of features proposed by Halle and Stevens for
characterizing both tones and segments has come under some
criticism (Lisker and Abramson (1971); Fromkin (1972);
Ladefoged (1973)). Ladefoged's own approach to glottic
features is more in accord with the principles outlined in
this essay for characterizing tone. Ladefoged distinguishes
"four distinct actions" of the larynx: (1) glottalicness,
(2) voice onset, (3) glottal stricture, and (4) pitch. Each

"action" constitutes a physical scale. For example, Voice
Onset is a scale of 1 to 3: (1) Aspirated, (2) Unaspirated,
(3) Voicing throughout, etc. The Glottal Stricture scale is
one which obviously plays a great role in tone-segment relationships:

1. spread
2. voiceless
3. murmur
4. slack
5. voice
6. stiff
7. creaky
8. closed

Hyman and Schuh (1974) have proposed a phonetic hierarchy of consonants ranked by their tone lowering effect
(in the terminology here this would be the "beginning pitch
level lowering" effect rather than "tone lowering effect"):

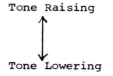

Tone Raising	implosive
	voiceless aspirated
	voiceless unaspirated
	sonorants
	voiced obstruents
Tone Lowering	breathy voice

While Ladefoged is likewise obviously aware of the
effects of glottic states such as breathy voice, aspiration,
voicing, murmur, etc., it is interesting that he sets up
pitch as a separate "action" from glottic stricture. However, though he did set up pitch as a separate state he put
this state "in parentheses":

> The use of the larynx in pitch variations in listed
> in parentheses because it is obviously an oversimpli-
> fication to suggest that there is only a simple
> linguistic feature which we may term pitch. (1973:
> 77)

For pitch features, Ladefoged simply proposes a scale of High,
Mid and Low. Nevertheless he does group these under two
"cover features" Raised and Lowered. The former is roughly
associated with aspirated and unaspirated voice onset, and
spread, voiceless and murmur on the glottal stricture scale.
However, he is quick to point out that while such features
as Raised and Lowered often do correlate with glottal stricture states, (e.g. high tones occur after voiceless aspirated
stops), the relationship is certainly not invariable:

> As we have seen, pitch and glottal stricture can
> sometimes covary, but they are often clearly in-
> dependent features. Most glottal strictures can
> occur on a wide range features (1973: 77).

12.5   Tone-Segment Redundancy

Given the above discussion, and especially Ladefoged's
characterization of tone, it would seem more appropriate to
characterize the interface of tone and segment not as some
sort of assimilation in one dimension (the Feature Assimilation approach) but as some sort of redundancy or phonotactics
between two different but related dimensions.

One facet of the tone-segment interface is definitely

intrinsic -- tone can only occur with voiced segments in
Chinese monosyllables. Since it is intrinsic, there is no
need for any sort of mapping. Especially, there is no need
for mapping one dimension onto the other. The interface is
better characterized by notions such as "linking" cr "coor-
dinating" the two dimensions rather than mapping one onto
the other.

For purposes of phonological representation tone could
certainly be associated with the _Final_ in Chinese just as
in traditional Chinese phonology. In the scheme proposed
in Chapter 7 ·tone would phonologically be associated with
$\overline{\overline{V}}$:[1]

If the initial consonant were voiced, say [m-] the tone
would intrinsically be associated with the [m] at the phonetic level. If the syllable ended in a voiceless stop,
the tone would intrinsically be shortened at the phonetic
level -- i.e. it could not occur simultaneously with the

----

1. The formalism here is adopted from Chomsky (1970) (see
especially p. 210-211) at the suggestion of John Bowers.
The brackets enclose a "complex symbol" such that the tone
(T) is not left or right branching from $\overline{V}$ but can be thought
of as extending into a third dimension. The effect of this
notation is that while tone is associated with the Final,
it is not related to the Final in the same way that segmentals are related to the Final and to each other.

voiceless stop.

Aside from the intrinsic relationships between tone
and segment which should be covered by universal redundancy
rules, there would also be a set of language-specific redundancy rules. These would be a function of the Local Constraints sub-component of the Surface Phonetic Component
(see Chapter 6). That is, such relationships are not "processes" as the Feature Assimilation approach suggests
(i.e. the "process" of assimilation) but rather cooccurrence
restrictions. The Feature Assimilation approach sought to
judge the naturalness of such relationships through using
the same set of features plus alpha-rules. The present proposal is that the naturalness of such tone-segment relation
ships be judged by the naturalness of the redundancy rules.
That is, I am suggesting using natural vs. non-natural redundancy rules rather than using distinctive features as the
way to evaluate tone-segment naturalness. Let us suppose
there exists a set of universal redundancy rules which state
that among other things, it is natural for beginning pitch
height of a tone to be lowered when the syllable begins with
a voiced obstruent. If the language has such a relationship,
e.g. Shanghai or Wenzhou, then this rule need not be specified for the language. Thus, the more redundancy rules
added to the Local Constraints sub-somponent, the more complex and less natural the relationship.

This appraoch is particularly appropriate with respect
to Chinese languages which do not have tone-segment relationships of this type. Recall that one consequence of following the Feature Assimilation approach is that even when there
is no segment-tone assimilation, tones are still represented
as segments -- thereby creating unmotivated complexity. In
the present framework, if we are describing a language like
Mandarin, then there will be no tone-segment redundancy rules
-- which is one measure of simplicity -- and there will be
no need to characterize tone as a feature of segments.

12.6 Diachronic Tone-Segment Relationships

The historical relation between tone and segment has
been discussed under the general term of "tonogenesis." I
will not discuss this facet in the present essay save to
suggest one more dimension of such diachronic tone-segment
relationships.

Recall that one function of the Surface Phonetic
Component is to indicate inherent syllable structure in
terms of strong and weak positions and in terms of consonantal strength. In Hooper's strength scale strengthening takes
place in syllable initial position and voiceless stops are
stronger than voiced stops. That is, part of the inherent
structure -- and therefore an inherent diachronic tendency

-- involves initial voiced consonants devoicing. Let us
examine what role this could have in the tone-segment interface.

Middle Chinese (ca. 600 A.D.) is said to have had
four distinct tone categories with two pitch shapes in each
category. Lower pitch shapes occurred only with syllables
having voiced initials. Wang (1967) provides the usual description of what is believed to have happened historically:

> When the voicing distinction was obliterated through
> historical change, as evidenced in most Chinese
> dialects today, the phonetic differences in the
> pitch shapes in certain cases became distinctive
> (p. 95ff)

The question is, how could a critical distinction such as
the voicing distinction be obliterated? The obvious answer
would be that the phonetically non-distinctive pitch heights
became distinctive so that the voiced-voiceless distinction
was no longer critical. But why would the phonetically non-
distinctive pitch heights become distinctive? Compare Ladefoged's glottic stricture scale, Hyman and Schuh's tone-
level scale and Hooper's strength scale:

Ladefoged	Hyman and Schuh		Hooper
1. spread	Tone	implosive	vl. stop
2. voiceless	Raising	vl. aspirated	vd. stop
3. murmur	↑	vl. unaspirated	vl. continuant
4. slack	↓	sonorants	vd. continuant
5. voice	Tone	vd. obstruents	nasals
6. stiff	Lowering	breathy voice	liquids
			glides

(Hooper column marked "strength" along the side, arrow pointing up)

Note that Hooper's strength scale with respect to voiced and
voiceless stops is parallel to Hyman and Schuh's tone-rais-
ing scale and to Ladefoged's increasingly more constricted
glottal stricture scale.

Hooper suggests that as an inherent facet of syllables the initial consonant strengthens. If we apply this to
the Chinese case then we have a principled reason for the
devoicing of initial voiced consonants -- namely "strengthening." Indeed, with respect to voiced and voiceless stops
this explanation is appealing. There are no cases of voiceless stops becoming voiced -- i.e. no cases of voiced initial
stops developing initially -- in Chinese languages. The
trend has been for initial voiced stops to devoice. If this
is the case, then the fact that pitch-height distinctions
became distinctive in various modern Chinese languages would
be due in some part at least to syllable-initial strengthening. As the voiced stop strengthened through an inherent
tendency, the pitch-height distinctions became contrastive.

Whether or not this is indeed the case remains to be
seen but the incorporation of the notion "inherent syllable
structure" should definitely have tonal consequences if it
is valid.

12.7 Summary

The latter chapters of this essay have been concerned

with how tone is to be characterized in relation to the
segmental syllable. I have proposed an approach in which
the tone and the segmental part of the syllable are characterized largely independently of one another -- each in
terms of its inherent qualities. To clarify the conceptual-
ization of my proposal, I have divided the syllable into
two programs. The Segment Program is concerned with what
we might call the gross articulatory gestures (places of
articulation) of the supraglottal chamber and the glottic
gestures inherently associated with these segments -- e.g.
voicing, segment duration, etc. The Tone Program is likewise concerned with glottic features but only as they are
inherent in tone characterization. The two programs must be
coordinated but this is largely intrinsic. In those cases
where there is a tone-segment relationship this is seen as
a linking of the two dimensions through glottic features.
Such a framework could be conceived as this:

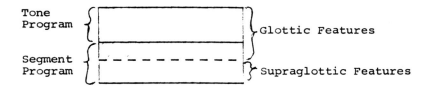

Nevertheless, while tone-segment relations may be rooted in
the interplay of glottic states, the two programs remain

largely independent. The interplay is then characterized
as a type of redundancy or phonotactics and is expressed in
the Local Constraints sub-component of the Surface Phonetic
Component.

The essence of this approach is that neither domain
dominates the other and neither domain is mapped onto the
other. Rather, there is room for mutual interdependencies.
The inherent duration of a tone may cause some vowels to be
phonetically longer; the inherent low fundamental frequency
of a voiced obstruent may lower the beginning state of the
pitch of a syllable. Thus, such an attempt suggests that
the realm of future research lies in attempting to account
for the interface of these two dimensions rather than in
trying to reduce one to the other.

However the interface of tone and segment is eventually resolved, it seems clear that this interface is only
a subset of the much more complex interface between prosodies, syllable constituents (onset, nucleus, coda) and
the accompanying segment specifications and syllable dynamics
(strong and weak position, etc.). Moreover, tone is only one
type of prosody and even if the tone-segment interface were
adequately characterized, we would still be faced with the
problems of relating other prosodies (e.g., breathiness,
glottalicness, nazalization, stress, intonation, etc.) to
the segment, as well as relating strong and weak· syllable

positions, consonantal strength and the like to specific segmental features in specific syllable positions.

Rather than pursuing the tone-segment interface any further in this chapter, it is perhaps more productive to turn to the larger issue, the interface or integration of the prosodic, syllable-dynamic and segmental components of the Chinese monosyllable. Given the discussion to this point, it seems safe to conclude that standard Generative Phonology is ill-suited to account for many of the proposals put forward earlier, much less to provide a format for this much more complex integration task. Thus, in the following chapter I shall examine some alternative approaches that might conceivably help resolve this more fundamental pro-sodic/non-prosodic interface.

Chapter Thirteen

THE PROSODIC, AUTOSEGMENTAL AND NON-SYNCHRONIZED APPROACHES
TO NON-SEGMENTAL PHONOLOGY

13.1   Introduction

The structure of the Chinese monosyllable presents
an interesting challenge to our traditional and modern
conceptions of the nature and role of the segment in
phonological theory. The case for filtering the continuous
phonic experience of speech in terms of discrete units
has been eloquently stated by Halle:

> The most important justification that could be perhaps
> offered for this stand is that almost every insight
> gained by modern linguists from Grimm's Law to
> Jakobson's distinctive features depend crucially on
> the assumption that speech is a sequence of discrete
> entities. In view of this fact, many linguists have
> been willing to postulate the existence of discrete
> entities in speech even while accepting as true the
> assertion of instrumental phoneticians that there
> are no procedures for isolating these entities.
> (1964: 325).

Anderson writing only ten years later echoes Halle's
defense of the segment but suggests that modifications of
our conception of this construct may be in order:

> .... it can still be asked what theoretical justifi-
> cation we have for making the segmental abstraction.

The only justification that can be given is a prag-
matic one; such a description, based on a segmental
structure imposed on the event by the analyst, has
been the basis of virtually every result of note
that has been observed in the field of linguistic
phonetics or phonology. As such, it will continue
to be employed until some deficiency is pointed out,
in the form of a linguistically significant generalization that is essentially unstatable if the
procedure of segmentation is adhered to. It is
fairly clear what sort of situation would furnish
such evidence and it is interesting to note that
some recent research in the area (appropriately
enough) of suprasegmental phonology indicates a
need for some revision of our notion of the segment.
(1974: 6).

In the present work I have attempted to provide
arguments using Chinese data to demonstrate that "some
revision of our notion of the segment" is indeed in order.
However, I question whether the evidence garnered herein
could be exclusively classified as "suprasegmental" since
this term often refers to segmental overlays such as palatalization and nasalization and to tone, duration and
stress phenomena. Evidence from "syllable dynamics" such
as strong and weak syllable position, consonantal strength,
internal segment bonding, etc. also suggests the need for
revision of our conception of the segment. Thus, I would
prefer to call all phenomena which lie outside the direct
domain of the segment as "non-segmental" and I would argue
that "non-segmental" phenomena provide the impetus for

revision rather than simply suprasegmental considerations.

Let us briefly review the evidence that has been
mustered in this essay with regard to revision of the
omnipotent status of the segment. Whereas the syllable in
Chinese is generally conceived of as a linear string of
equivalently weighted segments described by a column of
distinctive feature values, I have proposed that segments
in the syllable have a hierarchical configuration with the
result that segments are characterized by their structural
function, as well as by distinctive features. The "same"
segment will actually have a different specification
depending on its function within this hierarchy. For
instance, a bilabial stop in syllable-initial position
differs phonetically and in its tendency toward diachronic
change and synchronic intersyllable assimilation from the
same stop in syllable-final position. In the former case,
the stop is likely to be fortis (released, at least), but
in final position, lenis (often unreleased, as in Cantonese).
In initial position the stop seems more resistant to diachronic loss, as Chinese language history amply reveals,
whereas in syllable-final position, this consonant is very
prone to reduction to glottal stop and eventual disappearance, again as the language history demonstrates. In

intersyllable assimilation, the final consonant is more
apt to assimilate to the following syllable's initial
(strong) consonant, rather than vice-versa. As a voiced
initial, this stop is likely to be associated with an
initial non-high pitch (as in Shanghai), whereas consonants
in syllable-final position seem to have little effect on
the terminal pitch, at least as far as we know. On the
other hand, a stop consonant in the syllable-initial position seems to have little influence on tone duration,
whereas in syllable-final position, the same stop consonant
is generally associated with a short tone duration (as in
Shanghai and Cantonese).

Moreover, the bonding between the initial and final
portions of a Chinese syllable seems rather loose (this
may be true of syllable structures in all languages, see
Hockett (1955)), as is the bonding between the medial and the
rime, whereas bonding between segments within the rime seems
very tight (see Light (1974) for an exhaustive discussion
of this bonding in Cantonese). These facts of syllable
structure were discussed in the early part of this work
under the rubric of "syllable dynamics."

In the immediately preceding chapters, I have argued
that tone, while related to specific segmental features

in some Chinese languages (e.g., the Wu languages), cannot
be reduced to segments. In addition, I have not yet discussed other non-segmental features of the Chinese syllable
such as breathiness, gottalicness, nasalization, etc. as
described in Sherard's (1972) excellent study of the
Shanghai syllable. These phenomena will be considered in
this and the following chapter.

The Chinese data suggest that, as Halle stated, the
segment is necessary as a theoretical construct but that
it is not sufficient to account for the entire range of
phonic phenomena in the human language sound pattern, even
at the syllable level.

The problem is how to characterize these non-
segmental phenomena with the rigor that has been accorded
our approach to the segment. This chapter and the one
following are intended as a somewhat speculative, explora-
tory extension of the earlier chapters towards a comprehensive re-evaluation of the nature of the segment, of non-
segmental phenomena and of the relationship between the two.
No new data is here offered as constituting the critical
case. Indeed, the Chinese data presented thus far in this
work are of such complexity that no existing schema can
adequately characterize them. The data, I believe, have
long been with us. What is needed is a more powerful, more

precise approach to the same old problems.

13.2 Non-segmentals, Segments and Surface Phonetic Structure

There are many perspectives from which to approach the characterization of segments, non-segmental phenomena and their integration. In the Chinese case, the language itself dictates this perspective. I have already suggested that deep phonological approaches to Chinese, grounded in morphophonemics and the intricacies of rule ordering have not been particularly revealing about the nature of the Chinese sound pattern, except in the limited area of tone sandhi. As a consequence, the study of the Chinese sound system gravitates towards a study of surface phonetic structure. Diachronic change, first and second language acquisition, borrowing, native speaker judgments on syntagmatic patterning, the native Chinese analysis of the syllable, all seem overwhelmingly oriented toward surface phonetic rather than deep phonological structure. Thus, a meaningful approach to segmental and non-segmental speech features in Chinese must be phonetically rather than phonologically motivated. This is not to impugn the relevance of a more deeply phonological orientation to these same problems in other languages. For example, Goldsmith's

(1977) recent work on the morphophonological relationship between segment and tone seems very promising in describing certain processes in several African languages.

A surface phonetic orientation to segmental and non-segmental phenomena carries with it the constraints characteristic of a universal theory of surface phonetic, as opposed to deep phonological, structure. Four such constraints can be outlined below. A surface phonetic representation or scheme should:

(1) include the parameters and features necessary to differentiate utterances from one another in a given language. (Anderson 1974: 7).

(2) include a universal set of parameters and features for characterizing the differences among languages. (Anderson 1974: 7).

(3) serve as an abstract representation of commands to the vocal tract. (Chomsky and Halle: 1968; Postal: 1968).

(4) serve as a constraint on the nature of underlying phonological representation. (Chomsky and Halle: 1968; Postal: 1968).

In order to integrate the first half of the present essay which was concerned with syllable structure and dynamics into this approach, we would certainly want to add the following requirement:

(5) a surface phonetic representation scheme must
provide a set of phonetically grounded parameters for specifying the internal structure
of syntagms (specifically here, the syllable).

Examination of these five requirements reveals that some

parameters characterize segments, some, prosodic features

such as pitch and amplitude in tone, and some, syllable

features such as strong position, weak position, segment

bonding strength, etc. If we are to go beyond a simply

descriptively adequate account of the surface phonetics of

the Chinese syllable, that is, if we want to approximate

an explanation of the processes involved in diachronic

syllable change, segment change, tone change, language

acquisition, borrowing, and so on, then a sixth requirement

is necessary:

(6) a model of surface phonetic structure must
possess the machinery or devices to characterize the relationship within and among the
dimensions and parameters assumed in formulating requirements (1) - (5) above.

These requirements are designed to help formulate

a surface phonetic model but not a performance model of

speech. The former is not a physical account of speech

such that the model is isomorphic with speech events. The

former is not intended to specify neurological commands to

the vocal tract, to specific inherent muscle-mass resistance,

to specify real time parameters. A surface phonetic model,

since it depends critically on the recognition of discrete
entities such as segments, is by definition quite abstract.
Parameters are not equivalent to neurological and muscle
phenomena, but are rather abstract categories for specifying apparent physical phenomena. These parameters are
associated with abstract, rather than physical commands to
the vocal tract.

This distinction between surface phonetic structure
and a performance model has long been established. Yet,
the physical or performance oriented nature of the surface
phonetic level is all too easily invoked as a rationale for
dwelling on the non-phonetic, underlying facets of sound
structure. Here, I am re-articulating the claim that between
the level of abstract, sometimes phonetically ungrounded,
but logically constrained (e.g., rule schema and orderings)
phonological structure and the speech event, there exists
another quite abstract but quite phonetically grounded level
of phonological structure and that this level, in languages
such as Chinese, is an integral component of an adequate
phonological theory.

In the following chapter I will outline a model of
surface phonetic structure along the lines of the six
requirements listed earlier. But this should not be taken
as any sort of performance model. Before proceeding to
this sketch, however, it will be useful to review several

existing approaches to non-segmental phonology.

13.3 Non-segmental Phonology: the Prosodic, Autosegmental and Non-synchronized Approaches

There have been many theoretical attempts to account for such common non-segmental phenomena as tone, nasalization, retroflexion, lip-rounding, etc., but here I will examine only three such approaches which, because of inherent qualities or certain innovative characteristics, might be judged as appropriate for a surface phonetic rendering of the Chinese syllable. I will briefly examine and evaluate each approach with regard to the six requirements listed in the previous section, particularly requirements (5) and (6) since all three approaches could conceivably meet requirements (1) - (4) by simply adding straightforward phonetic detail to their existing formulations.

13.3.1 Prosodic Phonology

13.3.1.1 Description

Prosodic phonology as formulated by the British linguists of the Firthian School recognizes two domains, the phonematic and the prosodic. According to Robbins (1957) in Palmer (1970: 192):

> Phonematic units refer to the features or aspects
> of the phonic material which are best regarded as
> minimal segments, having serial order in relation
> to each other in structures. In most general terms
> such units constitute the consonant and vowel units
> or C and V units of a phonological structure.

Prosodies characterize what Robbins (1964: 107) has termed

"pleurisegmental" features such as stress, pitch, and voice

quantity, but he notes that "certain processes themselves,

though assignable to individual consonant or vowel segments

are often best regarded in this light." Such processes are

said to include lip-rounding, glollalization, retroflexion,

palatalization, velarization, nasalization, and vowel

harmony.

Prosodies are characteristic of and are assigned to

particular domains or "structures" and some types of pro-

sodies are seen as more pervasive in one domain than in

another. Taking Henderson's (1949, in Palmer 1970) analysis

of Siamese, we find at the highest level, the sentence

prosodies, that is, sentence intonation. Below this are

the sentence-part and polysyllabic prosodies which would be

length, stress, and pitch features. Then come the syllable

prosodies such as tone, quantity, labialization, labiovel-

arization, and yodization. The lowest level prosodies are

termed "prosodies of syllable parts" and refer to the pro-

sodies of syllable-initial and syllable remainder. The

former includes plosion, aspiration, voice, affrication,

friction, lateralization, rhotacization, and labialization.
The latter prosodies include "closure with plosion" and
"glottal." In this hierarchy, processes which cover
stretches larger than the segment and manner of articulation
features which seem characteristic of the onset or final
rather than of the specific segment, are progressively
factored out. Thus, the segmental or phonematic units (C's
and V's) are essentially only supraglottal place-of-
articulation indicators.

13.3.1.2 Evaluation

With regard to Chinese syllable structure, prosodic
phonology is appealing in two respects. First, at least
some prosodies, those at syllable level (and above) are
seen as independent of segments. There is no attempt, for
instance, to reduce tone to segments as has recently been
suggested (see above, Ch. 9, 10 and 11). Secondly, the
syllable is formally recognized and the recognition of
syllable parts and prosodies of syllable parts agrees in
some respect with the position of the present work towards
syllable dynamics. Notions such as fortis onset and lenis
coda are expressed and the division into initial and final
is somewhat in accord with the traditional analysis of the

Chinese syllable. It is interesting that such features as plosion, voice, friction, etc. are not seen as features of the initial segment itself but of the onset position. This analysis will be echoed below in Anderson's (1974) analysis.

However, this approach fails short of accounting for many of the phenomena present in the Chinese syllable. There is no recognition of the hierarchial or constituent structure of the syllable (requirement (5) above) that would show, for instance, that there is closer bonding between a nucleus and a coda than between an initial and the nucleus.

A more serious problem arises with respect to requirement (6) above which holds that an acceptable sur-face phonetic model must provide a means for revealing the relationships and interdependencies among the various seg-mental, suprasegmental, and syllable parameters. This requirement is not only necessary for an adequate synchronic description but for showing phonetic processes such as sound change, acquisition, etc.

In this theory, prosodies are extracted and labeled but the relationships among them, between them and the phonematic units and between them and syllable-level dynamics are all left unspecified. For example, nasaliza-

tion, breathiness, tone, and voice could all be extracted
as prosodies but the theory has no mechanism for showing
that tone pitch, breathiness, and voice may be closely
related and interdependent in, say, Shanghai, but that
nasalization has no such relationship. In other words,
prosodies are not classified by more atomic, physiological,
articulatory features even though they often share such
features. Thus, prosodies are somewhat analogous to segments which have not been characterized by atomic, arti-
culatorily based distinctive features. Since features,
rather than complex, indivisible bundles (segments) play
the critical role in both diachronic and synchronic
processes, the theory has provided only a gross taxonomy
of prosodies rather than a phonetic analysis.

For the same reason, this approach cannot show th-
relationship between syllable prosodies, such as tone, and
prosodies of syllable parts, such as voice. The fact that
in Shanghai, an initial low tone pitch is associated with
a voiced onset cannot be captured without a finer phonetic
grounding.

Without such phonetic grounding we are unclear as
to how prosodies arise, change, and exit historically and
of what role phonematic and syllable dynamics play in all
of this. In sum, Prosodic theory has the advantage, as its

appelation indicates, of treating suprasegmentals as such, rather than as features of segments and it does recognize the syllable and internal syllable structure. However, in separating out the non-segmental features of the speech stream, the theory fails to characterize these features in such way that the various prosodies can be related one with another and with segmental units. As a model of surface phonetic structure, prosodic theory is simply too abstract.

13.3.2 Autosegmental Phonology

13.3.2.1 Description

    The essential notions behind autosegmental phonology as formulated by Goldsmith (1976) seem to be these:

    (1) not all relevant phonological phenomena can be characterized as features of our traditional, alphabetic-sized segments.

    (2) as a consequence of (1), phonological phenomena may be characterized as occurring on different "tiers."

    (3) while at the most superficial level these tiers are portrayed as movements of independent articulators, at some more abstract level, psychologically real, indivisible segments corresponding to phonemes are postulated.

    (4) each tier will have its own linearly ordered segments though the term "segment" does not mean simply alphabetic-like segments but segments in other domains (such as pitch) as well.

(5) the segments, of different types on different
     tiers, need not be synchronized exactly, nor
     correspond one-to-one across the tiers. They
     are rather linked by Melodic Association Rules.

The parallels between Autosegmental and Prosodic phonology

are indeed striking, though Goldsmith (1976) only mentions

the latter in passing. The terms "Autosegmental" and

"Prosodic" reflect a view that phonematic or alphabetic-

sized segments play only one role in describing the speech

stream. Prosodies, such as nasality, pitch, stress, etc.

are practically identical to tiers. However, Autosegmental

phonology does provide the prosodic conception with some

needed formalism and does propose to link prosodies or tiers

in a specific, though quite abstract, way via Melodic

Association Rules.

13.3.2.2 Evaluation

     Autosegmental phonology seems to resolve a number

of dilemmas in standard generative theory: (1) the exis-

tence of contour-valued pitch features (e.g., rising tone)

on single segments; (2) the characterization of "stability"

where a pitch feature persists though its associated seg-

ment is erased; (3) a more precise account of grammatically

associated "melody levels;" (4) a characterization of

"floating" tone and (5) a characterization of unidirectional and bi-directional tone spreading. All these cases
seem to involve a change in a presumed one-to-one linkage
between a segment and a pitch feature. The processes
involved appear to be motivated by abstract, deep-level
morphophonemic considerations. Most of these phenomena
are restricted to African languages.

The theory, however, has surprisingly little to
offer, conceptually speaking, to the Chinese case and most
likely to the analysis of Sino-Tibetan languages generally.
This derives no doubt from Goldsmith's concern with phonological processes rather than surface phonetic description:

> .... we are here more interested in phonological,
> as opposed to phonetic kinds of analysis. Again,
> it will be a feature's behavior with regard to
> phonological rules that gives it away as a supra-
> segmental, not any phonetic facts. Ultimately,
> it will be extremely interesting to pursue the
> extensions of autosegmental representation to
> phonetics, but this will not be our good here.
> (Goldsmith 1976: 13).

Unfortunately, as noted many times, except for tone sandhi,
there will be few rules to "give away" a feature as suprasegmental in Chinese and the suprasegmental problem is
indeed rooted in surface "phonetic facts."

Autosegmental phonology is so close, conceptually,
though not formally, to Prosodic phonology that is shares

the criticisms forwarded with regard to the latter as discussed in the previous section. The Chinese case presents the problem of accounting for segmental-suprasegmental integration at the phonetic level and the resolution of this integration problem is restricted to "phonetic facts" rather than underlying rules.

Moreover, it is doubtful whether Autosegmental phonology reveals any new insights even when applied to the problem of relating one segment to a contour tone. In his preface Goldsmith states:

> The idea behind this thesis began with the reading of Will Leben's thesis on suprasegmental phonology, in which he argued that in some languages, even short vowels could have two successive tones.
> Impossible!
> ....Because inexplicable, in segmental terms. And yet the facts persisted; Leben's case was clear. How could we express two successive (level) tones on a single segment... (1976: 1).

Linguists dealing with Chinese phology and those whose work lies outside the strict confines of Praguian, segment-oriented standard generative theory may be somewhat puzzled by the presuppositions that (1) tone must be expressed in segmental terms and (2) that two successive tones cannot be expressed on a single segment. If the essential thesis of Autosegmental phonology in this case is that tone is in a separate dimension and that tone features

need not be tied in a one-to-one fashion to a single segment, then the Prosodists and Wang (1967) have already done
the "impossible" long ago. In both of these approaches,
tone is a syllable feature, even if the syllable is a
single segment. While Chinese tone has not always been
analyzed as sequences of level tones, this issue is conceptually divorced from the notion of separability of tone and
segment — once they are separate, other criteria determine
whether tone is analyzed as a unitary dynamic unit or
sequences of static pitch heights. The issue of how to
represent tone in this latter instance rests not with segmental phenomena but with tone processes.

The real problem is that Autosegmental, like Prosodic phonology, is so abstract that it can reveal little
about the phonetic level. One example will suffice to show
this. Goldsmith characterizes the English word "pin" as
having a falling tone:

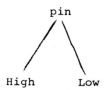

I would analyze this word, said without intonation, as
having a strong onset, high amplitude peak and a weak

or trailing amplitude off-glide:

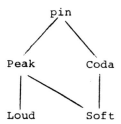

Pitch would be a redundant feature of the intrinsic amplitude contour. The literary reading for the Chinese word
meaning "to betrothe" which has a falling tone would be:

The amplitude is much stronger, initially, than in the
English monosyllable. At the surface phonetic level, we
want to indicate that tone in Chinese is lexical and is
apart from the natural amplitude curve of English monosyllables, whereas we want to indicate that the amplitude
curve in the English monosyllable is most likely an
instance of a universal process, but pitch is redundant.
In Autosegmental phonology, the abstract representations
of these two words would be identical. The problem is how

to reveal the inherent differences between the Chinese and
English sound patterns.

Goldsmith's approach is to "extend" Autosegmental
phonology to the phonetic level. The present work has
been based on the assumption that surface phonetic structure is not an "extension" of underlying phonology but a
necessary, somewhat independent, abstract level having its
own set of constraints which must be "extended" into the
underlying phonology. The discussion of "pin" directly
above is reminiscent of the phonologically oriented
approach to tone in Mandarin. This procedure eventually
led to the conclusion that when phonological tone was
extended into phonetics, we would "map" tone onto segments,
and if there were not enough segments there to carry the
tone, we would create them. The futility of this procedure
was discussed earlier. The top-to-bottom approach of Autosegmental phonology is not constrained by "phonetic facts"
as Goldsmith admits. It is constrained rather by formalism
and rule behavior. But surely a theory unconstrained by
phonetic structure is inadequate and surely constraints
which derive only from underlying rule behavior are insuf-
ficient for characterizing the complexity of sound systems.
Not being phonetically constrained, Autosegmental phonology
allows us to extract prosodies or tiers ad infinitum

without regard to the implications at the phonetic level.
Likewise, such an abstract orientation is not concerned
with inherent syllable structure, with the phonetic relationship among segmental and suprasegmental features, with
the relationship between tone and segment (such as the
voiced-initial, low initial pitch relationship) nor with
the factors at work in phonetic sound change, borrowing,
etc. (but see Goldsmith, Chapter 4, for an extension of his
work to first language acquisition). In sum, I would
suggest that a complete theory needs both phonetic and
phonological constraints and must recognize both the phonetic and phonological levels as somewhat independent
rather than one being "basic" and the other "derived."
Without the phonetic constraints we don't really have a
theory but only part of one.

13.3.3 Anderson's Non-synchronized Phonology

13.3.3.1 Description

Unlike the two approaches discussed so far, the
suggestions offered by Anderson (1974) are restricted to
the surface phonetic level. Thus, his approach, which I
have termed the "non-synchronized" approach, shares the
perspective of the present work.

Anderson's tentative framework can be summarized as follows:

(1) speech is decomposed into four channels: (1) an energy source (2) a laryngeal configuration (3) an oral configuration and (4) a nasal configuration.

(2) the energy source is laryngeally based, and a syllable would be characterized by a [- syllabic] initial consonantism, a [+ syllabic] syllabic peak and a possible [- syllabic] coda.

(3) while specifications from these four channels are usually synchronized, they need not always be (e.g., several laryngeal configurations may be realized during an oral articulation or a single nasal specification may extend over several oral articulations).

(4) in the spirit of (3), the larynx-based source features, [± syllabic] need not coincide with the boundaries of specific segments.

Anderson notes that his formulation necessitates a modification of the traditional view of the monolithic segment and thus, of phonological rules, since, if segment boundaries can be non-synchronized, then rules might be better seen as boundary shifts rather than feature changes. For example, assimilation would be characterized as a case of segment boundary shifts or boundary erasing so that one feature characterizes, say, two contiguous segments. Needless to say, Anderson's proposal is near-revolutionary with regard to the segment. Under his proposal we would

have literally four segments, one per channel, or equivalently, one segment, possibly unaligned in four different
tiers or channels.

13.3.3.2 Evaluation

Anderson's proposal has much to recommend it as an
approach to surface phonetic structure. There is an attempt
to account for syllable dynamics independent of segments in
a way reminiscent of the Prosodic conception of "prosodies
of syllable parts" and there is an attempt to relate the
various parameters, segmental and suprasegmental, by classifying them with respect to the same four phonetic channels.

Several problems remain, however. First there is no
recognition of the internal constituent structure of the
syllable, such that bonding is revealed (requirement (5)
above). Secondly, characterizing both the initial and the
coda as [- syllabic] fails to account for the fact that
the initial is fortis, and diachronically and synchronically
persistent, while the coda is lenis, and subject diachronic
and synchronic weakening (again, requirement (5) above).

In addition, Anderson attributes the "non-synchrony"
of specifications in the various channels to the nature and
latent response times of articulators. This might explain

nasalization in certain cases since the velum is not subject to fine tuning and does have a slower response time
than some other articulators. But what about variation in
voice onset time? The VOT for initial consonants is different for French, English, and Chinese, but this difference
could not be associated with latent response times of
articulators. The variation in the alignment of VOT with
oral closure is language determined. We would assume in
cases like this that different languages exploit the independence of various articulators in different ways. That
is French, English, and Chinese actually have different
voice onset "targets" and these various targets have nothing
to do with the inherent latent response times of articulators.

   More serious is Anderson's failure to allow for
suprasegmentals which are not directly related to segment
specifications. For example, how would this proposal
account for tone in Mandarin? Consider the syllable i
with dipping tone. The laryngeal specification must account
for the voice, amplitude, and pitch of the vowel but also
must provide a [low][low][high] pitch specification, a
soft-loud-soft amplitude contour, and a characteristic duration related to rate-of-pitch change. We would not want
to attribute these two different laryngeal configurations

(one for segments and one for tone) to the physiological
nature of the articulators or to latent response times.
Rather we have two different, unrelated programs relying
on one channel.

In brief, Anderson's approach, while preferable
phonetically to Prosodic and Autosegmental phonology fails
to allow for independent prosodies within a given channel.
This approach is, in a sense, too concrete.

13.4 Summary

In reviewing these various approaches as possible
candidates for a model of surface phonetic structure
capable of describing and integrating segmental and non-
segmental parameters, it would seem that each has advantages
and disadvantages. The Prosodic and Autosegmental theories
build in a potential separability of segmental and non-
segmental features necessary for analyzing the Chinese
syllable. Prosodic phonology has the added advantage of
incorporating some syllable structure features. Both
theories, however, are quite abstract and it is unclear
as to how they could be extended to the surface level without considerable alteration. The non-synchronized version
has the benefit of being phonetically concrete but fails

to allow for certain segment independent suprasegmental phenomena.

In brief, all these approaches fail to meet requirements (5) and (6) discussed in section 13.2 above. In the following chapter, I will formulate the essentials of a model which can overcome these deficiencies.

Chapter Fourteen

A Sketch of Polydimensional Phonology

14.1 Introduction

None of the approaches described in the preceding
chapter is satisfactory as a model for expressing the relationships between segments, suprasegmentals, and syllable
dynamics. Yet, each offers certain insights into the
characterization of these interrelationships. The present
chapter is an attempt to integrate these insights with the
proposals put forward earlier in this work so as to formulate, in very broad terms, a scheme of surface phonetic
structure which describes the nature of and relationships
between segmental and non-segmental phenomena.

14.2 Requirements for a Surface Phonetic Model

In the previous chapter (section 13.2) six requirements were given as basic for a surface phonetic model.
However, the proposals reviewed in the preceding chapter
suggest some refinements of requirements (5) and (6) which
deal with syllable structure and interrelationships among
segmental and non-segmental parameters, respectively.

It would seem that the necessary surface phonetic
framework should possess the following ingredients in

addition to requirements (1) - (4) listed in section 13.2:

(1) a mechanism for indicating the constituent structure or hierarchial nature of a syntagm (word or syllable).

(2) a mechanism for indicating inherent syllable dynamics such as fortis, and lenis syllable margins, weak and strong syllable positions, etc.

(3) related to (2) above, a mechanism for describing the distribution of energy across the syllable, not in terms of specific segments but in terms of onset, nucleus and coda.

(4) a conception of the segment as occurring in three modes, the nasal, the oral and the laryngeal but which allows for non-synchrony of segment specifications across these modes.

(5) a format which characterizes certain prosodies or suprasegmentals within a particular mode (nasal, oral, laryngeal) as common to or extending over two or more contiguous segments.

(6) a format which characterizes certain prosodies or suprasegmentals as arising from or related to a particular segmental specification but where such prosodies persist over non-contiguous segments (in contrast to (5) above).

(7) a format which allows some prosodies (such as lexical tone in Mandarin) to persist in a given mode over more than one segment (as in (5) and (6) above) but where the prosody does not arise from (synchronically) nor is tied to a specific segment specification (as in (5) and (6) above).

The necessity for requirements (1) and (2) have been discussed earlier and can be met by a Surface Phonetic Component (Chapter 6) which assigns constituent structure and defines syllable dynamics in terms of this constituent structure.

Requirement (3) follows Anderson's proposal concern-
the need for a source mode specification (he uses the feature
Syllabic) to indicate energy distribution over the onset,
nucleus and coda, and his proposal that the boundaries of
source-mode features need not line up exactly with oral/nasal
segment boundaries. Likewise, this requirement seeks to
capture the Prosodic School notion of "prosodies of syllable
parts."

Requirment (4) follows Goldsmith's (1976) notion of
low-level tiers and Anderson's division of the speech stream
into four channels. Such a phonetic taxonomy is widely
accepted and has its counterpart in Chomsky and Halle (1968)
and Ladefoged (1973). The lack of alignment at the phonetic
level has been discussed by Anderson (1974) and is implied
by Goldsmith's conception of non-aligned segments on different tiers at the phonological level.

Requirement (5) is concerned with the "feature
sharing ' of contiguous segments. Anderson has suggested
that assimilation be characterized as a type of suprasegmental where boundaries are shifted so that one feature, e.g.,
palatalization, characterizes two contiguous segments. This
view is also reminiscent of Campbell's (1974) persuasive
argument for "complex features" and of the American structuralist notion of "long components." What has been added

here is that such intersegmental feature sharing be specifically and formally grounded in either the nasal, oral or
laryngeal modes. Palatalization, for example, is feature
sharing in the oral mode, but voicing in consonant clusters
is feature sharing in the laryngeal mode.

Requirement (6) goes back to the Prosodic School
observation that some segmental features (as opposed to
syllable-wide features) persist throughout a word of syllable
though the feature is not necessarily shared by contiguous
segments only. For example, in vowel harmony all the vowels
of a given form may share height and roundness values even
though the vowels are not contiguous.

This requirement also allows for non-contiguous
"verticle" feature sharing. For example, in Shanghai, low
initial pitch is associated with voicing in the initial
segment or onset configuration. Here, a segment feature is
tied to a non-segmental tonal configuration.

Requirement (7), left out in Anderson's (1974)
account, covers prosodies which are independent of any
particular segmental specification. For example, nasalization in a syllable or word which has no nasal segments would
fall into this type of prosody classification as would tone
in Mandarin.

14.3 Polydimensional Phonology

14.3.1 Introduction

A model which incorporates these seven requirements
might be termed "polydimensional." The term is meant to
apply to the multidimensional nature of many of the theoretical constructs involved. A syllable, for example, is
not defined by just two dimensions, segmental and suprasegmental, but also by a third dimension, syllable dynamics
(strong and weak syllable positions, fortis and lenis
margins). The internal structure of the syllable is not
defined by a two-dimensional matrix of rows of segments and
columns of features but also by a third dimension, the
hierarchial arrangement or constituent structure of these
segments within the syllable. The segment is not classified
simply by place and manner of articulation but by specifications in three (or four, if the source-mode is included)
dimensions, the nasal, the oral, and the laryngeal. Prosodies do not exist in one dimension while phonematic units
exist in another. Rather, prosodies exist in three dimensions, the nasal, oral and laryngeal. Thus, the term
"polydimensional" is used to stress the complexity of the
composition of syllables (and by extension, words).

14.3.2 The Segment in Polydimensional Phonology

Halle (1964) and Anderson (1974) have summarized the arguments for the necessity of the segment in phonological theory and phonologists generally recognize the reality of the phoneme which is based on the notion segment. Fromkin's (1971) study of speech errors likewise supports the reality of the segment since entire segments are often mistakenly transposed.

However, Anderson (1974) has suggested that at the phonetic level, segment feature specifications do not necessarily line up exactly; specifications in one mode, for example, the nasal or laryngeal, may not line up exactly with the oral feature specifications of the segment.

If we are to recognize the validity of a polymodal segment, having separate nasal, oral, and laryngeal specifications, then we will need some reference point which has a firm set of boundaries in one mode from which we can characterize the non-alignment of feature specifications in the other modes. I propose that the oral mode specifications provide the "anchors" or reference points in the speech "stream."

This follows traditional practice which itself is likely based on certain unconscious, psycholinguistic factors. The oral place-of-articulation configurations are by far the most discrete, non-continuous facets of speech. The tongue does "stop" as it were or does come into contact with or approximate physical contact with other areas of the upper vocal tract. The lips do assume, even if momentarily, specific, discrete configurations which can be photographed. The tongue and jaw do approximate definite, observable, positions in producing vowels. Most of the upper tract oral configurations can be frozen, prolonged, or exaggerated.

These configurations are more directly observable both by others and by our internal kinesic feed-back mechanisms. We can see lip, tongue, and jaw movements rather directly and our kinesic feed-back seems more tangible and accurate with respect to the oral mode as compared to the movements of the velum and vocal chords. This kind of concreteness may lie behind the oral tract orientation of natively produced alphabets and their historical development.

If we accept the oral mode place-of-articulation configurations as basic, then the segment can be defined by those boundaries present in delimiting oral mode specifications. Nasal and laryngeal specifications can be seen to deviate from these boundaries. This ties in with Fromkin's (1971) observation that in some speech errors,

one feature of a segment may not be transposed or some but
not all features of a segment may be transposed. Thus, the
segment may be seen as consisting of independent specifications which normally coincide but which in speech errors
may actually manifest their independence.

14.3.3 Syllable Constituents and the Source Mode

Anderson (1974) proposes formal recognition of
syllable-margin and syllable-peak by the incorporation of
a source mode having specifications in terms of the feature
Syllabic. The Prosodists went even further in their proposal that certain features such as syllable-initial plosion
and syllable final glottalicness were not features of segments but of syllable parts, i.e., onset and final. Hooper
(1972) has argued that the syllable energy distribution
influences the nature and tendency toward change (diachronic
and synchronic) of segments in relation to this energy flow.

Since such features of the syllable are in a sense,
extra-segmental in origin and since they are not confined
to the segment as is obvious by overlay, it may make better
sense to consider these features as properties of the syllable margins and nucleus. I prefer the term "constituents"
for labeling the three traditional syllable positions of
onset, nucleus, and coda. Thus, Hooper's specifications of

"strong" and "weak" syllable position, characterized by
fortis and lenis articulations, Anderson's "energy distribution" and the Prosodic School's "prosodies of syllable
parts" (such as aspiration, voice, affrication, friction,
lateralization, etc.) are considered to be the features of
syllable constituents, that is, of onset, nucleus and coda.

Since both the laryngeal mode and the source-mode
are based on laryngeal configurations, it is a question of
specific language analysis as to whether a certain configuration is best considered as a source-mode constituent
feature or a laryngeal segment feature. For instance, in
Shanghai voice (or voice-onset) is probably more accurately
classified as a constituent feature. This will classify
the initial segment as voiced and will also more precisely
show the relationship of voice onset to low initial pitch.
However, in a language having an initial consonant cluster,
where, for example, one consonant is voiced and the other
is not, then it will be difficult to "factor out" voice as
a feature of the entire onset. Thus, these specifications
should be captured by laryngeal mode segment specifications,
not source-mode specifications.

Likewise, the source-mode can serve as the reposi-
tory of what Lehiste (1970) has termed segment-intrinsic
prosodies. As mentioned above (Chapter 12), Lehiste notes

that vowels have intrinsic prosodies: other factors constant, high vowels have higher fundamental frequencies,
lower vowels have lower fundamental frequencies. In the
Polydimensional format being outlined here, I would prefer
to characterize such features in terms of the nuclear
syllable constituent. Indeed, Lehiste implies this: "If
a pitch level is considered phonemic, it must be kept in
mind that its realization is determined to some extent by
the segmental quality of the syllable nucleus over which
it is realized" (Lehiste 1970: 70; emphasis mine).

Requirements (1) - (4) in light of the discussion
just above can be expressed for the Shanghai syllable laŋ
as follows:

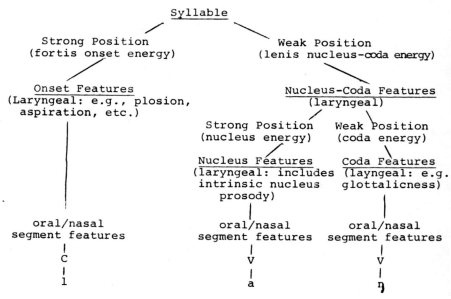

Thus, following the Prosodic approach, we factor out
certain syllable-part, larynx-based features before specifying particular segmental features. The fundamental constituent structure (including strong and weak syllable
position) is assigned by the Surface Phonetic Component
described in Chapter 6 above.

14.3.4 Modal Based Prosodies

So far, we have examined the notion of a polymodal
segment. Now we must turn to the prosodies. The British
School characterization of prosodies was criticized in the
previous chapter as having no phonetic, articulatory,
physiological grounding. Prosodies in that scheme are
extracted and labeled but since they are not grounded in
smaller, phonetic features, there is no formal mechanism
that can account for their relationship to one another nor
to segments.

In the Polydimensional framework, prosodies, like
segments, are characterized in terms of feature specifications in each of the four modes. Thus, there are nasal
prosodies, oral prosodies (such as lip-rounding, retroflexion, palatalization, vowel harmony, etc.), laryngeal
prosodies (such as voicing in constant clusters) and syllable constituent prosodies (such as initial plosion, aspira-

tion, etc.), or nucleus-coda prosodies such as glottalicness.

Here, too, it will be necessary to include inherent
nucleus prosodies, such as the high fundamental frequency
or pitch of high vowels. However, as Lehiste (1970), Ohala
(1973), and many phoneticians have discussed, there are
also transition prosodies between the initial constituent
and the nucleus and between the nucleus and the coda. For
instance, higher fundamental frequencies occur after a
voiceless initial consonant and lower fundamental frequencies
occur after a voiced initial consonant (Lehiste 1970: 71).
After voiceless consonants, especially fricatives, the
highest pitch occurs immediately after the consonant whereas
after a voiced consonant, particularly a resonant, the pitch
rises slowly and peaks with the nucleus (Lehiste 1970: 74).
Maran (1971) has suggested that tonal features in Jingpo
Burmese may have arisen from the transition prosodies
between the nucleus of the syllable and the following final
consonant such that final voiced consonants are associated
with low pitch and final voiceless consonants with high
pitch. This sort of relationship also seems apparent in
Haudricourt's (1954) analysis of tone origin in Vietnamese.

It is important that a model of surface phonetic
structure express these interconstituent prosodies since

they may play a role in tonogenesis and since they present
a more accurate account of the phonetic nature of segment-
pitch relationships in synchronic descriptive analysis.

14.3.5 The Nature and Classification of Prosodies

14.3.5.1 Defining Prosodies

Prosodic features have a variety of relationships
with segmental features ranging from total independence
(e.g., intonation; tone sandhi and tone in Mandarin) to
very intimate relationships such as segmental overlays and
consonant-pitch associations. Prosodies often seem to have
arisen from segmental features: lip-rounding of an initial
consonant before a rounded or back vowel, palatalization
of a consonant before a high vowel, nasalization of a
vowel before a following nasal consonant, and so on. Simply classifying prosodies by the mode (oral, nasal or
laryngeal) even though phonetically accurate and concrete
is still inadequate because we have failed to demonstrate
th e relationship between segment and prosody. Therefore,
in the Polydimensional scheme, I propose that prosodies be
defined not only with respect to their mode of origin but
also with respect to their interaction with modal-based
features of segments. Four types of prosodies will be recognized.

14.3.5.2 Asegmental Prosodies

Prosodies such as tone in Mandarin and nasalization where no nasal segment exists are termed Asegmental. That is, there is no relationship between the segmental and prosodic domains. There are two types of Asegmental prosodies depending on mode: Asegmental nasal prosodies and Asegmental laryngeal prosodies. In addition to tone as in Mandarin, the latter would include tone sandhi, word stress, phonological phrase, and sentence stress and sentence intonation.

By definition, there can be no Asegmental oral prosodies. Prosodies are defined by their relationships to the segmental domain and segments are further defined (as discussed earlier) by oral mode specifications. That is, oral place-of-articulation features constitute the fundamental reference points or "anchors" for alignment with nasal and laryngeal segment features but the notion "Asegmental" implies that place-of-articulation features are irrelevant and are not to be considered.

14.3.5.3 Pleurisegmental Prosodies

Prosodies which are based on feature sharing of contiguous segments are termed Pleurisegmental (the term is borrowed from Robbins 1964). Retroflexion, palatalization,

voicing, liprounding, nasalization, etc. across contiguous segments would fall under this classification.
This type of prosody would capture the idea of boundary
shifts proposed by Anderson (1974), the idea of complex
features proposed by Campbell (1974), the notion of "long
components" in American structuralist phonology and certain type of prosodies recognized by the Prosodic School.
Pleurisegmental prosodies would be sub-classified by mode
as nasal Pleurisegmental (e.g., vowel and following nasal
consonant share the feature nasal), oral Pleurisegmental
(e.g., a consonant and following vowel share tongue height
position as in palatalization), and laryngeal Pleurisegmental (e.g., voicing in consonant clusters).

14.3.5.4 Parasegmental Prosodies

Prosodies which are related in some fashion to particular segment specifications (or to a particular syllable
constituent specification such as the onset configuration)
but which persist beyond contiguous segments are termed
Parasegmental. Since such prosodies are not totally independent of segment specifications, they are not Asegmental.
Since they are not analyzable totally in terms of contiguous
segment specifications, they are not Pleurisegmental.
Rather, Parasegmental prosodies are in between Asegmental

and Pleurisegmental prosodies. They are partly independent of segments and partly determined by segments. These
prosodies can likewise be sub-classified as nasal, oral,
or laryngeal. A Parasegmental nasal prosody would occur
if a nasal segment were associated with the nasal quality
of a non-contiguous segment, say a final nasal segment
influencing the nasality of an initial consonant or vice-
versa. Vowel harmony would be an example of an oral Parasegmental prosody. Here each vowel segment receives a
unique characterization for some vowel features, yet other
vowel features such as, for example, tongue height, are
shared by a number of non-contiguous vowels. The "harmony"
is Asegmental in the sense that it persists regardless of
other vowel specifications. The vowels, however, are segmental in nature since they receive definite segment specifications for some features. The sharing of features among
non-contiguous segments is captured as a Parasegmental
prosody.

Laryngeal Parasegmental prosodies could be of two
types. One type would be the sharing of, for example, the
feature glottalicness by the initial and final consonants
of a syllable ending in a glottal stop. This seems to be
the case for some Shanghai syllables as described by Sherard
(1972). Breathiness also may extend its domain to influence

non-contiguous segments.

It is also possible to analyze those cases where a
segment specification (or onset specification) such as
voice is associated with low tone pitch as instances of
Parasegmental prosodies. While tone in Mandarin is
Asegmental, in Shanghai initial low pitch is associated
with an initial voiced obstruent, and duration (and thus
contour) is associated with a final glottal stop. In
this instance, tone is not totally Asegmental nor is it
totally segmental since some tonal features, e.g., contour in open syllables, are independent of segment
specifications. Thus, this partially segmentally determined tone would be an example of a laryngeal Parasegmental
prosody.

14.3.5.5   Interconstituent Prosodies

We have already discussed that a syllable nucleus has
an inherent prosody (high vowels manifest high pitch, etc.)
and that there are characteristic transition (high vowels
manifest high pitch, etc.) prosodies between initial consonants and the nucleus and between the nucleus and the
coda. In fact, phoneticians maintain that consonants are
perceptually identified in part with respect to these
transition prosodies. Since these prosodies do exist and
since they may play a role in the evolution of Pleurisegmental, Parasegmental, and Asegmental larynx-based prosodies,

they must be labeled and classified.

14.3.5.6 An Overview of Prosody Types

The discussion of prosodies to this point can be
diagrammed as follows:

NASAL MODE

Type	Specification	Example
Asegmental	Segment-independent	Nasalization (no nasal segment present)
Parasegmental	segment-related (non-contiguous overlay)	Nasalization of non-contiguous vowels where a nasal segment is present
Pleurisegmental	segment-bound (contiguous overlay)	Nasalization of contiguous segments where a nasal segment is present

ORAL MODE

Type	Specification	Example
Asegmental	(does not exist)	(does not exist)
Parasegmental	segment-related (non-contiguous overlay)	vowel harmony
Pleurisegmental	segment bound (contiguous overlay)	palatalization, retroflexion, lip-rounding, etc. of contiguous segments

LARYNGEAL MODE

Type	Specification	Example
Asegmental	Segment-independent	tone in Mandarin, stress, intonation in all languages
Parasegmental	segment-related (non-contiguous overlay)	glottalicness of initial segment in Shanghai; voiced initial consonant-- low initial pitch in Shanghai
Pleurisegmental	segment-bound (contiguous overlay)	voicing in consonant clusters
Interconstituent	Inherent nucleus prosody and onset-nucleus, nucleus-coda transition prosodies	high fundamental frequency in high vowels, low rise in fundamental frequency after resonant onset, etc.

Since the larynx figures in both source-mode syllable constituent specifications (onset, nucleus, coda) and in
laryngeal segment specifications, some features attributed
to segments in this diagram would in some cases be better
assigned to syllable constituents rather than specific
segments.

14.3.5.7 The Hierarchial Array of Prosodies

Prosodies are hierarchically arrayed by domain within the syntagm. In a case where the syntagm is a syllable
the following pattern emerges:

Syllable
|

Syllable-Wide (Entire Syllable) Prosodies
Nasal: Asegmental Prosodies

Laryngeal: Asegmental Prosodies

|

Initial-Final Prosodies
(Prosodies holding between the initial segment and the
remaining segments)

Nasal: Parasegmental Prosodies

Pleurisegmental Prosodies

Oral: Parasegmental Prosodies

Pleurisegmental Prosodies

Laryngeal: Parasegmental Prosodies

Pleurisegmental Prosodies

Interconstituent Prosodies

Onset Features

(Oral, Nasal, Laryngeal
Pleurisegmental Features
in consonant clusters)

|

Segment Features

Nucleus-Coda Features

(Oral, Nasal and Laryngeal
Para- and Pleurisegmental
Features and Laryngeal
Interconstituent Prosodies

Nucleus Features   Coda Features
(Intrinsic Nucleus (Oral, Nasal
Prosody)   and Laryngeal
                     Pleurisegmental
                     Features in
                     consonant clusters

| |

Segment Features   Segment Features

This diagram is suggestive at most. For instance, it may be that some language also has Parasegmental prosodies in the onset or the nucleus-coda or the coda alone if non-contiguous segments within any of these domains share a feature. For example, two non-contiguous consonants in an onset or coda cluster may share a feature which could be factored out of the cluster.

The diagram is simply intended to show, in Prosodic School fashion, that prosodies are factored out domain by domain until inherent, place-of-articulation segment specifications are all that remain. Unlike the phonetically abstract Prosodic School notion of factoring out prosodies, the current approach follows two principles: (1) prosodies are factored out with respect to mode (oral, nasal, laryngeal) and (2) prosodies are factored out with respect to their relationships with segments (Asegmental, Parasegmental, Pleurisegmental, Interconstituent). Since segments are also classified by modal-based features (nasal, oral and laryngeal), it is clear that both segments and prosodies are cross-classified by one and the same set of phonetically grounded features such that their synchronic and diachronic relationships are revealed.

14.3.5.8 Prosodic Programs

Earlier (Chapter 11) I suggested that the Chinese syllable was the confluence of three separate programs, a Tone Program, a Segment Program and perhaps a Syllable Program which linked the first two and provided specifications for syllable dynamics and constituent structure. This Program orientation can now be revised and extended as follows:

PROGRAMS

Segment Program: Specifies inherent segment features in all modes

Source Program: Specifies constituent structure, syllable dynamics (fortis, etc.), energy distribution and ties the segment program to Asegmental Programs

Asegmental Nasal Program: Specifies nasal features characteristic of an entire syntagm (e.g., syllable)

Asegmental Laryngeal Programs:

1. Syllable-tone Program
2. Word-tone Program (including tone-sandhi)
3. Word-stress Program
4. Phonological Phrase Tone Program (including tone sandhi)
5. Phonological Phrase Stress Program
6. Sentence-stress Program
7. Intonation Program

A "Program" in this sense is defined as a set of commands with respect to a set of targets such that the

targets are independent of (though linked to) other factors
in the speech stream.

14.4 The Role of Polydimensional Phonology in Phonological Theory

This scheme is not intended to provide endless phonetic detail. The intrinsic nasalization of vowels in the
context of nasal segments, or the intrinsic overlay of
aspiration of lip-rounding onto following segments may be
of more interest to the development of a speech synthesizer
than to the theory of phonetic or phonological structure.
Many such intrinsic properties may properly belong to a set
of universal phonetic phenomena which need not be characterized within language-specific descriptions. This
approach is intended, rather, to provide as precise a phonetic characterization as possible where such a characterization is necessary for analyzing phonetically based processes and synchronic relationships which are obviously
relevant to a language-specific analysis. It is an attempt
to bring all the complex phonetic parameters that are
commonly invoked in describing or explaining some narrow,
specific phenomenon into a structured, integrated framework.
Thus, the nature of one specific process such as pitch
lowering in the vicinity of a voiced segment is not seen as

an idiosyncratic relationship, but rather as a process
which follows general principles of a phonetic nature and
as a process which is not unrelated to the other relationships and phenomena present in a speech event.

Diachronic sound change, language acquisition, etc.
must be defined, at least in some cases, with reference to
the phonetic nature of certain limited parameters and their
interplay. Where do tones come from? Where do prosodies
come from? How are prosodies affected by syllable dynamics,
by other prosodies, by segments? How do prosodies and syllable dynamics affect segments? Surely, the answers to
these questions require some sort of detailed, coherent
phonetic framework in addition to an understanding of deeper
phonological processes.

Likewise, many phonological rules and processes are
phonetically motivated. What are the phonetic pressures
behind these processes? What parameters and parameter relationships are involved? How do deep phonological rules
affect the interplay of the parameters?

The Polydimensional conception offers nothing more
than a more elaborate and precise taxonomy of surface phonetic structure. Yet, the application of this taxonomy
should have consequences in accounting for both diachronic
and synchronic language processes.

14.5 Polydimensional Phonology and Phonological Rules

A formal system can be described as a set of primes
and the operations which characterize relationships among
these primes. If we change the nature of the primes, we
may be forced to change the nature of the operations which
apply to the primes. A change in the traditional conception
of the segment and of prosodies may well require a revision
of the nature of phonological rules. The traditional phonological rule which changes the features of traditionally
defined segments may be adequate only for describing the
relationships among the rather gross parameters of oral-
tract place and manner articulations. Other types of rules
and redundancy conventions may be necessary for characterizing the interaction of polymodal prosodies with polymodal
segments and both of these with syllable dynamics.

The Polydimensional taxonomy suggests the use of
scalar parameter values, of directional tendencies, perhaps even of a probabilistic or variable-rule approach to
phonetic phenomena. Strong and weak syllable positions,
fortis and lenis syllable margins, a sonority classification
of consonants (see Hooper 1972) all suggest a system of
scalar values and hierarchical ratings. Prosodies may be
better classified by their strength and direction. For
example, it may be worthwhile to indicate that a prosody is

moving from Pleurisegmental to Asegmental as the latter
takes over features from a progressively weakening final
nasal segment (i.e., nasalized vowel plus final nasal consonant becomes nasalized vowel only) — a process wide-
spread in Chinese languages. We may need to indicate that
a Parasegmental tone is "strengthening" by breaking loose
from segment specifications and that it is moving towards
realization as an Asegmental prosody — modern Mandarin
obviously underwent such a stage when initial voiced
obstruents devoiced and syllable-initial low pitch moved,
in some cases, to a higher pitch range.

Briefly put, if we refine and redefine the parameters which characterize phonetic structure, it seems only
natural that a refinement and redefinition of processes
which involve these parameters is in order.

14.6 Implications and Advantages of Polydimensional Phonology

14.6.1 Parameter Integration

The nature of the segment and of segment-change processes has been extensively studied in modern phonology
whereas non-segmental phenomena have received much less
attention. Simply the volume of published literature focus-
ing on the former as opposed to the latter supports this

observation. Lehiste (1970) in her work on suprasegmentals notes the consequences of this situation:

> During the twentieth century, prosodic phenomena have become a part of linguistics that most linguistic schools have attempted to incorporate into the theory... Yet a certain degree of vagueness seems to characterize most discussions of prosodic features. They seem more elusive than segmental features, and their incorporation into a linguistic system seems to strain the limits of an otherwise coherent framework. (Lehiste: 1)

The main reason for this state of affairs, I believe, is that the segment has been defined totally in segmental terms from the outset and then linguists have attempted to force the characterization of prosodic phenomena into this pre-existing but ultimately ill-suited framework, hence the "strain" on the "otherwise coherent framework" to which Lehiste refers. In the present approach I have suggested that prosodic features be considered from the outset in formulating our conception of the segment. The resulting advantage is that segments are defined in such a way (by mode-base; in terms of constituent structure and features of syllable dynamics; by allowing non-synchrony among the modes, etc.) that their relationship with prosodies are more clearly delimited from the beginning. At the same time, prosodies are defined by the same rather than by different parameters (as has traditionally been the case)

so that their relationship to segments is likewise more
precisely defined in formulating the basic framework.
Moreover, unlike the Prosodic and Autosegmental approaches,
these relations are based on concrete phonetic features of
the speech stream rather than on underlying and more abstract phonological features. Thus, the hypotheses underlying the establishment of the fundamental framework are
more open to empirical testing from the outset.

14.6.2 Phonetically Based Classification of Prosodies

There is a natural tendency to group Asegmental
prosodies together simply because they are unrelated to
segments. For instance, using Goldsmith's tier approach,
we could postulate a nasal tier, a vowel harmony tier, and
a tonal tier. At the more abstract levels of deep phonology
these tiers are rather similar in their nature and in the
way that they relate to segments via Melodic Association
Rules. However, at the surface level, when these prosodies
receive particular modal specifications, it becomes clear
that they are not truly equivalent either in their "nature"
or in the way in which they relate to segments. For example,
nasal and vowel harmony prosodies seldom go beyond the
domain of the word. Asegmental laryngeal prosodies, on the
other hand, are not so restricted and range from the

syllable (tone), to the word and phrase (tone sandhi, stress), to the sentence (intonation).

Furthermore, this difference in phonetic mode may require different types of rules. There are tone change rules, for example, which are very complex and seem different in nature from the standard segment-change rules. Brown (1972) and Anderson (1974) have already noted the unique formal nature of tonal perturbation rules as compared to the usual segment change rules. It is doubtful whether there are perturbations in the nasal mode or in the case of vowel harmony, in the oral mode, which are similar to those processes based in the laryngeal mode. Do the "segments" of Goldsmith's nasal and vowel-harmony tiers affect and perturb each other in the same fashion that "segments" within the tonal tier affect each other? The evidence suggests a negative answer: there seem to be no "nasal perturbation rules" nor "vowel harmony perturbation rules" which resemble tonal perturbation rules.

Each mode has a certain uniqueness defined by the phonetic nature of the articulators involved. The nasal mode seems more prone to overlay phenomena and is perhaps less amenable to fine tuning. Vowel harmony is quite different from Asegmental nasal prosodies because, as I have argued here, it is actually a Parasegmental rather than Asegmental prosody. The laryngeal mode is perhaps the most unique simply by virtue of its versatility and amenability to extremely fine tuning. Due to the physiological structure of the larynx and its proximity to the energy source, we find that it can simultaneously serve many functions. It provides the fundamental frequency for intrinsic vowel quality and the transition prosodies among consonants and vowels, which apparently helps the listener perceive consonant quality. It provides intrinsic vowel amplitudes and an amplitude curve for the entire syllable. At the same time, the larynx, in conjunction with the energy source provides the amplitude and pitch associated with stress (though duration is also involved). But beyond these segment oriented features, the larynx also provides, simultaneously, for syllable, word, phrase, and sentence tone and for tonal perturbations within these domains.

If we are to arrive at the "coherent framework" mentioned by Lehiste above, it would seem that these modal idiosyncracies must be recognized and formally included in the formulation stage. The second stage would be discover the implications of these idiosyncracies as regards deeper phonological processes. This approach is just the reverse of that proposed by Goldsmith (1976) and that implied by the Prosodic School's treatment of prosodies. The a priori

establishment of deep-level, phonetically abstract parameters seems only to result in endless ad hoc patchwork
at the surface phonetic level. The advantage of the Polydimensional framework in this respect, then, is that such
ad hoc and ultimately unsuitable adjustments are prevented
by the initial recognition of the phonetic nature of prosodies (oral, nasal, laryngeal, interconstituent), of
segments (oral, nasal, laryngeal specifications), and of
their relationships (Asegmental, Pleurisegmental, Parasegmental).

14.6.3 Pitch-Segment Relationships

The segmental orientation of standard generative
theory has led to certain problems in expressing pitch-
segment interaction. Recall that Halle and Stevens (1971)
and Maran (1973) attempted to use one set of laryngeal
features to characterize both segments and pitch such that
the feature Low when applied to consonants captured the
feature Voice but when applied to vowels captured the
feature Low Pitch. Thus, the relationship between voiced
initial consonant and low pitch can be seen as a case of
assimilation. However, if a syllable has only one vowel
and if the pitch shifted to high at the end of the contour,
then an additional vowel segment would have to be added to

carry the specification High. This approach proved cumbersome and counterproductive (see Chapter 10 above).

The Polydimensional framework provides formal recognition of the syllable constituents onset, nucleus and coda. If the feature Low applies to the onset rather than the initial segment and if tone features are ascribed to the syllable nucleus (and interconstituent transitions) rather than specific vowels, then the Halle-Stevens-Maran feature assimilation scheme can be retained. Low applies to the onset, Low plus High to the nucleus, and we have a case of onset-nucleus assimilation rather than consonant-vowel assimilation. Thus, the problem of adding specific vowel segments is totally avoided.

Wang (1967) has discussed a case in Foochow Chinese where high tones raise vowels in morphophonemic processes and Lehiste (1970) discusses a case in Vietnamese where one tone influences the first formant of vowels occurring with this tone. The present approach possesses the machinery to capture such segment-pitch relationships by recognizing inherent nucleus prosody as a necessary specification and by the use of Programs. In this framework the nucleus constituent receives an intrinsic pitch specification, e.g., Mid and the Tone Program likewise specifies certain pitch specification, .e.g., High. The Source Program and

the Tone Program thus share a feature in such cases, via
assimilation of the nucleus specification (<u>Mid</u>) to the
pitch specification (<u>High</u>), but the two programs are definitely independent: pitch is not reduced to a segment
specification nor vice-versa. Such nucleus-pitch assimila-
tions are an instance of a Parasegmental prosody since the
Tone Program is not totally independent of segment (or
nucleus) specifications, i.e., the Tone Program is not
Asegmental (as, for example, in Mandarin).

14.6.4 <u>Prosodies and Perception</u>

     Little has been said of perception in this essay,
yet the Polydimensional framework does suggest certain
implications with regard to perception. Whether or not
these implications are substantive is quite questionable at
the present time, but the issue is worth a brief examination.
     The Polydimensional conception may offer a better
orientation to an eventual perception model than most
existing approaches. The Prosodic School justified the
extraction of prosodies partly with regard to perception.
For example, Prosodic School linguists contended that the
listener perceived palatalization as a prosody rather than
as a feature of a consonant segment followed by a feature
of a vowel segment. The Prosodists did not seek to charac-

terize a feature of one segment as distinctive and a feature of a contiguous segment as redundant and criticized the American phoneme-allophone dichotomy on just these grounds. To the Prosodists the entire prosody was distinctive.

The present model suggests, in a similar fashion, that the listener extracts prosodies as holistic units in a hierarchical manner from larger to smaller domains. For example, a listener may extract syllable-wide prosodies such as tone and syllable-part prosodies such as Voice Onset Time, breathiness; glotticness, etc. in a separate and different sort of operation than he extracts discrete segmental place-of-articulation specifications. In fact, this model implies that the listener actually extracts only prosodies and infers from this extraction what the segmental specifications must be. This ties in with the assumption among phoneticians that vowels are perceived by their fundamental frequency and formant specifications and that consonants are identified by their transition configurations into and out of one another and into and out of the nucleus.

14.6.5 Language Acquisition

Most emphasis on phonological acquisition seems to have been on how segments are acquired, which ones are acquired first, in what order and so on. One can easily

imagine that prosodies are likewise acquired in a pre-
scribed order both in regard to one another and in regard
to segment features.

That Asegmental prosodies may be acquired first is
implied by the early use and recognition of intonation
patterns by children. The Polydimensional approach suggests
that holistic prosodies would be acquired in a domain to
domain fashion and most likely in an Asegmental to segmental manner through the intermediate Parasegmental and
Pleurisegmental stages and that all such prosodies are
acquired prior to specific, well-formed segment specifications. While highly speculative, it may turn out that the
child acquires Asegmental, large-domain prosodies because
they are phonetically more gross and holistic and require
less fine tuning than individual segment specifications.
In this scheme, the child would continue to make refinements,
first in syllable level features, then syllable part
features (onset, nucleus, coda) and, finally, in terms of
more precise oral and nasal tract segment specifications.
Obviously, the larynx would play a primary role in phonological acquisition within this framework.

This account must be backed by empirical research
but it does seem plausible since intonation (an Asegmental,
laryngeal prosody) apparently is acquired first and since

some specific segment specifications are acquired quite
late. It may be that second-language acquisition works
along the same lines, but this is quite a different process since the learner has already mastered one system of
precise segment specifications and thus may employ a much
more sophisticated, segment-oriented strategy (backed up
in some cases with heavy training in alphabetic writing and
segmentation).

14.6.6 Diachronic Change

The formal recognition of different types of prosodies and of syllable dynamics gives a clearer view of
sound change. Again, traditional emphasis has been placed
on how segments change rather than how prosodies and syllable configurations change. In Chinese, for example,
there seems to be certain uni-directional tendencies in the
evolution and change of prosodies. We might assume that
at one stage of evolution, pitch prosodies of the syllable
consisted of only the inherent nucleus vowel pitch and the
non-distinctive interconstituent prosodies between onset
and coda and the nucleus. As syllable dynamics exerted
pressure on syllable margins, these intrinsic redundant
prosodies became Pleurisegmental and Parasegmental and likewise became distinctive as compensation for changes in

syllable-margin configurations. By this time some facets
of the Tone Program, such as contour, may have become
totally independent of segments while other facets such as
initial pitch and duration may have remained tied to the
voicing of the onset configuration and the presence of a
final stop, respectively. Finally, in langauges such as
Mandarin, the tone became totally Asegmental as it divorced
itself from segments, which themselves had lost many features (e.g., onset voice) or all features (e.g., final
stop disappears) due to syllable-dynamics (syllable-initial
strengthening and syllable-final weakening). If it should
turn out that prosodies are most readily perceived than
specific segment features, we can surmise that this fact
greatly aided and hastened the rise of prosodies and the
decay of segment features.

Syllable dynamics also seem to have exerted unidirectional pressures in the evolution of syllable-types in
Chinese. Final consonants are steadily dropping and initial
consonants seem to be steadily strengthening (in Hooper's
terminology). That is initial voiced consonants tend to
devoice and not vice-versa.

The Polydimensional model of prosody change in
Chinese could be diagrammed as follows:

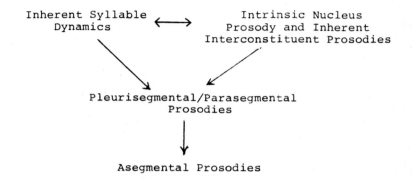

Of course, such a scheme unrealistically assumes that segments gradually give up features to prosodies such that
segments would disappear altogether. While a tremendous
number of segments have disappeared in the evolution of
Chinese, even since 600 A.D. and while a great number of
segment features (such as voice in initial segments and
place-of-articulation in final nasals and the like) have
also been lost, we must assume that there is an upper limit
on the number and kinds of prosodies which can exist in
proportion to the number of syllable types defined by segment sepcifications. However, evidence from Mandarin dialects suggests that segments are continuing to diminish
in number and that this trend is offset, not by intrasyl-
lable compensation, but by the grouping of different
syllables into phonologically more distinct entities such
as compound words.

14.6.7   Typological Classification

Chinese languages are often classified typologically
by the inventory and types of segments, tones, and syllable
types since syntactic features are, relatively speaking,
quite similar. The syllable types and syllable structures
for each language are generally given in dialect studies.
These often provide information as to the linear and positional arrangements of consonants and vowels within the
syllables of the given language or dialect. However, aside
from Sherard's study of Shanghai syllable types, there has
been little attention devoted to showing the unique interdependencies of tonal, segmental, and syllable constituent
parameters characteristic of and unique to each language
and dialect.

The present framework suggests that the traditional
classification be enriched by including information on
the relationships between segments and prosodies. For
instance, Chinese languages and dialects can be additionally
classified with respect to the interaction of tonal and
segmental features on a scale revealing the strength of
tone-segment bonding. On one end of the spectrum would be
Mandarin which is an Asegmental tone language; tones and
segments are independent. Cantonese would be a case of a

slightly Parasegmental language since final stops are
associated with short tones. Shanghai, on the other hand,
would be at the other end of the spectrum as a heavily
Parasegmental tone language since initial pitch is associated with voiced obstruents and final glottal stop is
associated with short tone duration. Other dialects and
languages would manifest intermediate classifications
between totally Asegmental and heavily Parasegmental.

This same classification scheme would presumable be
useful in characterizing syllable types in non-Chinese
tone languages and dialects where variable segment-tone
relationships exist. If the relationship between segments
and non-tonal prosodies are included, then an even more
detailed picture of syllable types can be revealed. For
example, Shanghai and many Wu dialects are characterized
by the presence of Asegmental nasal prosodies and by Parasegmental and Pleurisegmental breathiness and glottal
prosodies. Simply the total number of Asegmental, Parasegmental, and Pleurisegmental prosodies in a given language
or dialect can be considered as information relevant to
typological classification and as a gauge of evolutionary
developmental tendencies.

At the same time, this sort of enriched syllable
classification framework provides a more precise character-

ization of syllable formation within a given language.
The formulae for the canonical shape of syllables in a
given Chinese language do not nearly give the whole story.
For instance, as Sherard (1972) perceptively demonstrated,
Shanghai syllables are best characterized by the overall
internal relationships between segmental and prosodic features rather than by their linear segmental composition
alone. Such a description not only provides a more accurate
phonetic account of Shanghai syllable structure but also
seems, according to Sherard, more in agreement with the
native speaker conception of syllable structure. Of all
the parameters used in describing the Shanghai syllable,
native speakers seem less comfortable and less concerned
with segment-sized units.

In the format suggested here we could say that
Shanghai has one heavily Parasegmental tone syllable-type:
syllables having a voiced obstruent initial and a final
glottal stop. The syllable tone in such cases is entirely
predictable from segmental features (or constituent-onset
and coda-configurations). Shanghai has two fairly heavy
Parasegmental tone syllables: those having a voiced initial
or a sonorant initial but having a glottal stop coda.
Finally, the language has two Asegmental tone syllables:
those having a voiceless or sonorant initial and no final

stop. Sonorant initials may or may not be associated with low initial pitch.

The basic notion put forward here is that whether for language typology or synchronic description within a given language or dialect, tone, and other prosodies are best classified with respect to their relationship to the total syllable configuration rather than as independent parameters.

14.6.8 Syllable Sandhi

In Mandarin, tone perturbation exists independently of segmental configurations. But in Shanghai, as Sherard has demonstrated, certain tonal and non-tonal prosodies of the initial syllable of a phonological word persist through the following syllables of that word. Non-tonal features include, in this instance, breathiness and glottalicness. Many of these prosodies are associated with either the onset or coda configuration of the initial syllable of the phonological word. Since this phenomenon is obviously much more complex than tone-sandhi in the usual sense, it might be better termed "syllable-sandhi" — the tendency of features of a given syllable to affect features of other close-knit syllables. The Polydimensional taxonomy should help to bring such processes into focus and to provide a suitable

phonetic framework for characterizing such processes.
For instance, if breathiness is a feature of the onset
configuration of the initial syllable of a phonological
word and if it persists through the following syllables
of the word, then we could classify this phenomenon as a
polysyllabic or word ·Parasegmental prosody. If low pitch
is associated with the breathiness and likewise persists
over following syllables, this would likewise be a case
of a Parasegmental word prosody. Such features would then
be realized as a part of the Phonological Word Program.
If tone in Shanghai monosyllables should become Asegmental,
then we would expect Shanghai syllable-sandhi to evolve
into Mandarin-like Asegmental tone sandhi.

14.7 Summary

At least three types of relationships could conceivably hold between segmental and non-segmental phenomena:
(1) they are independent and unrelatable; (2) they are
not independent but are reducible to one another, and (3)
they are independent but nevertheless relatable. The conception of the segmental— non-segmental relationship seems
to have evolved in just this sequence in modern phonological theory. American structuralist phonology and the
Prosodic School adopt position (1) above by dividing the
speech stream into segmental and suprasegmental (or

phonematic and prosodic) domains and describing the characteristics of each domain without regard to the other.
Standard generative theory, as discussed in earlier chapters,
seems to have adopted the second position above in trying to
reduce features of the non-segmental domain to features of
segments. Autosegmental phonology opts for the third position.

However, with regard to position (3) above, the manner
in which segments and non-segmentals are related depends on
whether the relationship is defined in phonological or in
phonetic terms. The former approach, characteristic of
Autosegmental Phonology, is restrained more by the formal
nature of dynamic processes such as morphophonemic change
rules whereas the phonetic approach is constrained by the
static relationships among the parameters involved at the
surface level.

In the present chapter, I have proposed a sketch in
line with position (3) above with a phonetic approach which
seems necessary to complement the abstract orientation of
of Autosegmental phonology. This outline is admittedly
speculative. It is offered as a perspective rather than
as a fully developed formal system. The essence of the
proposed framework is that segmental and non-segmental
features of the speech event are independent but relatable
by virtue of being defined by one and the same set of

phonetic parameters (laryngeal mode, oral mode, nasal mode)
and by the assumption that a finite number of relationships
hold between these parameters (e.g., Asegmental, Pleurisegmental, etc.).

14.8 Conclusion

From the outset, this essay has been concerned with
two major issues, one descriptive and one theoretical.
On the descriptive side, it has been argued that an analysis
of the primary, typologically defining features of the
Chinese sound pattern must be based on the internal structure of the Chinese monosyllable as it is manifested at the
surface phonetic level. On the theoretical side, I have
attempted to demonstrate that no single current theory or
theoretical approach, be it structural, prosodic, generative, or revised generative (e.g., Natural Generative
Theory, Autosegmental Theory) is sufficiently powerful to
characterize the defining features of Chinese phonological
structure. The bulk of this study has, consequently, been
devoted to the interplay between these two concerns.

The initial seven chapters were concerned with a
systematic analysis of the non-prosodic features of the
Chinese syllable. Here, arguments were made that the
syllable is most appropriately analyzed at the surface

phonetic (rather than at the abstract, underlying) level
and that the syllable is not simply a linear sequence of
segments but rather a hierarchial configuration of constituents (onset, nucleus, coda) which manifest a variety of
relationships among themselves and with syllable boundaries.
Segment-like units do appear but only as defined in terms
of these constituents. With regard to theory, it was shown
that Morpheme Structure Conditions, Positive Conditions,
Syllable Structure Conditions, Surface Phonetic Constraints
and other formal devices recently proposed are incapable of
assigning structure but are rather only suitable for interpreting and filtering pre-existing structure. Thus, a
Surface Phonetic Component which assigns hierarchial structure was proposed to align theory and data more coherently.

The second part of this study (Chapters 8-11) was
concerned with the prosodic domain of the monosyllable.
Three fundamental claims were made with regard to the
essence of this prosodic domain: (1) lexical tone is of
such complexity that a set of distinctive features geared
largely to pitch, while useful, cannot capture all the
relevant facets of Chinese tone; (2) while an abstract,
underlying representation tone is necessary to account for
tone sandhi (when syllables are combined into larger units),
a surface phonetic account of tone is also necessary to
characterize the integration of prosodic features in

isolated syllables, and (3) the relationship between the
prosodic and non-prosodic features of the syllable is much
too complex to assume that the former can be "mapped"
onto the latter at the surface level. From the theoretical perspective, it was demonstrated that any approach
which failed to take the complexity of lexical tone and
tone-segment relationships into account (e.g., the Sonorant
Segment and Feature Assimilation approaches) would eventually prove unsatisfactory. Thus, the Tone Program was
offered as a richer and yet more constrained approach to
the characterization of Chinese tone.

The third and final part of this essay focused on
the integration of the non-prosodic and prosodic features
of the monosyllable. Chapter 12 presented a perhaps
rather orthodox attempt to integrate these two dimensions.
Chapters 13 and 14, however, go far beyond this initial
attempt at integration and offer a rather less orthodox,
much more speculative orientation to the non-prosodic—
prosodic interface. This orientation is offered in light
of several theoretical models which lie outside the confines of standard Generative Theory. Yet again, I have
forwarded the view that these particular approaches,
Prosodic, Autosegmental and Non-Synchronized, simply cannot
account for the relevant data as it has been interpeted

in the earlier parts of this study. As a step towards
resolving this data-theory dissonance, I have presented
a tentative alternative under the rubric of "Polydimensional Phonology."

As is often the case in theoretical inquiry, the
revisions, requirements, and formulations proposed in this
sutdy, even when taken in their totality, are less likely
to disprove the validity of certain theoretical tenents
than to effect shifts in what constitutes the appropriate
subject matter of linguistic analysis. The nature of
the Chinese sound pattern and of the native Chinese tradition surrounding its description provide an impetus for
just such a shift in the current perspective of phonological structure, a perspective implicit in the present-day
candidates for the most appropriate theoretical orientation to the characterization of human sound systems.
Thus, my purpose in undertaking this study will have been
well served even if I have only made a plausible case for
revising our perceptions and consequently our theories,
as to what constitutes the valid linguistic generalizations
of the Chinese sound pattern.

APPENDIX

1. Shanghai Data

The following phonetic data is drawn from the
Chinese work <u>Jiangsusheng he Shanghaishi Fangyan Gaikuang</u>
(<u>Outline of the Dialects of Kiangsu Province and Shanghai</u>).

2. Consonants

	Bilabial	Labio-dent.	Dental	Alveolar	Palatal	Velar	Glottal
Stops:							
Voiceless Unaspirated	p		t			k	ʔ
Voiceless Aspirated	p'		t'			k'	
Voiced Unaspirated	b		d			g	
Fricatives:							
Voiceless		f	s		ɕ		h
Voiced		v	z				ɦ
Africates:							
Voiceless Unaspirated				ts	tɕ		
Voiceless Aspirated				ts'	tɕ'		
Voiceless Unaspirated					dʑ		
Nasals:	m			n	ñ	ŋ	
Liquids:				l			

3. <u>Vowels</u>

	Front		Central		Back	
	UR	R	UR	R	UR	R
High	i	y				u
Intermediate High		Y				
Half-High	e	ö	ə		ɣ	o
Mid						
Half-Low	ɛ					
Intermediate Low						ɔ
Low	a (ã)					ɒ̃

The so-called "apical vowel" represented in the syllabaries
as i̇ is not shown in the above table. See Walton (1971)
for a discussion of the nature and phonetic interpretation
of such vowels.

4. <u>Tones</u>

Tone	Contour	Description
1	53	High Falling
2	34	Mid Rising
3	14	Low Rising
4	5	High Level (Short)
5	2	Low Level (Short)

5. <u>Tone - Initial Consonant Relationships</u>

		Final				
		Non-glottal			Glottal	
	Tone:	53	34	14	5	2
Initial						
Voiceless Obstruent		+	+		+	
Nasal and liquid		+		+		+
Voiced Obstruent				+		+

BIBLIOGRAPHY

Anderson, John. 1969.
"Syllabic or Non-Syllabic Phonology?" Journal of
Linguistics 5: 136-42.

Anderson, Stephen R. 1974.
The Organization of Phonology. New York: Academic
Press, Inc.

Ballard, W. L. 1966.
"The Wu Dialect: Outline of Initial and Tonal System." Berkeley, California: Unpublished Ms.

Bloomfield, Leonard. 1933.
Language. New York: Holt, Rinehart and Winston.

Bowers, John.
"Phonological Structure." In preparation.

Brosnahan, L. F. and Bertil Malmberg. 1970.
Introduction to Phonetics. Cambridge: W. Heffer
and Sons, Ltd.

Brown, E. Wayles III. 1972.
"How to Apply Phonological Rules." MIT Quarterly
Progress Report 105, pp. 143-146.

Cairns, C. E. 1969.
"Markedness and Universal Redundancy Rules."
Language 45: 863-885.

Campbell, Lyle. 1974.
"Phonological Features: Problems and Proposals."
Language 50: 52-65.

Chafe, Wallace. 1968.
"The Ordering of Phonological Rules." I.J.A.L.
34: 115-136.

Chao, Y. R. 1931.
"Eight Varieties of Secret Language Based on the
Principles of Faanchieh." Bulletin of the Institute
of History and Philology, Academia Sinica, II, No. 3:
312-354. (In Chinese).

Chao, Y. R. 1934.
"The Non-Uniqueness of Phonemic Solutions of Phonetic Systems." Bulletin of the Institute of History and Philology, Academia Sinica, Vol. IV, part 4, 363-97. Also in Martin Joos, ed., Readings in Linguistics, 1957: 38-54.

Chao, Y. R. 1948.
Mandarin Primer. Cambridge, Mass.: Harvard University Press.

Chao, Y. R. 1968.
A Grammar of Spoken Chinese. Berkeley and Los Angeles: University of California Press.

Chen, Matthew. 1970.
"Vowel Length Variation as a Function of the Voicing of the Consonant Environment," Phonetica 22: 129-59.

Chen, Matthew. 1973.
"Cross-Dialectal Comparison: A Case Study and Some Theoretical Considerations." Journal of Chinese Linguistics 1: 38-63.

Cheng, Chin-chuan. 1973(a).
"A Quantitative Study of Chinese Tones." Journal of Chinese Linguistics 1: 93-110.

Cheng, Chin-chuan. 1973(b).
A Synchronic Phonology of Mandarin Chinese. Monographs on Linguistic Analysis No. 4. The Hague: Mouton.

Cheng, R. L. 1966.
"Mandarin Phonological Structure." Journal of Linguistics 2: 135-58.

Cheng, T. 1968.
"The Phonological System of Cantonese." Project on Linguistic Analysis (2nd series; Berkeley) 5: C1-C85.

Chomsky, Noam. 1965.
Aspects of the Theory of Syntax. Cambridge, Mass.: MIT Press.

Chomsky, Noam. 1970.
"Remarks on Nominalization" in Jacobs, R. A. and
Peter Rosenbaum, ed., pp. 184-221. Waltham, Mass.,
Toronto, London: Ginn and Company.

Chomsky, Noam and Morris Halle. 1968.
The Sound Pattern of English. New York: Harper and
Row.

Fromkin, Victoria. 1968.
"Speculations on Performance Models." Journal of
Linguistics 4: 47-68.

Fromkin, Victoria. 1971.
"The Non-Anomalous Nature of Anomalous Utterances."
Language 47: 27-52.

Fromkin, Victoria. 1972.
"Tone Features and Tone Rules." Studies in African
Linguistics 3: 47-76.

Fromkin, Victoria. 1974.
"On the Phonological Representation of Tone." The
Tone Tome (UCLA Working Papers in Phonetics 27), pp.
1-17.

Fudge, E. C. 1967.
"Syllables." Journal of Linguistics 5: 253-86.

Goldsmith, John A. 1976.
Autosegmental Phonology, MIT dissertation, reproduced
by Indiana University Linguistics Club.

Halle, Morris. 1959.
The Sound Pattern of Russian. The Hague: Mouton.

Halle, Morris. 1964.
"On the Bases of Phonology." In The Structure of
Language, Fodar, Jerry A. and Jerrold Katz, editors,
pp. 324-333. Englewood Cliffs, New Jersey: Pren-
tice Hall, Inc.

Halle, Morris. 1971.
"Theoretical Issues in Phonology in the 1970's." In
Proceedings of the Seventh International Congress
of Phonetic Sciences, Montreal. The Hague: Mouton.

-339-

Halle, Morris and Kenneth Stevens. 1971.
"A Note on Laryngeal Features." M.I.T. Quarterly
Progress Report 101: 198-213.

Hanyu Fangyan Cihui. 1964. Peking: Wenzi Gaige Chubanshe.

Harms, Robert T. 1968.
Introduction to Phonological Theory. Englewood
Cliffs, New Jersey: Prentice-Hall, Inc.

Hartman, Lawton M. 1944.
"The Segmental Phonemes of the Peiping Dialect." In
Joos 1957: 116-123.

Haudricourt, A. G. 1954.
"De l'origine des tons en vietnamien." Journal
Asiatique 242: 69-82.

Hempel, Carl G. 1966.
Philosophy of Natural Science. Englewood Cliffs,
New Jersey, Prentice-Hall, Inc.

Hoard, James E. 1971.
"Aspiration, Tenseness, and Syllabication in English."
Language 47: 133-140.

Hockett, Charles F. 1947.
"Peiping Phonology." In Joos 1957: 217-228.

Hockett, Charles F. 1955.
A Manual of Phonology. Bloomington, Indiana:
I.J.A.L. Memorial.

Hooper, Joan B. 1973.
Aspects of Natural Generative Phonology. Los Angeles:
U.C.L.A. dissertation.

Hooper, Joan B. 1974.
"The Archi Segment in Natural Generative Phonology."
Unpublished Manuscript. Buffalo, New York: State
University of New York.

Hyman, Larry M., ed. 1973.
Consonant Types and Tone. Los Angeles, Southern
California Occasional Papers in Linguistics I.

Hyman, L. and R. Schuh. 1974.
"Universal of Tone Rules: Evidence from West Africa."
Linguistic Inquiry 5: 81-113.

Jiangsusheng he Shanghaishi Fangyan Gaikuang. 1960. Peking:
Jiangsu Renmin Chubanshe.

Joos, Martin. 1957.
Readings in Linguistics I. Chicago: University of
Chicago Press.

Kiparsky, Paul. 1973.
"Abstractness, Opacity, and Global Rules." Paper
delivered at the Indiana University Conference on
Rule Ordering, April 1973.

Kisseberth, Charles W. 1970.
"On the Functional Unity of Phonological Rules."
Unpublished mss. (A later version appears in
Linguistic Inquiry 1: 291-306.)

Kozhevnikov, V. and L. Chistovich. 1965.
Speech: Articulation and Perception. Joint Publications Research Service 30: 5443.

Kratochvil, Paul. 1968.
The Chinese Language Today. London: Hutchinson.

Ladefoged, Peter. 1964.
A Phonetic Study of West African Languages. Cambridge,
Mass.: Cambridge University Press.

Ladefoged, Peter. 1967(a).
Linguistic Phonetics. Working Paper in Phonetics 6.
UCLA.

Ladefoged, Peter. 1967(b).
Three Areas of Experimental Phonetics. London:
University of Oxford Press.

Ladefoged, Peter. 1973.
"The Features of the Larynx." Journal of Phonetics
1: 73-83.

Leben, W. R. 1973.
"The Role of Tone in Segmental Phonology" in Hyman,
ed., Consonant Types and Tone, pp. 115-150.

Lehiste, I. 1970.
"Suprasegmental Features, Segmental Features, and
Long Components." In Actes du Xe Congres Interna-
tional des Linguistes. IV. 1970, 1-6. Budapest.

Lehiste, Ilse. 1970.
Suprasegmentals. Cambridge, Mass.: MIT Press.

Lenneberg, Eric H. 1967.
Biological Foundations of Language. New York:
John Wiley.

Liberman, A. M., F. Cooper, D. Shankweiler and M. Studdert-
Kennedy. 1967.
"Perception of the Speech Code." Psychological
Review 74: 431-461.

Light, Timothy. 1974.
Phonological Relativity and Constituent Analysis:
Evidence from Chinese Syllable Types and Traditional
Chinese Analyses. Ithaca: Cornell University
dissertation.

Lister, Leigh and A. Abramson. 1971.
"Distinctive Features and Laryngeal Control."
Language 47: 767-785.

Lyons, John. 1968.
Introduction to Theoretical Linguistics. Cambridge,
Mass.: Cambridge University Press.

Lyovin, Anatole. 1973.
Review of D. L. Gao, Structure of the Syllable in
Cantonese. Language 49: 954-961.

Malmberg, Bertil. 1963.
Phonetics. New York: Dover Publications.

Malmberg, Bertil. 1964.
"Stability and Instability of Syllabic Structures."
In Proceedings of the Fifth International Congress
of Phonetic Sciences, Munster. Basel/New York.
pp. 403-408.

Maran, La Raw. 1969.
The Syllable Final in Tibeto-Burman. Unpublished
Ms. Cambridge, Mass.: Massachusetts Institute of
Technology.

Maran, La Raw. 1971.
Burmese and Jingpo: A Study of Tonal Linguistic
Processes. Occasional Papers of the Wolfendon Soc-
iety on Tibeto-Burman Linguistics 4. Urbana, Ill.:
Center for Asian Studies. University of Illinois.

Matisoff, J. 1970.
"Glottal Dissimilation and the Lahu High-Rising Tone:
A Tonogenetic Case Study." Journal of the American
Oriental Society 90: 13-44.

Matisoff, James A. 1973.
"Tonogenesis in Southeast Asia." In Hyman, ed.,
Consonant Types and Tone, pp. 71-96.

McCawley, J. D. 1968.
The Phonological Component of a Grammar of Japanese.
(Monographs on Linguistic Analysis, 2). The Hague:
Mouton.

McCoy, John. 1966.
Szeyap Data for a First Approximation of Proto-
Cantonese. Unpublished doctoral dissertation.
Ithaca, New York: Cornell University.

Nida, E. A. 1949.
Morphology: The Descriptive Analysis of Words. Ann
Arbor, Michigan: University of Michigan Press.

Ohala, John J. 1973.
"The Physiology of Tone." In Hyman, ed., Consonant
Types and Tone, pp. 1-15.

Palmer, Frank Robert, compiler. 1970.
Prosodic Analysis. London, Oxford University Press.

Pike, Kenneth Lee. 1947.
Phonemics: A Technique for.Reducing Languages to
Writing. Ann Arbor, Michigan: University of
Michigan Press.

Pike, Kenneth L. and Eunice Pike. 1947.
"Constituent Analysis of Mazeteco Syllables."
I.J.A.L. 13: 78-91.

Postal, Paul M. 1964.
Constituent Structure: A Study of Contemporary
Models of Syntactic Descriptions. Bloomington,
Indiana: Indiana University Publications in
Folklore and Linguistics.

Postal, Paul M. 1968.
Aspects of Phonological Theory. New York: Harper
and Row.

Pulgram, Ernst. 1970.
Syllable, Word, Nexus, Cursus. The Hague: Mouton
and Co.

Robins, R. H. 1964.
General Linguistics: An Introductory Survey.
Bloomington, Indiana: Indiana University Press.

Romeo, Luigi. 1964.
"Toward a Phonological Grammar of Modern Spoken
Greek." In Papers in Memory of G. C. Pappageotes
(Supplement to Word 20: 3), edited by R. Austerlitz
et al., pp. 60-78.

Sampson, Geoffrey. 1970.
"On the Need for a Phonological Base." Language 46:
586-626.

Saporta, Sol and Heles Contreras. 1962.
A Phonological Grammar of Spanish. Seattle, Wash-
ington: University Press.

Saussure, Ferdinand de. 1949.
Course in General Linguistics. New York: Philo-
sophical Library.

Scholes, Robert J. 1966.
Phonotactic Grammaticality. The Hague: Mouton.

Sherard, Michael. 1972.
Shanghai Phonology. Ithaca: Cornell University
dissertation.

Shibatani, Masayoshi. 1973.
"The Role of Surface Phonetic Constraints in Generative Phonology." Language 49: 87-106.

Stanley, Richard. 1967.
"Redundancy Rules in Phonology." Language 43: 393-436.

Stanley, Richard. 1968.
"The Formal Character of Redundancy Rules in Phonology." Project on Linguistic Analysis (2nd. Series; Berkeley), No. 6, S1-S31.

Trubetskoy, N. S. 1971.
Principles of Phonology. Translated by Christiane A.M. Baltaxe. Berkeley: University of California Press.

Walton, Ronald. 1971.
Phonological Redundancy in Shanghai. Ithaca: Cornell University M.A. Thesis.

Wang, William. 1967.
"The Phonological Features of Tone." I.J.A.L. 33: 93-105.

Wang, William. 1968.
"Vowel Features, Paired Variables and the English Vowel Shift." Language 44: 695-708.

Woo, Nancy. 1970.
"Tone in Northern Tepehuan." I.J.A.L. 36: 18-30.

Woo, Nancy. 1972.
Prosody and Phonology. Bloomington, Indiana: University of Indiana Linguistics Club publication.

Yen, Sian-L. 1965.
Studies in the Phonological History of Amoy Chinese. Urbana, Ill.: Unpublished doctoral dissertation.

Zwicky, Arnold M. 1973.
"The Strategy of Generative Phonology." Working Papers in Linguistics No. 14. (Studies in Phonology and Methodology). Columbus, Ohio: Department of Linguistics, The Ohio State University.

CORNELL UNIVERSITY EAST ASIA PAPERS

For information on ordering the preceding publications
and tapes, please write to:

EAST ASIA PAPERS
China-Japan Program
Cornell University
140 Uris Hall
Ithaca, NY 14853-7601